DAN DURYEA

HOLLYWOOD LEGENDS SERIES
CARL ROLLYSON, GENERAL EDITOR

DAN DURYEA

HEEL WITH A HEART

MIKE PEROS

University Press of Mississippi • Jackson

www.upress.state.ms.us

Designed by Peter D. Halverson

The University Press of Mississippi is a member of the
Association of American University Presses.

First printing 2016

∞

Library of Congress Cataloging-in-Publication Data

Names: Peros, Mike.
Title: Dan Duryea : heel with a heart / Mike Peros.
Description: Jackson : University Press of Mississippi, 2016. | Series:
Hollywood legends series | Includes bibliographical references and index.
Identifiers: LCCN 2016014275 (print) | LCCN 2016024278 (ebook) | ISBN
9781628462326 (hardcover : alk. paper) | ISBN 9781496809933 (epub single)
| ISBN 9781496809940 (epub institutional) | ISBN 9781496809957 (pdf
single) | ISBN 9781496809964 (pdf institutional)
Subjects: LCSH: Duryea, Dan, 1907–1968. | Actors—United States—Biography.
Classification: LCC PN2287.D875 P48 2016 (print) | LCC PN2287.D875 (ebook) |
DDC 791.4302/8092 [B] —dc23
LC record available at https://lccn.loc.gov/2016014275

British Library Cataloging-in-Publication Data available

For Barbara

CONTENTS

DAN DURYEA

CHAPTER 1

A Duryea Overview

LATE IN HIS LIFE, DAN DURYEA MADE A RESERVATION AT A WILSHIRE Boulevard restaurant called the Egg and the Eye. He was expecting a telephone call from his wife, Helen, and informed the pretty girl at the reservation desk. "Look," she warned, "don't be mad if I mix up wives a little. Today we have reservations for Dan Duryea, Dan Dailey, and Bill Daily." Duryea loved it. It gave him his story for that week. This anecdote reveals a lot, not only about Duryea's sense of humor, much of it self-effacing and occasionally self-deprecating, but also about how Duryea tends to be either forgotten or confused with somebody else. When I would tell people I was working on the first biography of Dan Duryea, the initial response would be "Dan *Dailey*?" After I mentioned *The Little Foxes* and perhaps *Scarlet Street*, I'd finally get the smile of recognition that I was seeking.

Whenever I look at Dan Duryea's body of work, one question comes to mind: why hasn't there been one single major literary effort that has addressed the entirety and variety of his career? A comprehensive look at Dan Duryea's films and television career (not to mention his radio and theater work) is akin to taking a journey through a largely undiscovered country, and one that is long overdue. This biography seeks to correct this grievous oversight. Dan Duryea is probably best known for the slimy, scheming villains that he compellingly portrayed in films throughout the 1940s, '50s, and into the '60s. Consider the three films that comprise his cinematic partnership with Fritz Lang. *Ministry of Fear* casts Duryea as a tailor with a very menacing pair of shears; his appearances are fleeting throughout but his very presence heightens the danger for beleaguered hero Ray Milland, as well as the audience. In *The Woman in the Window*, he insolently swaggers into kept woman Joan Bennett's apartment after she and Edward G. Robinson believe (mistakenly) that they've managed to remove all traces of what had been a killing in self-defense. As the victim's presumed bodyguard, Duryea challenges Bennett to call the police, and later threatens to blackmail the hapless couple—even as he's putting the make on Bennett (money is money, but Duryea's characters also hold out for the promise of sexual satisfaction). When Lang and his three stars reunited the following year for *Scarlet Street*, many critics commented that it was just a redo of *Woman in the Window*. It is in fact a far darker film than its predecessor, as Duryea is joined by Bennett as predators par excellence who fully deserve each other as they lead the hapless Robinson inexorably to a special dance of death (and one which wreaked havoc on the Production Code).

Film noir is the ideal genre for Duryea's patented blend of menace, sleaze, confidence, and superficial charm that leads his characters to believe they're God's gift to women. 1949's *Criss Cross* pits Duryea's silky smooth Slim Dundee against working-class, blinded-by-love Burt Lancaster's Steve for the prize of a satchel of cash and the alluring Yvonne De Carlo. Lancaster and De Carlo turned a lot of filmgoers' heads in the 1940s, but when Duryea is on the screen, all eyes are on him. *One Way Street* is one-third of a good film—at least the third that Duryea appears in as a big-time crook thwarted by his physician James Mason. Yes, Doc Mason takes Duryea's money—but when he makes off with Duryea's woman (Marta Toren), there will be hell to pay. 1949's *Manhandled* presents Duryea as an ex-cop-turned-sleazy-private-eye who nevertheless ingratiates himself into naïve Dorothy Lamour's life and improvises a scheme to steal some valuable jewels. While not a great movie, Duryea is in rare form as a conniving, confident chiseler, especially in contrast to the rather desultory leads (including Sterling Hayden).

Westerns also provide a scenic backdrop to Duryea's villainy. *Along Came Jones* is a comic Western in which Gary Cooper is mistaken for notorious outlaw Dan Duryea, and while Coop is his usual lanky, diffident self, it's Duryea who provides some much-needed punch to the proceedings. In *Winchester '73*, Duryea makes a late entry as Waco Johnny Dean, but once in, the screen is his. Yes, James Stewart is looking for the villain who stole his prized Winchester, but when Waco enters, needling, smiling, and shooting, he almost swipes the gun and the film from a marvelously obsessed Stewart. Allan Dwan's *Silver Lode* presents Duryea as Marshal McCarty, an obsessive lawman who rides into town with a warrant for well-liked John Payne, in what was interpreted as a Western allegory about the Hollywood witch-hunts of the 1950s.

Yet Duryea's impeccably portrayed villainy in films that have generally grown in stature over the years doesn't begin to prepare one for the variety and shadings in his characterizations. This ability could be detected early on with his official film debut, recreating his stage role as the transparent, good-for-nothing Leo in *The Little Foxes*; as comic gangster Pastrami in *Ball of Fire*; as sportswriter Walter Brennan's naysaying but likable sidekick in *Pride of the Yankees*; as the enterprising, forever-wagering radioman for Humphrey Bogart's cut-off tank unit in *Sahara*. All these well-etched supporting characters were of inestimable service to films which later became classics.

This versatility would manifest itself throughout Duryea's career, much of which was spent at Universal but would eventually include a freelance option, which Duryea took full advantage of. By the time of 1946's *Black Angel*, Duryea had already completed his Lang trifecta, but in Roy William Neill's initially underrated noir, he is low-key and moving as an alcoholic pianist carrying a torch for his murdered wife, while trying to help the young heroine solve that murder. 1950's *The Underworld Story* uses Duryea's established persona as a heel to keep his costars and the audience guessing in this powerful, unsung drama of a disgraced news reporter who moves to a small town and quickly latches onto a sensational case involving murder, corruption, and racial prejudice. It's a pretty daring film for its time, and Duryea is superb in it. The little-known *Chicago Calling* is probably Duryea's most atypical film, and the one he's on the record as saying he's proudest of. Duryea is intense and heartbreaking throughout this gripping little film; his anguished depiction of a flawed man desperately trying to find out what happened to his daughter is a career highlight. 1953's *Thunder Bay* presents Duryea as James Stewart's good-natured buddy and partner who provides the much-needed voice of reason, as opposed to Stewart's obsessive oilman.

Everything I've discussed so far is only a precursor to the deeper characterizations to come. The 1950s saw Duryea widening his range while continuing to dabble in his trademark villainy. By now, a certain world-weariness and vulnerability began to creep into Duryea's characters. The actor had aged somewhat since his entry in 1941, and Duryea's character, heroic or not, felt largely out of synch with a world that was changing too fast and too far. Robert Aldrich's 1954 *World for Ransom* provided Duryea with one of his best roles as a private eye in Singapore with a yen for his best friend's wife and the ability to get himself jammed up while trying to help his duplicitous best friend avoid disaster. Duryea exudes an air of weary nobility throughout but always keeps his edge, never descending to the maudlin—even when his character is plumbing the depths of despair. 1957's *The Burglar* casts Duryea as a master thief with an attractive ward (Jayne Mansfield), and hounded by a corrupt, murderous cop who wants the loot. Duryea manages to convey the cagey exterior, the suppressed longing, and the fatalistic attitude that makes him an ideal David Goodis (novel and screenplay) hero.

What makes Duryea so remarkable, besides his sheer versatility, is his vast body of work, not only in the movies, but as a prime player in television drama, mainly from the late 1950s on . . . all the while maintaining his standing in motion pictures. He starred as the adventurer *China Smith* for two seasons, first in 1952, then for a return in 1955. Duryea became a fixture in episodic drama on anthology shows like *The Cavalcade of America* and *Climax*, as well as weekly dramas that were more than generous to their guest stars, many of them movie actors of varying degrees of stardom (or post-stardom). These shows provided opportunities for the guest stars to put their formidable talents on display while the regular cast members graciously (or not) stepped back. Duryea starred in classic episodes of *Twilight Zone*, *Bonanza*, *Wagon Train*, and *Rawhide*, among others. I say "starred" on purpose because his characters were invariably the "leads," and the evidence of this is apparent in the number of DVD boxed sets of these titles, as well as exposure on various streaming sites like Hulu, Amazon Instant Video, and YouTube, which have helped provide easy access to these classic appearances.

In his late fifties, when many movie actors might have eased up (not by choice), Duryea remained as prolific as ever, and with some of his most interesting work. *The Bounty Killer* showcased Duryea as a tenderfoot who evolves into a disreputable bounty hunter. A reunion with Robert Aldrich and James Stewart in *Flight of the Phoenix* provided Duryea with a warmhearted supporting role in an all-male, all-star tale of survival. Duryea also tried his hand at the spaghetti Western, playing a wily old gunman who aids the revenge-driven hero in *The Hills Run Red*. One of Duryea's last outings was in a TV movie directed by Don Siegel, *Stranger on the Run*, as the lone rational man in a relentless posse hunting down Henry Fonda. I remember watching this movie when I was a boy (*NBC Saturday Night at the Movies*), and had to dig around a bit in order to find a copy, but it's a film that deserves to be better known. Duryea's last major work would be on the popular prime-time soap opera *Peyton Place*, filming nearly sixty episodes and stealing most of his scenes as the wily conman Eddie Jacks.

Duryea worked right up to his death, and while some of his final motion picture choices were a little dubious, the demand for his services never waned. Would he have liked to have been offered more humane roles? Definitely, especially when you read a number of his interviews and profiles from the 1950s. Duryea seemed to have a lot riding on the comedy *Kathy O'*, and while it was a moderate success, it didn't provide the career breakthrough he had been hoping for. But maybe actors aren't necessarily the best judges of their own careers. Look at Edward G. Robinson and James Cagney: to hear them tell it in their respective autobiographies, Robinson was monotonous and *Scarlet Street* was second-rate Fritz Lang, while to Cagney, *White Heat* was "just another cheapjack job." As I examine Duryea's output, although Duryea never had that big "breakthrough" (at least in his own eyes), he was continually testing the boundaries by effectively integrating portrayals of heroism, vulnerability, and integrity alongside his patented villainous rogue's gallery.

If the sheer scope of Duryea's career weren't enough for Duryea to merit his own biography, there's another thread I'll pursue throughout: the contrast between his screen image as one of cinema's nastiest scoundrels and the reality of his life as one of Hollywood's most honorable and decent men, a faithful husband and devoted father. Duryea remained married to the former Helen Bryan from 1932 until her death in 1967. Their early years together had been fraught with difficulties and heartbreak, from Dan's breakdown while putting in long hours in advertising (not quite his chosen profession) to Helen's losing their first child. However, by all accounts, it would ultimately be a happy, fulfilling union and they would have two sons, Peter and Richard. Dan Duryea proved to be an attentive, proud father, just as his own father, Richard, had been to him. He and Helen took an active role in raising their children, joining the PTA and the Cub Scouts, with Duryea serving as a scoutmaster. Duryea publicly lobbied for more recreational opportunities for children, to keep his neighborhood free from environmental hazards and proposed superhighways. Duryea may have been consciously combatting his screen image of the bad man, but he also genuinely cared about his family, his friends (most of whom were not in the Hollywood community), and his town. While Duryea was fiercely proud of being an actor, he had many other outside interests, such as gardening and building sailboats, pursuits which he shared with his sons. Duryea generally avoided the party circuit, and as soon as finances would permit, he bought a second home seventy miles north in Lake Arrowhead, where the family would spend their entire summers, as well as weekends in winter.

Throughout the course of Duryea's career, however, his nasty screen persona would clash both with his gentle off-screen life and with the kinds of parts that he wanted to undertake. Duryea knew villainous roles were what the public expected of him; the more he slapped women around, the more he received approving letters from female fans. There would be a public backlash if these fans read an article depicting what a stand-up guy Duryea was in real life—or if they saw a movie where he played a friendly fellow.

It frustrated Duryea that he couldn't be completely successful at breaking the typecasting (his younger rival and heir apparent Richard Widmark would be more successful in this regard). The role and movie closest to his heart, that of the desperate father in *Chicago Calling*, did virtually no business. At least television would provide more variety, and Duryea was savvy enough to capitalize on the small screen's growing prominence. He was among the first to understand that the proper use of television could extend the actor's staying power, even enhancing an actor's film career.

The end of Duryea's life is not far from Hemingway's idea of "grace under pressure." Having suffered the loss of his beloved Helen in 1967, Duryea plunged headlong into his work, managing to complete a season of the popular soap opera *Peyton Place*, as well as a few movies, all the while coping valiantly with the onset of cancer. There were some columnists who were aware of his plight, but such was their esteem for Duryea that they refrained from going public with their knowledge, until after his death in 1968.

The book you are about to read, *Dan Duryea: Heel with a Heart*, is a labor of love but it's by no means a whitewash of Duryea's career. Like any actor, Duryea would sometimes choose unwisely, whether it was a movie, a role itself, or how he would portray it. In the course of my research, I was able to view all of Duryea's films (some were harder to track down than others), so any opinion you read about his films will be mine—unless I've quoted a reviewer to note the response at the time of a film's release. In addition, thanks to streaming services like the afore-mentioned YouTube and Amazon Instant Video, as well as DVD releas-es (official and unofficial), I was able to locate a substantial number of Duryea's television and radio performances, so what you'll read here is a fairly complete portrait of Duryea's life and career. The amount of work is astounding, but given Duryea's talent, it wasn't surprising. Duryea was a consummate actor and a gentleman until the end.

CHAPTER 2

From White Plains to Broadway

"YOU SEE, I HAD ALWAYS WANTED TO BE AN ACTOR. BUT MY FATHER had pointed out quite sensibly that it's very hard to earn a living as an actor. Therefore, he had suggested that if I wanted to get married and raise a family, I'd better go in for something at which I could earn a steady buck. That's what I had done. That's why I was pounding the pavements selling advertising space. Then came my heart strain . . ."

Upon reading Dan Duryea's own words from a 1951 article, you might think that his early life was marked by equal measures of passion and compromise—and you would be right. The young Duryea would put aside his creative ambitions and instead seek job security and a certain degree of happiness. Since the years in question encompass the late 1920s and the early years of the Great Depression, it's natural to assume these would be trying times.

These difficult times didn't occur during Dan's childhood—as a matter of fact, Dan's early years were fairly normal, largely devoid of any earthshaking events or emotional scars (great for Dan, not so good for a prospective biographer). He was born Daniel Edwin Duryea on January 23, 1907, in White Plains, New York, the second son of proud parents Mabel Hoffman and Richard Duryea. The Duryeas had been married in Brooklyn in 1902 but later moved to White Plains shortly before Dan's birth. The elder Duryea had a successful career as a textile salesman for the Deering-Milliken Woolen Company, working there until his retirement.

By all accounts, Richard and Mabel Duryea were loving, caring parents. Richard, in particular, tried to instill in young Dan not only the value of hard work and responsibility, but a number of other lessons as well, such as cultivating outside interests apart from school and work. As Dan would remember in a 1957 interview: "My father taught me long ago to have a hobby. I grew up with the idea of not devoting my whole life to work. Having a solid family life to me is a sound, intelligent way of living. I know this isn't the answer for many people—everyone has a different get-up—but it works best for me."

Dan's school years in White Plains were fairly uneventful; he had followed his older brother Hewlett through the White Plains public school system. Hewlett was an honors student throughout his school years, which resulted in teachers making the inevitable comparison between Dan and his big brother. According to Duryea's son Richard, Dan and Hewlett (whom most people, including Dan, called "Duke") were on friendly terms, but were not especially close, especially after they reached adulthood. Dan prided himself on being erudite and literary even during his high school years; when a teacher asked him what books (poetry and prose) he would take to a desert island, he replied the Bible and *Pippa Passes*, which led the teacher to question Dan about his honesty or lack thereof—resulting in a public, undeserved humiliation that still rankled him many years later. While there isn't much on record about Dan's school days, he would speak about them later on, and not always in the most flattering manner. In a 1950 interview with columnist Hedda Hopper, Dan would reflect on his unsatisfactory educational experiences when he discussed how he had prepared for his roles: "I thought about some of the people I hated in my early life . . . like the school bully who used to try to beat the hell out of me at least once a week . . . the one I used when I had to slap around women was easy. I was slapping the overbearing teachers who would fail you in their 'holier than thou' class and enjoy it."

Dan's interest in drama began at an early age. His first stage appearance was at a church social in White Plains, in which the six-year-old Dan was dressed as an ink bottle. Though it's hard to believe, this experience may well have helped pique his interest in acting. Dan would appear in a number of dramatic productions throughout grammar and high school, including a featured role in *Adam and Eva*, not necessarily distinguishing himself but not embarrassing himself at any rate. One of his high school drama teachers would later remember Dan as being talented and "a little above average"—certainly not the qualities that would seem to augur a later successful stage and screen career.

After Dan graduated from White Plains High School in 1924, he entered Cornell University's College of Arts and Sciences. He spent much of his academic career taking business and humanities classes while working his way through school by waiting tables at the fraternity house. When he wasn't occupied with studying or working, however, he developed an extensive interest in dramatics. There would be a number of future theatrical luminaries among his Cornell classmates, including actor Franchot Tone and playwright Sidney Kingsley. Duryea quickly earned some stature among his peers as a reasonably talented young man with an ability to interpret and execute a variety of parts, regardless of stature, whether in modern entertainment (at the time) such as George M. Cohan's *Seven Keys to Baldpate*, or in a classical, albeit comic, turn as Flute in Shakespeare's *A Midsummer Night's Dream*.

Dan would ultimately succeed Franchot Tone as president of the Cornell Dramatic Club in 1927, and as one could see while perusing many of the old Cornell programs, the Cornell Dramatic Club was a formidable institution. During Duryea's senior year at Cornell, the Dramatic Club staged no fewer than eight major productions, as well as thirty-three one-act plays. Dan took his position as president seriously, leading by example. He scored some starring roles, but did not consider himself above taking a few bits and supporting roles, and when Dan wasn't acting or presiding (as a president is wont to do), he was also active in set construction (for those who are not familiar with the theater, working set is a necessary evil for actors—and one avoided by many).

In 1928, Dan was elected to Sphinx Head, one of Cornell's two senior honorary societies. Duryea never severed his ties with Cornell; he was a noted contributor to its endowment and scholarship funds, regularly attended alumni reunions, and would occasionally appear in alumni productions. One such production, *The Perfect Alibi*, featured Dan as the murderer and provoked this response from a local reviewer named Livingston Larner. In a review entitled "The Imperfect Alibi," Larner noted somewhat presciently that "the thing we most admire about Dan is the ability to make a mean part win you over to him."

Upon graduating with a Bachelor of Arts degree in 1928, Dan thought about furthering his interest in acting by making it a full-time career. He asked a number of people for advice, but he found their answers somewhat discouraging. It wasn't that Dan was perceived to lack talent, but that people told him on more than one occasion of the difficulties in sustaining a career as a professional actor—and that the average yearly salary for a New York actor hovered around the not-too-princely sum of $300. It certainly wasn't enough to build any kind of life—especially when Dan was entertaining thoughts of love and marriage (neither of which were in the picture yet—but, still, he had thoughts).

Dan's father, Richard, suggested something more practical, and something befitting Dan's thespian talents: a job in advertising, pounding the pavements and selling ad space for N. W. Ayer for $35 a week. His work ethic paid off as he proved to be fairly successful on his rounds, with the guaranteed salary eclipsing, for now, his desire to test the uncertain theatrical waters. As this meant commuting by train from White Plains to New York City, he got into the habit of riding with an older gent who was also a commuter. One night, upon arriving in White Plains, the stormy weather was doing a number on the homeward-bound commuters. The older gent, Mr. Bryan, asked Dan if he might like a ride home; Dan accepted and saw a lovely, lively brunette at the wheel. Mr. Bryan said, "Dan, I'd like you to meet my daughter, Helen." The young lady was not only attractive; she was quite intelligent, with a razor-sharp wit. While Helen was born in Scarsdale, she was raised in White Plains, and graduated from St. Mary's Episcopal Convent in Fishkill. Before the ride was over, he'd gotten a date with Helen for that weekend. According to Dan, it was love at first sight—at least for him. But there were a few obstacles. As he recalled later: "She had to keep me off for a little while—on general principles . . . and there were a number of blokes around I had to get rid of." But after those gents were dispersed, Helen and Dan embarked on a whirlwind courtship, getting engaged within a year.

In the meantime, Dan changed jobs and joined the Katz Advertising Agency at $45 a week. A year later, Dan's salary was raised to a whopping $50 a week, and with his upcoming nuptials, Dan was on top of the world. Since Helen and Dan were both from White Plains, they had a large church wedding in 1932 with family and friends in attendance. There was some chaos on the wedding day itself, as the limo driver inadvertently took them to the wrong church, but order was eventually restored, and the ceremony would eventually take place, followed by a reception at a local hotel. They then took their '29 Ford roadster to New York City, beginning their honeymoon while dancing to the strains of Guy Lombardo's band at the Roosevelt Hotel. Afterwards, they continued their honeymoon in Ithaca, before returning to build a new life for themselves.

Then, reality began to intrude. The country was now in the throes of the Great Depression. Dan still had his job and his respectable salary of

$50 a week, which his bosses at Katz would soon increase to $55. Helen and Dan rented a small house—"three rooms so small you could scarcely turn around," according to Dan. However, almost as soon as they had gotten settled, word came that the highly regarded Dan had to go to Philadelphia and open new offices for the company. This meant more work and more responsibility under adverse conditions as most major industries were taking huge hits at this time; oddly enough, advertising was one of the few industries doing rather well, since struggling companies relied on securing space to promote their products and keep their firms afloat. This translated into increased business and added pressure for advertising firms such as Katz. Duryea certainly did his best to keep up with the hectic pace. There were enough worries to go around—the worry of keeping his job, keeping the companies' competitors at bay—but there were also worries of a more personal nature. The move to Philadelphia had the effect of forcing the newlyweds to start their lives among strangers; moreover, there would be another mouth to feed since Helen was expecting their first child.

Although the blonde, brown-eyed Dan considered himself reasonably fit, with his 6'1" frame bearing a relatively trim 160 pounds, all the pressures mounted to such an extent that he suffered a complete breakdown. Dan recalled that it began slowly: becoming winded after a routine game, becoming fatigued later at a dance, then finally, taking a walk on a Philadelphia street, on his way to work, and gasping for breath as his knees were buckling. Some authors have referred to it as a heart attack, but that might not have been the case. Duryea himself contributed to the confusion. On some occasions, he would refer to it as "heart strain," and on others, a collapse; on a few occasions, perhaps when he wasn't in the mood to discuss it, he would dismiss it as "not important." Duryea's son Richard would say that whenever this difficult period was referred to, there was never any reference to a "heart attack" among the members of the Duryea household—it was, indeed, a complete physical and nervous collapse. Doctors said he had strained his heart through stress and overwork, and his weakened condition was also complicated by a blood clot that had developed in his left leg.

Dan's doctors advised him to take to his bed and get plenty of rest, while the pregnant Helen did everything she could to facilitate his recovery, giving little thought to herself in the process. When the time came for Helen to have her baby, a very shaky Dan drove her to the hospital. He would recall that "the nurses told me that when we got to the hospital, they wondered who the patient was—Helen or I." After

Helen's caesarean, the doctors informed them that Helen would be all right, but that the baby was stillborn. It was devastating news for Helen and Dan; Dan felt primarily responsible, believing that Helen's condition resulted in part because of the sacrifices she had made in order to take care of *him*.

After ten days, Helen was out of the hospital, but there was still Dan's work situation and recovery period to deal with. His doctors urged him to stay away from the workplace, to get at least three months' worth of rest. Florida, with its warm weather and aura of serenity, was deemed the place to go to bring about a complete recovery. As Dan and Helen were not independently wealthy (and this was in the midst of the Depression), he thought this might be an insoluble problem. Dan went to his boss, Mr. George Katz. Katz reassured Dan that his job would be there, and that he would keep Dan at half-salary for as much time as Dan needed. Dan was never one to forget a kindness, remembering Katz as "a fine man. Whenever I go east, I look him up. He's part of the miracle that happened to me, a wonderful guy and a great friend."

Dan and Helen drove to Florida, where they found a frame shack with a sign asking for $25 a month. "We had ten dollars left," Dan remembered. "I knocked on the door and asked for the owner . . . I said 'we'll take the place now if you can let us have it for $20. I'll pay you $10 now and $10 next week.' He could have gotten $25 for it, if he'd held out for another tenant, but he took the $10."

Dan and Helen stayed in Clearwater for about six months, during which time he felt his strength and energy return. Dan was even cautiously optimistic about returning to advertising; after laboring at his old job for about a week, he knew that the whole unpleasant experience might be repeated. Mr. Katz, out of concern for Dan's welfare, told him, "You'd better get out of this business"—which brought back the question of what business to get into. While the country was slowly recovering from the Depression, there weren't other kinds of businesses clamoring for Dan's talents—and he wasn't even sure of what his marketable talents might be. He thought again of turning to the acting profession, consulting his dramatic coach at Cornell, Alexander Drummond. Drummond advised him against trying for a career, agreeing with Dan's father that "he was right—the chances are all against you." Dan would finally turn to Helen, who told him essentially that if he wanted to give acting a try, she would support him every step of the way. "We'll manage somehow," she would say, perhaps thinking that life would be better with a poor but happy actor, than with a wealthy but miserable advertising man. In any case, Dan would always credit Helen for giving him the courage to take a chance on the only career he really wanted.

Meanwhile, the Duryeas needed a place to live, and lucked into a cottage in Westport where they could stay rent-free, in exchange for minding the property. It was here, while clearing the grounds (part of the deal), that Dan developed what would become a lifetime interest in gardening and flowers. In 1935, he managed to land some paying gigs in summer stock, the first being at the County Theater in Suffern, New York, among some mighty heady company. *Caesar and Cleopatra* starred stage and screen actress Helen Hayes, under the direction of Joshua Logan; Dan appeared as "the boatman" in a production that ultimately didn't garner too many favorable notices. Wrote Brooks Atkinson of the *New York Times*: "Nearly every part requires an impulse beyond the skill of these actors." Better luck was not to be found in his next stage appearance; in Dobbs Ferry, Duryea landed a major supporting role as Langford in the Washington Theater's production of *White Cargo*. A local reviewer was not impressed with Dan, saying he "seemed to be too weak a character as presented." Duryea's next appearance for the Washington Theater was in the madcap comedy *Why We Misbehave* (opposite Natalie Schaefer, known for her stagecraft long before earning fame as Mrs. Thurston Howell on *Gilligan's Island*). This garnered him some positive notices, with the same reviewer now admitting a growing admiration for Duryea.

Buoyed by this newfound respect for his acting abilities, Dan figured he would try New York City. Having found a place in his hometown of White Plains, Dan decided he would go in to the big city at least three times a week in an attempt to find paying work; consequently, he found himself pounding the New York City streets even harder than when he was in advertising. He was a little disheartened when he perceived the theatrical world wasn't exactly waiting for the talents of Dan Duryea, Cornell pedigree and recent regional credits notwithstanding. In the end, it would be Duryea's Cornell connections that would open another door in his quest to achieve a degree of theatrical success. Duryea discovered that his old friend and fellow Cornell alumnus Sidney Kingsley had written a play with a large cast that was about to go into production on Broadway; it was called *Dead End*. Dan went to Kingsley's office and told him he was looking for a job. The supportive Kingsley sent Dan to his manager, where he secured a few small parts—mostly walk-ons and bits like the "second federal agent." However, the pay was $40 per week, and *Dead End*, when it opened in October 1935, turned out to be a resounding success.

There were some hitches on opening night: as one of the G-men, Dan was called upon to be involved in a climactic gun battle, but the prop man had forgotten to fill the revolvers with blank cartridges, leaving the rather surprised but undaunted actors with revolvers that refused to go off on cue. Of course, the play drew some attention to "the tale of two cities" that was New York then and now, with high-rise buildings skirting the edges of the projects; it also spawned the Dead End Kids, and the subsequent 1937 film adaptation would be a defining moment in Humphrey Bogart's career. For Dan Duryea, the play would be a boon to his burgeoning career; *Dead End* ran for 85 weeks, providing guaranteed employment in uncertain economic times. Moreover, during the course of the run, he progressed into bigger parts. Toward the end of the run, in May 1937, he was awarded the major role (at the rate of $50 per week) of Gimpty, the frustrated architect—a slightly altered, more romantic version of the role would be portrayed by Joel McCrea in the film.

After *Dead End* finished its run in the spring of 1937, it was time for Duryea to find other parts, but Broadway has a habit of not responding right away, so he joined the Westport Country Playhouse for *Retreat from Folly*. It starred Margaret Anglin, a theatrical diva of her time, who might have given the impressionable Duryea some valuable lessons on how *not* to behave on the set. Anglin was a star who liked to lord it over those around her, including fellow actors, the director, and not least of all, the writer. She did a lot of unauthorized revising of the text—so much so that according to a not-so-admiring reviewer, the line "I don't think I can stand much more" acquired a double meaning. Duryea followed this unfortunate experience with *Lysistrata* and *The Virginian*, starring Henry Fonda, an Omaha Playhouse alumnus, and a role in *The Petrified Forest*— alas, not as the infamous Duke Mantee, but in the lesser role of Commander Klepp.

Duryea was able to make it back to Broadway in October 1937 with the play *Many Mansions*, as Bob Edwards, a young crusader in a play that could be seen as an indictment of the present-day Catholic Church. Duryea's rendition was well-received in a play that ran for only 157 performances, closing in March 1938. From there, another stint at the Westport County Playhouse for Sidney Howard's play *Ned McCobb's Daughter*. In a cast that included Mildred Natwick and Van Heflin, Duryea was featured as George Callahan, the shiftless husband of Natwick's Carrie. It was a role that earned him some good notices; one critic said he "brings out all the slime" in his character.

Another person who took notice of young Duryea's skills was the playwright Elizabeth Ginty, who had written an upcoming Broadway play about Jesse James called *Missouri Legend*, to be produced by Guthrie McClintic. Ginty was impressed by Duryea and brought him to the attention of McClintic, who proceeded to cast him as Bob Ford ("the dirty little coward who shot Mr. Howard and laid Jesse James in his grave"). *Missouri Legend* starred Dean Jagger as a respectful Jesse James, only robbing banks because of that darned government and the Civil War; featured among the cast were notables and future notables such as Dorothy Gish, Jose Ferrer, Karl Malden, and Duryea's wife from *Ned McCobb*, Mildred Natwick. The play opened in September 1938, garnering mixed reviews but Duryea acquired plenty of positive attention for his role as Bob Ford. Brooks Atkinson of the *New York Times* wrote that "Duryea plays a treacherous tinhorn with horrible validity," while Ward Morehouse of the *New York Sun* honored Duryea (after the play's closing on October 29) for his valiant service in the production.

Fortunately, Duryea didn't stay idle for long; his turn as Bob Ford earned him the chance to audition for producer/director Herman Shumlin's latest production, Lillian Hellman's play concerning greed in the old South, *The Little Foxes*. Hellman's play about the Hubbard clan, a family that profited from the South's misfortunes during the Civil War and is now primed to add to their substantial fortunes (through subterfuge and undercutting the competition by paying their workers substantially less than their competitors—sadly, it's a play that never dates), already had a sterling cast. Tallulah Bankhead led the players as Regina Giddens, a Hubbard at heart though married to the town's leading banker, Horace Giddens (Frank Conroy). Charles Dingle was Ben Hubbard, the craftiest Hubbard brother—although ultimately no match for Regina, he remains good-natured about it. Carl Benton Reid was Oscar, Ben's staid but venal brother, seemingly concerned for his son Leo's fortunes, but really looking out for number one, much to the despair of his long-suffering wife, Birdie (Patricia Collinge). Into this nest of vipers, Duryea found himself cast as Oscar's son Leo, a scheming, cowardly, would-be ladies' man bank teller who nevertheless sets the plot in motion when he intimates that he can secure the "loan" of some bonds (integral for the Hubbards' nefarious schemes) by surreptitiously swiping them from the decent, long-suffering Horace Giddens's safe deposit box.

Duryea knew how lucky he was to have scored this role alongside such august company as Shumlin, Hellman, and Bankhead. In 1965, when he was working on *Flight of the Phoenix*, he would pause to reflect on his good fortune with *The Little Foxes*: "I wish I could once again have Hellman's words come out of my mouth. I haven't had words like those, or scenes like those, since then. Tallulah is fantastically the greatest woman I've ever known. The stamina she had to go through this every night. That is top quality . . ."

When *The Little Foxes* opened on Broadway, on February 15, 1939, the play received rave reviews, not only for Hellman's searing indictment of greed and capitalism and Shumlin's taut direction, but also for the flawless acting. Bankhead received her fair share of praise for her withering depiction of Regina, as did other members of the Hubbard clan; Patricia Collinge received some particularly strong notices as the kindly but addled Birdie. Duryea was not lost among the praise for the predators; he received a number of fine reviews for his "smooth, telling portrayal" of a "swinish adolescent." Duryea stayed with the show for the entire Broadway run, followed by a post-Broadway tour, including stops in Pittsburgh, Maryland, and Boston. On one of these stops, he received a letter from Elizabeth Ginty, his *Missouri Legend* benefactor, who praised him while "wondering if you'll ever play a nice guy again."

All kinds of people took notice of Duryea's uncanny skill in believably bringing to life such a contemptible character, so much so that the line between acting and real life would become constantly blurred. Duryea noted that while "Carl [Benton Reid as Oscar, Leo's father] and I shared the same dressing room, there was nothing admirable about the character Carl depicted but people were civil to him, whereas I was regarded with complete aversion." In an interview with powerful columnist Hedda Hopper (with whom Duryea subsequently developed a long-standing friendship), he remarked that people would come backstage to see Tallulah Bankhead and "when they looked at me, I could see the loathing in their eyes. They thought I was a heel in actuality. I was both surprised and gratified by their attitude." Surprised and gratified . . . Duryea knew he had made an indelible impression—but was it the kind of role he truly wanted to be identified with, perhaps forever? He confessed to having some misgivings, saying to interviewers at the time: "I hope I don't get too identified with this type of role . . . after all, you know it's only a part you play, you know you really aren't that way, but after a while you begin to wonder." This was in spite of Duryea's lifelong belief in the art and artifice of acting; he didn't think an actor should really lose himself in a role. He maintained that one can't get away from the fact "you're still someone else although you're putting everything you've got into a role."

It was only natural that a success such as *The Little Foxes*, with its year-long run on Broadway, and subsequent yearlong tour, would attract the attention of Hollywood heavyweights. Samuel Goldwyn, prestigious producer of such classics as *Dead End* and *Wuthering Heights*, bought the rights to the play, engaging the services of William Wyler, the director of those highly regarded films. Furthermore, it was decided that most of the cast would make the transition to film as well: Carl Benton Reid, Charles Dingle, Patricia Collinge, and Duryea himself were all contracted to recreate their stage roles. Teresa Wright was hired to play Regina's daughter Alexandra, as Goldwyn had been impressed with her work onstage in *Life With Father*. Of the other major players, only Tallulah Bankhead and Frank Conroy were not signed; the role of earnest hubby Horace would be taken by Herbert Marshall. Meanwhile, Miriam Hopkins had been courted by Goldwyn for the coveted part of Regina, but Wyler was adamant about not working with her again (after his travails with Hopkins's diva-esque behavior on the 1936 film *These Three*), so Goldwyn successfully borrowed Bette Davis from Warner Bros., thereby reuniting the potent combination of Davis, Marshall, and Wyler from the 1940 classic *The Letter*. The young Dan Duryea couldn't have asked for better conditions with which to make his big-screen debut.

CHAPTER 3

Studio to Studio, Finding His Footing

WITH THE SCREEN VERSION OF *THE LITTLE FOXES*, DURYEA HAD AN opportunity that most actors could only dream about: to make his official screen debut in a prestige film from one of Hollywood's most powerful producers, directed by one of its most respected artists, and with most of his major scenes among players with whom he had already established an easy rapport, not to mention a sense of intimacy. Although Bette Davis was the most prominent new cast member, Duryea would remember her as "a great gal. She felt in her heart that Tallulah Bankhead should do the movie, but Bette was a movie personality. I said to her I felt shy about doing a picture with her. She said, 'How do you think I feel playing with you? You've done the play on Broadway and know so much more about it than I do.'"

In spite of this mutual admiration, the movie itself did not have the smoothest of shooting schedules. The main trouble stemmed from a clash of wills between Bette Davis and William Wyler. Davis hadn't seen the Broadway production and Wyler insisted, perhaps foolishly in retrospect, that she should. After having seen it, it appears that Davis agreed with Bankhead's interpretation of Regina as a ruthless, conniving schemer who practically wore her venality on her sleeves; Wyler agreed with the conniving part, but argued that Regina should be more charming and feminine, as befitting a Southern belle who has a certain way with men. This clash would never fully be resolved, leaving both parties dissatisfied. Wyler would later lament that he never quite got the performance he wanted; Davis would say it was one of her unhappiest experiences, confident that she had never really nailed Regina. She either came to believe that Bankhead's interpretation was the only correct one, or that, having seen Bankhead's interpretation, she strove to create something different.

Looking at the film seventy years later, one thing becomes clear: neither Davis nor Wyler had anything to regret concerning their version of *The Little Foxes*. Davis's Regina may be a compromise between her vision and Wyler's, but what a splendidly realized compromise it is. She manages to convincingly portray a most unholy blend of feminine charm, thwarted ambitions, and heartless scheming, with the occasional nod toward parental concern. Hellman's writing might verge on the melodramatic, but Davis's interpretation is suitably grounded and makes for compelling viewing. As for Wyler, the inability to engage and control his headstrong star ultimately led to a rift between them; they would never work together again. Even so, Wyler's direction is assured and fluid throughout, eliciting fine, restrained interpretations from all (which could have been a problem considering that most of the actors had been portraying these characters on stage for two years), while bringing out the meaning and occasional irony in Hellman's text. The pacing and camerawork, combined with the opulence of the settings (this was after all, a Goldwyn production), helped create the illusion that one is not seeing just another filmed play.

As for Duryea, the character of Leo was perhaps one of the biggest beneficiaries in *The Little Foxes'* move from stage to screen. In the stage version, the action takes place all on a single set; it is certainly a well-utilized set, but a one-setting play it is. Hellman's screenplay creates new scenes that take the play beyond the realm of Regina's home. There is a sequence involving a train trip for Regina's daughter Alexandra (Teresa Wright) to bring home her ailing father; and, more important, for Leo (and for Duryea), there are now a number of scenes at the bank, where we see Leo's character in all his scheming, albeit dimwitted, glory. In the film version, and in Duryea's skillful rendition of the part, everyone is on to the shiftless Leo, although he thinks he's putting something over on everybody else. Leo's father, Oscar, admonishes him for his laziness and tardiness; upon his arrival at his Uncle Horace's bank, Duryea's Leo is all smiles and glad-handing, while the bank manager sternly advises him to "try to put in a good day's work—*all* day."

Later in the movie, after Leo has "borrowed" Horace's bonds from his safe-deposit box to finance Ben and Oscar's unsavory business dealings (thereby excluding Regina, who cannot raise her share due to resistance from Horace), he is unsettled by Horace's inopportune return to the office—and his request to see "the box." Duryea brilliantly conveys Leo's immediate discomfort, his transparency (as when he purports to have interrupted Horace by claiming he's concerned with the actions of another employee), as well as his relief when he believes Horace is putting the box away (little does he realize that his delaying tactics have caused Horace to remember to go through "the box"). After Duryea departs the office, Herbert Marshall's Horace remarks that perhaps Leo was hazy on his facts, while a colleague responds, "It ain't the facts that's hazy, it's Leo." Duryea plays this new scene for maximum impact, creating the template for his seemingly self-confident conniver, superficially charming and repugnant at the same time—and one whose actions and motivations fool practically no one.

In one of Wyler and Hellman's most talked-about departures from the play, a pivotal scene between Oscar and Leo takes place within the cramped confines of their bathroom, as opposed to Regina's spacious living quarters. Oscar is concerned because he and Ben haven't managed to acquire the necessary funds for their unscrupulous financial scheme. Leo has sauntered into the bathroom, a little worse for wear; both are shaving (Duryea had to learn how to shave with a single-edged razor for this scene) in their respective mirrors. As filmed, Oscar is facing the viewer while Leo is framed by his reflection. Leo is prattling on about their lack of funds—Horace's $90,000 in unused bonds which are languishing in his safe deposit box—and what he would do if *he* had all that money. When Oscar (a subtle, quietly lethal Carl Benton Reid) asks Leo how he knows about the bonds, Duryea's Leo moves seamlessly from glib and boastful at having seen the bonds, to quivering and outright defensive about how he saw them ("it was the other boys, I—I just went along—word of honor!"), before finally, after being prodded by his father, admitting that he alone looked into Uncle Horace's box. As Duryea plays Leo, there is a degree of self-awareness on his part; when asked if Horace would give him the bonds, he responds with a chortle, "Lend *me* the bonds?"

There are other touches that mark Leo as a singular Duryea creation. Watch Duryea as Alexandra remarks she could imagine what Leo could do in a big city and he responds with an ear-to-ear leer, "Oh no, you couldn't!" (As written, perhaps Leo has one saving grace, and that's his refusal to be goaded into an affair with his unwilling cousin Alexandra—though it's probably not scruples, but instead the fact he doesn't find her attractive). See him twirling about in Horace's wheelchair as Horace quite probably lies dying. Watch how he looks through a box of cigars, carefully choosing one that will make him a full-fledged member of the vipers' den. In the end, watch Duryea's reaction as Leo hastily plans to betray them if and when he is flung out to dry—followed by Ben's smashing of that carefully chosen cigar right in Leo's face.

A future colleague of Duryea's, Patricia Morrow, who would play Duryea's daughter in the popular television drama *Peyton Place*, was well acquainted with Duryea's special abilities, especially the way he could use his voice. Duryea could pitch it lower, and be equally effective whether he was projecting compassion or menace, and he was also quite expert at pitching it a little higher. Morrow explains, "Dan could pitch it . . . his voice could be one note above his speaking voice, and this made his character a little slippery. Just pitching it one note higher made his character a little more shallow." If one views Duryea's Leo closely, as he is wheeling and dealing, unsuccessfully attempting to project cleverness while trying to stake his claim to some Hubbard riches, one can see the template on which Duryea would build on, and which would come into use again and again, right up until the end. Duryea also made reference to his distinctive voice on occasion, as in this comment to an interviewer in 1965: "Take my voice. It's too high but that highness in some way makes me more mysterious, even malevolent to the public. It can't quite fathom me or what my motives are."

Duryea's sniveling, malicious, cowardly Leo proved to be quite popular with reviewers and audiences. One reviewer's opinion reflected many others when he remarked that "it would be difficult to conceive of a more interesting performance than Duryea's as the weakling son who embezzles at the suggestion of his corrupt father." In terms of Duryea's impact on film audiences, as with stage audiences, they both hated him and loved to hate him. He made such an indelible impression that the audiences didn't know—or didn't want to know—that off the screen, Duryea was a devoted husband and recent, proud father. Five years after her miscarriage, Helen had given birth to Peter in July 1939, finally providing Duryea with the chance to be the family man he had always wanted to be. Duryea's onstage aunt, Tallulah Bankhead, as fond of Dan as he was of her, would be Peter's godmother, giving Peter a large silver engraved cup to celebrate the event. (According to Peter's brother, Richard, Peter would give this same silver cup to Richard's son Derrian.)

Matters were improving on the professional front as well. While a working Broadway actor could sometimes wait months until his next engagement, a screen actor's fortunes could rapidly accelerate, particularly if a certain powerful producer took an interest. Samuel Goldwyn was so impressed with Duryea that he signed the actor to a term contract.

His first assignment was in another film that has since acquired "classic" status, a comedy called *Ball of Fire* (it's hard to fault Goldwyn for his taste during this time). It was to be directed by Howard Hawks, who had presided over the madcap antics of *Bringing Up Baby* and *His Girl Friday*. The writers were none other than Charles Brackett and his screenwriting partner, Billy Wilder, the latter of whom would soon be directing his own screenplays. And in a cast that included Gary Cooper as Professor Bertram Potts, Barbara Stanwyck as Sugarpuss O'Shea, and Dana Andrews as head gangster Joe Lilac, Dan Duryea was given a plum supporting part as Lilac's chief henchman, Duke Pastrami (as I've said before, this was a comedy).

The premise of *Ball of Fire* is a 1940s riff on *Snow White and the Seven Dwarfs*, with the seven dwarfs consisting of Gary Cooper and his fellow sheltered academics (among them Richard Haydn and Henry Travers) laboring over a dictionary of slang, without ever having ventured into the swinging, beboppin' modern world. Snow White is in the form of Stanwyck's Sugarpuss, a nightclub singer seeking shelter (unwillingly at first) from both the law and Big Bad Joe Lilac, who wants to marry Sugarpuss to keep her quiet about his unsavory underworld affairs. However, since this is a romantic comedy, Stanwyck and the lanky, goofy Cooper slowly become enamored of each other, while the other professors look on in an ultimately approving manner.

Where does this leave Duryea's Pastrami? He is featured in one of the film's most memorable scenes, as Pastami and his fellow henchman hold the professors hostage in their own study in order to keep them from interfering with his boss Lilac's wedding plans. Pastrami's cat-and-mouse game with the professors, as they contrive to have the sword of Damocles (in the form of a loosely hanging painting) fall on his head is both amusing and mildly suspenseful. Apart from this sequence, Duryea is both funny and menacing throughout. He adeptly delivers dialogue that wouldn't be out of place coming from a Damon Runyon gangster ("He gets more bang out of you than any dame I ever knew"; "Stay close to the Ameche!"), all the while managing to be somewhat likable—at least until Pastrami uses the professors for some William Tell-like target practice. Duryea also was a willing student, as Stanwyck and Cooper were both extremely solicitous toward the newcomer, offering sage advice about film technique and career options—and even the occasional line delivery. Duryea would work with both of them again—one much sooner—and frequently acknowledge their guidance.

It's not too surprising that *Ball of Fire* would receive some terrific reviews, and amidst the star wattage of Cooper and Stanwyck, Duryea received some good notices in praise of his skills at comedy. However gratifying the notices were, along with Goldwyn's interest in advancing Duryea's career, Duryea was nonetheless more than a little concerned about the direction his career was heading. He didn't want to be typecast as a heavy, but those were the only kinds of roles Goldwyn was assigning him. To a columnist at the time, Duryea said, "I told Goldwyn I wanted to stop being repulsive, let me get some sympathy." Goldwyn attempted to assuage Duryea by considering him for a role as a columnist in an upcoming movie.

Goldwyn's offering turned out to be another prestigious film, the famous biography of Lou Gehrig, *Pride of the Yankees*, directed by Sam Wood. In this idealized version of Gehrig's life Gary Cooper would star as the baseball great who ultimately succumbed to the debilitating disease that would later bear his name, then known under the clinical term "amyotrophic lateral sclerosis." In this somewhat fanciful rendition of Gehrig's life, his meddling family urges him to quit dreaming about baseball, and instead become an engineer. In truth, the way Gehrig plays baseball (at least as portrayed by Cooper), he might have done better to become an engineer. Yet this is Hollywood, and if everyone says Cooper's Gehrig plays the hell out of the ball, you can bet it will appear that way (thanks to the magic of cutaways and reaction shots).

As for the rest of the cast, Teresa Wright (also a Goldwyn contract player after *The Little Foxes*) would portray Gehrig's supportive wife, Eleanor, while frequent Cooper costar Walter Brennan (they had been teamed in Frank Capra's *Meet John Doe* and for Goldwyn in William Wyler's *The Westerner*) was cast as a sagacious newspaper columnist. Duryea shared many of his scenes with Brennan as his fellow sportswriter, both likable and cynical, with Duryea playing the naysayer opposite Brennan's experienced, perceptive, and somewhat optimistic reporter. Duryea delivers his lines with an appropriate edge, as in his remark after an early Cooper/Gehrig stumble: "You ought to have a nurse around." He and Brennan make for congenial colleagues, and near the end, Duryea expertly portrays the columnist's growing (albeit grudging) respect for Gehrig.

Duryea's success in these showy supporting roles coincided with an increasing sense of fulfillment in his family life. Shortly after Duryea made the move from Broadway to Hollywood, the Duryeas bought a house overlooking the San Fernando Valley, 7621 Mulholland Drive. It was a two-story Mediterranean-style house with commanding views on both sides. There was also enough property—five acres—so that Dan could indulge his interests in flowers and gardening, as well as carpentry. As for Duryea's family, there would be cause for more celebration; in July 1942, Helen gave Duryea a second son, Richard. When Dan wasn't at the studio or on location, he was generally at home with his wife and young sons.

These were difficult times, as World War II was raging abroad, and the United States had recently entered the fighting. Many Hollywood actors (Clark Gable and Tyrone Power, to name a few) either enlisted or found themselves drafted. Those who didn't or couldn't enlist (Duryea had been classified 4F) found other ways to serve, whether it was through acting in the escapist and patriotic films that were created during this time, or through contributing their time and energies in different ways. Duryea had obtained a degree of freedom when, quite unexpectedly, Goldwyn didn't renew Duryea's contract. It's hard to understand why, since Duryea had been so impressive in his debut and hadn't disgraced himself in his next two Goldwyn productions. It's quite possible that other Goldwyn stars, like Dana Andrews and David Niven, were monopolizing Goldwyn's attention, or perhaps Duryea didn't fit into Goldwyn's plans (Goldwyn tended to sign troubled, sincere types like Andrews and Farley Granger). Whatever the reason, his release gave Dan the opportunity to offer his talents elsewhere, and he managed to find receptive bidders. In this way, Duryea was somewhat able to do his duty by acting in films that either promoted the war effort or provided an escape from the war in a reasonably entertaining manner.

It's regrettable that Duryea's first film away from Goldwyn did neither. 1942's *That Other Woman*, which Duryea made for 20th Century Fox, might charitably be called a lame attempt at a screwball comedy. Directed by Ray McCarey (Leo McCarey's younger brother), the film is one of those inane concoctions wherein the womanizing boss (James Ellison) neglects his very attractive, long-suffering secretary (Virginia Gilmore) who is in turn pursued by an earnest, if heavy-handed suitor (an uneasy Dan Duryea in the Ralph Bellamy role). There is not much one can say about this fatuous so-called romp except that the pace is leaden, the lines land with a thud, and Ellison is perhaps one of the more charmless leads to have graced a production of this sort. While Gilmore gives it the old college try, Ellison remains so clueless that one wonders why she bothers. As for Duryea, he seems uncomfortable much of the time, with a middling Southern accent that comes and goes within each scene (accents would never be Duryea's forte). He does get to do some broad comedy and has several well-timed double takes, but in the end *That Other Woman* does everyone in.

Duryea's next film was much better, the wartime classic *Sahara*, released in 1943 by Columbia Pictures. Directed by Zoltan Korda with an all-male cast, the film starred Humphrey Bogart as Lieutenant Joe Rossi, who, cut off from the Allies along with his crew and Lulu Belle, their trusty tank, retreats across the unforgiving desert from advancing Germans, fighting both time and thirst. They encounter some other soldiers along the way—mostly a melting pot of our then-Allies, as well as a few nebulous individuals who may or may not want to sabotage their efforts.

Although Bogart starred as the pragmatic, heroic tank commander, this was an ensemble piece, a "to-the-last-man" saga with all the requisite questions intact: Who will survive? Can these parched, beleaguered soldiers find a rumored well? Will the blistering sun get them before the Germans do? And what about those Germans—aren't they also thirsty? *Sahara*'s cast proved to be an imposing assemblage, comprised of established stars like Bogart and Rex Ingram, sturdy character actors like J. Carrol Naish, and some up-and-comers like Bruce Bennett, Lloyd Bridges, and Duryea himself. Duryea is Bennett and Bogart's pal Jimmy, an affably cynical lad always ready to make a bet on something or other, including whether the tank will move or whether his friend Bennett will make it through the scorching desert to reinforcements. This last bet, which Duryea takes reluctantly, has him remarking to Bennett, "It's a sucker's bet," yet always showing concern for his friend. After the Germans shoot one of Bogart's men while under a flag of truce, Duryea says what must have been on everyone's minds at the time: "You're right, we don't know the Nazis—they did shoot him in the back."

Sahara turned out to be a big hit for Columbia, and Bogart's reluctant tank commander became the exemplar of the brave, resourceful everyman who was forced by circumstances to become a hero. For Duryea, however, the film was a mixed blessing. It provided further proof that his capabilities extended beyond villainy, and he was satisfied with his own work. Indeed, when Duryea started allowing his sons to see his own movies, *Sahara* was the first he would allow them to see. But it bothered Duryea at the time, more than he would let on, that his likable role would go relatively unnoticed by both the critics and the public.

He would reflect later that *"Sahara* is a picture which practically no one remembers my being in . . . one of the pictures I didn't play a heel and maybe for that reason."

Duryea's next role was in another home-front morale-booster, *Man from Frisco.* Directed by Robert Florey for Republic Pictures, the film was inspired by the life of Henry Kaiser, whose notions about prefabricated shipbuilding wound up being a huge asset to the Allied war effort. For this fictionalized version of Kaiser's efforts, Michael O'Shea (who had recently portrayed a brawling Jack London) was borrowed from 20th Century Fox to play the rough-and-tumble Matt Braddock, an engineer who alienates the beloved manager (Gene Lockhart) of a shipbuilding company, its workers, and an entire town when he insists that ships can be made using already constructed pieces. Braddock's innovations don't sit too well with the manager's daughter Diana (Anne Shirley) or his right-hand man Jim Benson (Duryea)—and in true Hollywood fashion, both men are in romantic pursuit of the fair, headstrong Diana.

Complicating matters is the fact that Braddock has arranged for new workers to be transported into town, thus crowding what had been a peaceful village. He also continues to encounter fierce opposition from his workers and the townspeople, all while facing increased pressure from navy brass—particularly the need to hasten production after the attack on Pearl Harbor. Duryea's Jim Benson is caught in the middle, playing a fundamentally good man led momentarily astray, mainly because he suspects his gal is falling for the burly roughneck with grandiose ideas. Duryea is creditable as a disillusioned swain whose gaffe contributes to a disaster on demonstration day. Chastened, he rallies the men to help Braddock's dream become a reality—knowing that he'll lose Diana in the process. It's interesting that in this stage of his career, Duryea would be called upon to engage in romance and redemption, and again, though some reviews were complimentary, the major studios would have different ideas about how to develop Duryea's talents.

A case in point is Duryea's first film for Metro-Goldwyn-Mayer, *Mrs. Parkington*, which was based on a work by Louis Bromfield (whose earlier novel *The Rains Came* became a success for 20th Century Fox in 1939) that originated as a *Cosmopolitan* piece and eventually became a novel. MGM wasted no time in securing the rights as a vehicle for Greer Garson and Walter Pidgeon. Along with Duryea, the cast included a mix of established and up-and-coming talents, including Edward Arnold, Cecil Kellaway, Gladys Cooper, Tom Drake, Hugh Marlowe, and Frances Rafferty, in a plush production directed by Tay Garnett. The story concerns a wealthy family gathering together on Christmas Eve to pay tribute to its erstwhile matriarch (Greer Garson). This privileged family can barely exert the energy to be anything beyond civil to each other; in the opening frames, it's clear that only two are capable of any warmth, the aged Mrs. Parkington herself and her great-granddaughter Jane (Frances Rafferty), who is about to elope with an employee (Tom Drake) at her crooked father's (Edward Arnold) investment firm. News of this development, along with Arnold's questionable financial dealings—which have put the comfort of the family at risk—causes Mrs. Parkington to reflect on her life with her late beloved (albeit short-tempered and rakish) Mr. Parkington (Pidgeon). Most of the film consists of an extended flashback to Garson's tumultuous coming-of-age, marrying the wealthy, uncompromising Parkington, becoming the belle of society, while tolerating her husband's occasional, sometimes flagrant indiscretions.

Duryea's presence, while limited to the film's present-day sections, certainly is felt throughout. As Edward Arnold's son, Duryea exudes an aura of casual disdain over his fellow family members (particularly his father) while he displays a polite regard for his great aunt. Throughout the film, Duryea quietly twirls a pocket watch as the others try to come to grips with the revelation that Arnold's investments may either send him to jail or possibly bankrupt the family. Duryea incorporated this watch-twirling business with the approval of Tay Garnett, communicating an air of disregard and contempt throughout the proceedings. At one point, when asked if his father's difficulties have aroused any feelings of compassion on his part, Duryea can only reply, "You see, Father, I never really liked you." Duryea's languid delivery of this line, accompanied by the twirl of the watch, helps create a memorable character—albeit one limited to a few scenes. This ability to create a great deal out of very little did not go unnoticed; MGM and Tay Garnett will seek Duryea's talents a year later for another lavish Garson epic. In the meantime, an émigré' director named Fritz Lang was about to embark on a screen adaptation of a Graham Greene novel for Universal Pictures. Lang would need someone like Duryea, who could make the maximum impact with minimal screen time; their resulting collaboration would be a landmark in cinema history.

CHAPTER 4

Lang and Duryea—Made for Each Other

FRITZ LANG WAS AMONG THE DIRECTORS WHO MADE HIS NAME IN the cinematic world we now refer to as film noir, although he was a master of the art form long before some critics affixed a sobriquet to it. Lang's *M*, filmed in Lang's homeland of Germany and anchored by Peter Lorre's star-making turn as a pathetic child-murderer, was a harbinger of the darkness soon to engulf American cinema. Not long after Lang and such fellow Hollywood émigrés as Billy Wilder and Edgar G. Ulmer arrived in America, the screens were overtaken by bleak, despairing looks at America, with crime and betrayal at the forefront, and the innocent victimized and hunted down at every turn. Lang built on his earlier success with such films as 1936's *Fury*, starring Spencer Tracy as a happy-go-lucky everyman who gets caught up in mob hysteria, and 1937's *You Only Live Once*, starring Henry Fonda and Sylvia Sidney as a young couple caught up in crime and overwhelmed by bad breaks and some unfortunate choices. By late 1943, Lang had already been given the "star director" treatment at 20th Century Fox, but after hits like *Man Hunt* and some atypical forays into the American West (via *Western Union* and *The Return of Frank James*), Lang would discover he was no longer the golden boy at Fox (reported clashes with some Fox stars such as Henry Fonda may have also contributed to Fox's disillusionment with Lang).

At the same time, Dan Duryea was trying to make some headway within the Hollywood studio system. Duryea had started off with a bang in *The Little Foxes*, but he hadn't yet managed to find a follow-up role that approximated the kind of impact he had made with Leo. The villain roles were pale shadows (although they had earned Duryea some good notices), whereas the comic and kindhearted roles seemed to escape the critics almost entirely.

As it happened, the two men were about to cross paths. Lang was contracted by Paramount Pictures for the film version of the Graham Greene novel *Ministry of Fear*. Aided by a taut script by Seton Miller, and with admirably atmospheric cinematography by Henry Sharp, Lang created a nightmarish thriller set in wartime England. Ray Milland stars as a recently released asylum patient (incarcerated because of his role in the death of his terminally ill wife) who is on his way to London and stops at a carnival, where he wins a contest and a cake. Since this is a tale of intrigue, it doesn't take the intelligent viewer long to realize that the cake was meant for someone else. That someone else happens to be Duryea, cast as a sinister figure (complete with cane) who discovers that, much to his chagrin, this all-important cake has fallen into the "wrong" hands. This being World War II, it doesn't take a physicist to figure out that there is something in that cake besides cake, but newly released Milland drops his guard and lets a blind man take the cake, which leads to all kinds of pursuits, complications, romantic entanglements, and even a séance.

This is where Duryea makes his second appearance in the film; a séance presided over by Hilary Brooke (who enjoyed some success at Paramount before becoming Lou Costello's statuesque foil on *The Abbott and Costello Show*) leads to his apparent demise, which results in Milland being framed and hounded for Duryea's "murder." But it's later in the film that Duryea makes his biggest impact, having "returned from the dead," in a climactic encounter with Milland, when Milland's character, Stephen, unwittingly visits the clothing emporium that bears the name "Travers," only to slowly come to the realization that this "Travers" is the same person he saw both at the carnival and as the eventual "victim" at the séance. Duryea only has a few minutes of screen time, but he makes the most of it, wielding a large pair of shears and calmly informing a customer over the phone that "when you've worn it once, the garment will settle," a line delivered in a perfectly smooth manner that also hints at the nature of the seemingly ill-fitting garment (i.e., the microfilm embedded within). Once Duryea's Travers takes stock of Milland, he flees into the backroom, after which Milland finds Travers impaled by his own monstrous scissors.

Duryea was always proud of his ability to do a great deal with relatively small roles. His exquisitely timed appearances in *Ministry of Fear* contribute to the sense that he has a much larger role. From the intensity of his initial entrance to his unctuous pleasantries delivered at the sé-ance, through to his final deserved demise, Duryea creates a character that stays in the mind and belies his limited screen time. The critics, such as the reviewer at the *Hollywood Reporter*, found that Duryea "comes through with one of his excellent characterizations." More important, director Lang was enamored of Duryea, collaborating with the actor in finding new bits of business. Lang expressed disappointment with the movie itself in several subsequent interviews (one should note that Lang was perhaps his own harshest critic and rarely found anything to praise in his own work), but held that Duryea's handling of the role (to say nothing of the scissors) was exceptional. Moreover, Lang left Duryea with the distinct impression that he would direct him again—and soon.

Simultaneously, over at RKO, the playwright Clifford Odets, known for his hard-hitting, occasionally sentimental forays into the small victories and huge hardships endured by the ordinary working class, had adapted the Richard Llelewyn novel *None but the Lonely Heart*, whose main characters were London counterparts to those depicted in Odets's stage work. RKO studio head Charles Koerner had bought the rights for Cary Grant and considered several potential directors (including Alfred Hitchcock) before handing over the reins to Odets himself. It was the first film Odets directed, and he had a distinguished cast at his disposal. Grant, in a departure from his smooth, assured romantic leads, was the itinerant Cockney dreamer Ernie Mott, wishing to better himself in a ravaged London, hoping not to disappoint his loyal mum (a superb Ethel Barrymore) while becoming entangled with the underworld. Jane Wyatt and June Dupree were the two women (good and shady, respectively) in Grant's life—this isn't a customary romantic comedy for Grant but he still has his pick of the ladies—while Barry Fitzgerald was his boozy confidant and George Coulouris was a prominent member of London's underbelly.

Where does Duryea fit in all of this? Certainly not as a shady member of London's gangland; rather, he was cast as Lew Tate, co-owner (along with his mum) of Tate's Fish Shop. It was not a role that Duryea would have wanted to include in his highlight reel, should anyone have asked. For one thing, accents were still not Duryea's strong suit. In fact, the Cockney accent that Duryea employs as the friendly yet wary Tate is a little jarring and would probably not be out of place in a miscast high school production of *Oliver*. Consequently, his admiration of Ernie's ill-gotten gains, clouded by a degree of suspicion as he urges Ernie to "be safe," comes across as callow and insincere.

Duryea's unsteady accent and fleeting appearances resulted in little career damage; elsewhere, amidst the doom and gloom that pervaded *None but the Lonely Heart*, there was plenty for reviewers to praise. Grant received some of his best reviews for his earnest playing in the atypical role of Ernie, eventually receiving his second (and final) Oscar nomination, while Barrymore won a Best Supporting Actress Oscar as Ernie's loving, long-suffering mum. Odets's work on *None but the Lonely Heart* also garnered a great deal of praise, as the movie itself was nominated for Best Picture. Despite the almost-universal acclaim, Odets wouldn't direct a picture for another fifteen years, with the 1959 courtroom drama *The Story on Page One*, starring Rita Hayworth, who was beyond her prime but still potent. As for Duryea, he was lucky that his personal Cockney calamity was barely noticed, since he was ready for a movie that played to his strengths.

Fortunately, Lang meant it when he said he wanted to use Duryea again in all due haste. Lang was to direct the film version of J. H. Wallis's novel *Once off Guard*, which had been adapted by writer/producer Nunnally Johnson and became known as *The Woman in the Window*. Edward G. Robinson is Richard Wanley, an erudite, married law professor whose wife has deserted him for the summer (to the country, with the children). After an evening of drink and merriment with two friends at their genteel club, during which Wanley rails against the staid solemnity of middle-age malaise, he has a chance meeting with Alice Reed (Joan Bennett, in a role that Merle Oberon had been seriously considered for), the "woman in the window," or, rather, the model whose portrait he has admired. This encounter, followed by a platonic date and late-night cocktail—in Alice's apartment—is spoiled by the untimely arrival of her violent so-called lover, Claude Mazzard, whom Wanley dispatches in self-defense with a pair of scissors supplied by Alice. Wanley, afraid of being implicated in what at the very least would be a scandal (and, at the worst, pre-meditated murder), convinces Alice to help him dispose of the body, presumably preserving both their freedom and respectability. This sequence, with the milquetoast Wanley taking charge, dragging the body, and then trying to transport it, is nimbly enacted by Robinson and directed for maximum tension (laced with dark humor) by Lang. The way Robinson, Johnson, and Lang present it, Wanley seems to be almost unconsciously seeking to incriminate himself, as when he drives Mazzard's corpse around in a car with a headlight out, attracting the attention of a motorcycle officer. But all ends well, at least temporarily, as Wanley and Alice make a pact never to see each other again.

Yet since this is film noir, we can't help but observe the noose slowly tightening. The newspapers report there is a missing millionaire who bears a striking resemblance to the man Wanley killed, followed by the discovery of the body (by proud Boy Scout Spanky McFarlane, late of the Little Rascals). Wanley's good friend, a district attorney (Raymond Massey), invites him to the crime scene, where Wanley walks unguided in the direction of the site of the corpus delicti. This leads to an amused reaction from Inspector Jackson (played by Thomas Jackson, fifteen years after playing the relentless policeman who hounded Robinson's Rico Bandello in *Little Caesar*), who remarks, "Professor, eh? You think we ought to look into this?" He then goes on to assure Wanley that the police "rarely arrest people for knowing where the body was." Still, one notices that Massey's character is intrigued but not concerned, while Robinson's Wanley can barely contain his anxiety.

Enter Duryea as the inevitable blackmailer—by design, in more ways than one. Lang was undeniably impressed with Duryea's devilry in *Ministry of Fear*. Having already cast Robinson and Bennett in two lead roles, Lang wanted to incorporate a younger cast member who would be able to keep pace with the veteran performers (as well as add a bit of box-office insurance). In *Ministry of Fear*, Duryea had to make his presence felt with limited footage spread throughout the film, but here he makes his first entrance after more than an hour and then dominates the movie for its remaining thirty minutes. As the ill-fated Mazzard's bodyguard and chauffeur, Duryea knocks on Alice's apartment door, threatening to go to the police, equipped with a confident smile that says he knows what he's getting into. Sizing up Bennett (a good match for Duryea as an actor, even if her character is no match in the treachery department), he casually mocks everything she says with a "Come now, Miss Reed," and proceeds to go through her apartment with a calm assurance, as if he had done this many times in the past. He is first bothered by such things as the absence of fingerprints (as he says, "even in places where they would normally be") and then by the discovery of some items belonging to Wanley. He makes his demand of $5,000 sound like he's doing her a favor: "You're a lot better off dealing with me than the homicide squad." Later, he brazenly attempts to elicit a degree of understanding by insisting she's "gotta look at it my way, don't you see."

It's during these encounters with Bennett that the Duryea persona, or at least the one most familiar to audiences, critics, and movie executives, takes hold: the patented confidence, the smoothly malevolent tone that exudes both insolence and insinuation, and a fondness for women that both alleviates and fuels his baser impulses. When Duryea returns for his money, he is offered a lesser amount—just enough for him to think that someone else is pulling her strings. In spite of this (and this is where his not-so-pure romantic tendencies take over), Duryea offers to take Bennett away with him and free her from her indebtedness—provided she come along. It's to Duryea's credit that he makes this offer seem almost magnanimous. Unbeknownst to Duryea, however, Bennett's character has conspired with Wanley to rid themselves of the blackmailer through a poison-laced drink. Her insistence that Duryea take the drink reveals her intentions, resulting in Duryea's sudden flash of temper followed by a vigorous search of the premises. Duryea's recovery of the pocket watch bearing Mazzard's initials "CM" leads to a memorable Duryea line: "You . . . *amateurs!*" The line is delivered with a perfect disdainful tone. Unfortunately, this also means the presumably romantic getaway is canceled, as well as any attempts to gain mercy from Duryea. He verbally and physically pummels Bennett, and informs her he'll be back for even more money tomorrow.

For those unfamiliar with *The Woman in the Window*, the hurried remaining scenes lead to a major twist that has divided audiences and critics alike: the revelation at the end that the events of the evening (following Wanley's night out with "the boys") have all been a dream. Critics have said this ending greatly diminishes the impact of all that has gone before, as the inhabitants of the "dream" turn out to be previously unseen employees of the gentlemen's club. Lang, however, said that he insisted on this ending (over Johnson's strenuous objections), that Robinson's character shouldn't be punished for being "once off guard." Despite the coda's inclusion, *The Woman in the Window* remains a thoroughly entertaining drama that easily sustains repeated viewings, and Duryea's sly malevolence was no small factor in the film's success and enduring appeal.

Before Duryea could reunite with Lang for a third and final time, there would be a number of relatively minor films that would utilize his presence without fully realizing his talents. MGM's *Main Street After Dark* is the first of six Duryea films released in 1945—and a strong contender for the nadir of Duryea's screen career. Written by Karl Lamb and John Higgins and directed by Edward Cahn, it was one of these "Crime Does Not Pay" films that MGM kept churning out in the 1940s. These were cautionary tales that would let you know what would happen if you (or a loved one) turned to a life of crime. The big difference is that most of the earlier films were shorts, twenty minutes in length, and occasionally padded at that, while *Main Street After Dark* somehow stretched its way out to fifty-seven minutes, and a fairly long almost-hour it is. With working titles such as *Telltale Hands* and *Paddy Rollers*, *Main Street After Dark* relates the story of the Dibson clan, a family of pickpockets in a small town that serves as a departure point for servicemen. The Dibsons are awaiting the arrival of the eldest son, Lefty, after his release from prison. Ma (Selena Royle) would like Lefty to pick up where he left off, while she fends off the entreaties of a local pawnshop owner (and stealth underworld mastermind) Hume Cronyn, who is pressuring Ma into purchasing some of his guns, presumably for illegal use. Edward Arnold is a dedicated, crafty police inspector who tries to discourage Lefty from resuming his life of crime by implying a dark future for him and his siblings, Rosalie and Posey. Only Arnold is too late; Lefty is already planning a theft far beyond the pesky and petty profession of pickpocketing.

In a scenario like this, one might think Duryea would make a perfect Lefty; instead, Lefty was assigned to the colorless, charmless Tom Trout. Duryea was relegated to the comparatively unrewarding role of the whining younger brother, Posey, who, with the help of Lefty's wife, Jessie (Audrey Totter), robs a few servicemen and sets in motion the events that will eventually spell doom for the Dibson clan, and for Duryea's unfortunate Posey in particular, courtesy of a misplaced, fatal bullet fired in the struggle between Inspector Arnold and Lefty. Thus ends this insistently moralizing endeavor, and not a moment too soon.

If Duryea was looking to escape the weakling roles and low-budget efforts, you wouldn't know it from his next film. *The Great Flamarion* features Duryea as an alcoholic former dancer who works alongside his faithless wife (Mary Beth Hughes) and a sharpshooter (Erich von Stroheim, twenty years after *Greed* and a few years before *Sunset Boulevard*). The movie, mostly told in flashback by a dying von Stroheim, shows what happens when the sharpshooting Flamarion (von Stroheim) develops an insatiable obsession with Duryea's wife—a fixation so complete that it leads Flamarion to contemplate murder. And since this was made in the very noir 1940s, murder ceases to be mere contemplation and eventually becomes reality that assures tragedy for all of the major characters.

The Great Flamarion is among Duryea's more visible efforts because it fell into the public domain when the original copyright lapsed (as did several noirs of the period, including *DOA* and *The Strange Love of Martha Ivers*). One can surmise that director Anthony Mann would have been unhappy with this increased visibility for *Flamarion*, since he has gone on record in interviews as saying there is very little of value here. Despite Mann's displeasure with the end result, there is a lot to enjoy in this not-altogether *Great Flamarion*. For one, von Stroheim seizes the part of Flamarion with a blend of bravado and melancholy, and retains the audience's sympathy, even after being caught up in Hughes's machinations. For her part, Hughes is fine as the femme fatale—perhaps a little too obvious, but at that time, what femme fatale wasn't (except to the chumps they manipulated)? This brings us to Duryea himself, as Hughes's soon-to-be "late" husband. Unsteady on his feet, battling alcohol and the wavering affections of his wife, Duryea is credible throughout, whether threatening Hughes if she leaves him (a threat she doesn't take at all seriously) or sharing a tense scene with von Stroheim in which Duryea declares, "The Wallaces stick together." The movie, in spite of some narrative lapses (such as the dying von Stroheim relaying events he could not possibly have been aware of), sustains interest throughout. *The Great Flamarion* is certainly not prime noir by any means, but even Mann later admitted that one good thing had come out of it: the chance to work with Duryea, whom Mann would grow to admire and would use in two later films. On both these occasions, Duryea would deliver memorable—and very different—characterizations.

After this journey down poverty row, Duryea's return to MGM would put him in the midst of some pretty good company. He would appear in the period romance *The Valley of Decision*, again under the direction of Tay Garnett and starring the lovely Greer Garson. This time, however, the male lead was not the inestimable Walter Pidgeon, but the rising star Gregory Peck, borrowed from 20th Century Fox for the occasion. The movie itself came to represent what might have been the Garson template for box-office and critical success, as it was based on a popular novel (in this case, by Marcia Davenport), fortified by a sterling cast (including Lionel Barrymore, Donald Crisp, Reginald Owen, and a young Jessica Tandy), with a plot that combines narrative sweep with a poignant romance. Set among the mills of 1873 Pittsburgh, Garson is Mary Rafferty, an Irish immigrant living with her bitter father (Barrymore, playing to the balcony), who has become wheelchair-bound because of an accident at the mills. Not unexpectedly, Mary causes some grief within her family by taking a job as a maid at the home of the mill owner Scott (the always excellent Donald Crisp). Yet before long, Mary has managed to endear herself to key members of the Scott family—namely, the father, his wife, Clarissa (Gladys Cooper), daughter Constance (Marsha Hunt), and especially son Paul (Peck), a man of ideas who plans to modernize the mill.

A romance develops, and naturally it cannot be consummated because Mary doesn't think it would be right, given their respective backgrounds. Concurrently, family friend and romantic rival Louise Kane (a pitch-perfect Jessica Tandy) takes every opportunity to cast a steely glance and a tart remark towards Mary, whom the glacially cool Louise perceives to be a tart on the make.

While Duryea stands on the periphery of the romantic sections (as his character has an all-consuming interest in business—or, rather, money), he does have effective moments throughout, playing an instrumental role in the unfolding events (rather than being a passive, caustic observer, as in *Mrs. Parkington*). Duryea's role is that of William, Jr., one of Scott's other sons (the third being the weak-willed, alcoholic Ted, played by Marshall Thompson). In stark contrast to Paul's idealism regarding both the mill and the poorly treated workers, Duryea's pragmatic William contrives (unsuccessfully) to sell the mill to the highest bidder. After the workers begin their long strike, William hires a gang of thugs to act as strikebreakers—in direct opposition to the peacemaking efforts of Paul, Mary, and an acquiescent Scott. As a result of Duryea's misbegotten actions, bloodshed ensues, and what might have been a tenuous peace is shattered—at least for a time. Mary distances herself from the Scotts, especially Paul, leaving the field clear for the predatory Kane to get her hooks into Paul.

Years pass, and Paul has sired a young son (Dean Stockwell) while growing increasingly discontented with Louise, who realizes (not inaccurately) that his heart will always be with Mary. Meanwhile, Paul's mother has also never lost her affection for Mary, and soon after their scene of reconciliation (exquisitely played by Garson and Gladys Cooper), the mother dies, leaving her share of the mill to Mary and setting the stage for the final showdown. Duryea wants to sell the mill for a substantial sum, and is intent on persuading the rest of his siblings to do likewise. It appears all the Scotts are in his favor (except for Peck, who can't see the family not being involved with steel)—until Garson prevails upon a wavering Constance to break the deadlock and affirm her faith in mill and family. Duryea excels in this scene, and throughout, as a smooth-talking capitalist who is reluctant to let family stand in the way of making a profit. His trenchant portrait should have shown MGM a glimpse of what Duryea is capable of—specifically, commanding attention opposite such daunting competition as Crisp, Garson, and an increasingly assured Peck.

The acting isn't uniformly superb, since Barrymore ventures beyond believability as the overbearing, practically demonic father who will brook no opposition. Duryea would have done well to observe the damage that could be inflicted when a good actor is allowed to overindulge—especially since Duryea would be guilty of some egregious displays of overacting himself in the 1950s. The poor reaction to Barrymore's on-screen hysterics during previews led the studio to do some hasty reshooting and re-editing. In the end, even Barrymore's bellowing couldn't keep a good film down, for *The Valley of Decision* proved to be one of Garson's biggest hits, as well as a movie that gave Duryea a chance to shine in a major undertaking.

Even after impressive turns in two out of the three films Duryea worked on for MGM, the free-spending studio (at least for production values, perhaps not so much for the talent) was not forthcoming with a long-term contract. Luckily, Gary Cooper, Duryea's early mentor, had decided that after toiling for the studios as an employee, he would produce his first (and only) film. It would be a lighthearted Western that would poke gentle fun at Cooper's stoic, heroic on-screen persona while allowing him opportunities for romancing and a little action—but not much shooting, as his character is a notoriously poor shot. Based on Alan Le May's novel *Useless Cowboy*, the film's working title would be the more equivocal *American Cowboy*, with the final release being called *Along Came Jones*. Having worked with Duryea previously on two successes (*Pride of the Yankees* and *Ball of Fire*), Cooper took a liking to the actor, particularly his easygoing professionalism. Cooper awarded Duryea a major supporting role alongside the already-cast Loretta Young and William Demarest.

As adapted by the prolific Nunnally Johnson, *Along Came Jones* presents a long-haired Duryea as Monte Jarrod, a notorious wanted outlaw, while Cooper is Melody Jones, a soft-spoken, gun-shy cowpoke. Through a series of misunderstandings—namely, that Jones's saddle bears the same initials as Jarrod's—he and his crusty sidekick (William Demarest—who else?) are mistaken for Jarrod and his half-witted sidekick, Uncle Roscoe. The bewildered Jones finds himself first courted by the terrified citizens of Payneville, then protected by a tough-talking, very lovely Cherry (Young) when some of those very citizens decide they want a taste of the reward offered for Jarrod. Little does Jones know that Cherry is really Jarrod's girlfriend, and that Jarrod is hiding out nearby—wounded but still no less dangerous, and quite jealous of Cherry's attentiveness to the gentle Jones. A series of complications ensues involving some larcenous individuals who try to get Jones to divulge the whereabouts of his (really *Jarrod's*) loot, while Jarrod indulges in some cold-blooded, murderous acts and pins them on Jones. This leads Cherry to realize that her heart belongs not to the increasingly unstable Mr. Jarrod, but to the likable, reliable (if a bit slow on the uptake) Mr. Jones.

As this was Duryea's first Western, there were a number of skills Duryea had to master in order to convince as the outlaw Jarrod, primarily shooting and horseback riding. For an actor who subsequently performed in dozens of Westerns on film and on television, he was not comfortable with either activity. As far as horses went, Duryea was always slightly spooked by them, and it always took a little bit of encouragement to get him to ride; he was also put off by the occasional breakneck speed. For as long as he was in the saddle, Duryea would always be a little tentative around horses, yet one would never know it from his (simulated) ease. He would tell a reporter later: "They *know* I'm afraid of them. They sidle up to me to allay my sensible fears, and then, when I begin to relax, they step on my nearest foot."

In terms of guns, despite effortlessly embodying many nasty (and not-so-nasty) gun-wielding tough guys, Duryea was decidedly not a gun fan. This probably had its origins in a long-ago incident in which his father inadvertently shot off his uncle's hat—with what he presumed was an unloaded gun. Duryea would credit Gary Cooper with helping him develop some sort of facility at handling weapons. Cooper patiently tutored the neophyte bad man on how to draw, shoot, and even twirl his gun. On set, the growingly assured Duryea would bark orders, kick a door shut, and, on one unfortunate occasion, drop his own gun, causing one chamber to discharge, resulting in no small measure of mortification for the so-called desperado.

Cooper's tutoring nevertheless proved to be quite beneficial, as Duryea acquitted himself quite well as Jarrod. Critic Archer Winsten would say that Duryea "turns his villainy to horse-opera style as if to the cactus born." Duryea is at his best when sparring with the charming Young, trying to assure her that he's open to mending his ways while dropping enough hints (both to Young and the audience) that change is not really part of Jarrod's vocabulary. In one key scene, Cooper and Duryea square off, with Duryea training his gun on Cooper while sizing up what he considers to be his ill-fated competition for the concerned Young. It's a tense scene laced with some laconic humor, one in which Duryea delivers his lines with a great deal of bite.

Along Came Jones would emerge as a very likable, slightly meandering Western. There are some lulls, and for a Western that was filmed on the Iverson ranch in California as well as in scenic parts of Arizona like Tucson and Nogales, there is an overreliance on rear-screen projection, so much so that one could make a case that Cooper, Demarest, and their would-be horses never made it off the soundstage. Yet Cooper and Young are winning throughout, Demarest is in good form, and Duryea manages to be quite plausible in his first outlaw role.

It's quite possible that Duryea was a little too persuasive for certain audience members—namely, a certain six-year-old son, his eldest, Pete. Pete by now had been playacting fairly regularly on his own, so Duryea thought there was no harm in letting Pete see his latest film role. Yet toward the end, when Cooper and Duryea faced each other, Pete shouted at the screen "Don't you dare shoot my daddy!" This heartfelt plea reminded Duryea of the potential for audiences, old and young, to suspend their disbelief to such an extent that they would practically surrender to the so-called realism of the screen. It would be a few years before he would let Pete see another one of his films. In fact, the only Duryea movie he had allowed his son to see prior to this was *Sahara*, where his part had been somewhat smaller—but his character had been much more agreeable.

Duryea's next film might have been another he would have allowed Peter to see. Universal signed him to appear in support of their reigning musical comedy star, Deanna Durbin, in *Lady on a Train*. Now, you might be thinking, Dan Duryea in a *musical*? Well, yes and no. Even though Durbin had made her career in frothy musicals, usually baubles where she reunited her parents or fell in love with a would-be heartthrob, *Lady on a Train* would be a little different. In 1944, Durbin had made a little noir called *Christmas Holiday*, appearing with Gene Kelly (cast against type as a charming murderer). After the film received polite reviews (and managed to sell some tickets), Universal would soften the formula and let Durbin take another noir-ish journey—one that allowed room for a number of songs (including some in character as a would-be club singer) while surrounding her with a sturdy cast of rising stars and character actors.

Lady on a Train has Durbin coming to New York by train for Christmas and witnessing, from her train compartment, the murder of an old man by a mysterious figure. Her investigations (she is a murder-mystery aficionado) lead her to the mansion of the murdered man in question and his eccentric family—namely, Duryea and Ralph Bellamy as two of his sons, and the prime suspects. They have convened for a reading of the will, and most members of this not-too-happy family are angling for the late patriarch's wealth. After sneaking onto the property, Durbin is discovered and later mistaken for the dead man's fiancée, a nightclub singer—a convenient plot device that affords her the opportunity for several song interludes. Durbin is abetted in her search for the killer by a mystery writer (David Bruce) and here is where the film goes astray; in its determination not to follow the doomed romance formula of *Christmas Holiday*, Universal seemed intent on disfiguring this work by including several presumably humorous complications involving Bruce and Durbin. The problem is Bruce is both bland and unfunny, so this viewer roots for more screen time to be granted to the real actors in the cast, especially Bellamy and Duryea.

As the two brothers, Bellamy and Duryea manage to steal whatever is worth salvaging. Bellamy is quite good as the seemingly befuddled brother who is obliging toward Durbin (until plot machinations make him act otherwise). Duryea does a fine job as the brother whom Durbin perceives as the guilty party, and the actor was cast based on audience expectations. His last few roles were as villains, so why not try to subvert audience expectations? Duryea is good throughout, graciously flirting with Durbin in the early scenes, gradually becoming "wise" to her, and then confronting her in a car, where for at least a few minutes—especially as he works that expressive lower register—he most certainly appears to be "taking Durbin for a ride." When it becomes clear that someone else is the real murderer, Duryea tries to protect Durbin—but the romantic comedy conventions of the time force the hero role to fall to the hapless Bruce. Durbin would wind up with Bruce, but Bellamy and Duryea would get the notices.

Around this time, the anticipated Duryea-Lang teaming would materialize, and because of his sterling work in his recent ventures, not to mention Lang's interest in utilizing Duryea, a new period would begin in Duryea's life—one during which he would be considered a star.

CHAPTER 5

A Universal Man

DURYEA'S WORK IN HIS LAST FEW FILMS, NOTABLY *ALONG CAME JONES* and *The Woman in the Window*, did not escape the attention of a number of studio executives, but Universal was the first to offer Duryea a lucrative long-term contract. This meant a number of things: for one, Duryea would be given the big studio build-up, along with the requisite number of press releases and publicity material as befitting a new star. Duryea would be quickly known around town as a good interview, graciously giving his time to columnists, even occasionally contributing a byline of his own (the better to make use of his Cornell degree). Another would be the opportunity to occasionally escape the villainous roles and make his mark as a leading man, thereby widening his appeal. Finally, as opposed to the uncertain world of freelancing, Duryea would be able to provide financial security for Helen and their sons, Peter and Richard, for Duryea was in every way the family man, and a far cry from the unsavory individuals he frequently portrayed.

Duryea's first film under his new contract—although not the first to be released—was the much awaited (on all sides) reunion with not only Fritz Lang, but Edward G. Robinson and Joan Bennett. *Scarlet Street* was a remake of *La Chienne*, a 1931 French film starring Michel Simon and directed by Jean Renoir, which itself had been based on *The Poor Sap*, by French novelist Georges de La Fouchardiere. The road to filming *Scarlet Street* was not an easy one. The original already had a sordid reputation, due to its perceived seamy storyline involving obsession and murder, aided by several unhealthy helpings of sexual innuendo. Director Ernst Lubitsch had tried to get the movie made, but he and his screenwriter had been unable to produce an acceptable script—namely, one that would appease the censors. Lang was undeterred by the potentially unsavory material, and he and screenwriter Dudley Nichols worked for months, finally coming up with a script that would be approved by the censors. In order for Lang and Nichols to get the film made, Lang formed Diana Productions with Joan Bennett as treasurer, Bennett's then-husband Walter Wanger as vice president, and Lang himself as president.

Scarlet Street would prove to be a far darker film than its predecessor, *The Woman in the Window*, and one that would continue to have a difficult journey, during and after filming. Edward G. Robinson plays Christopher Cross, a clerk of long-standing, one of those "mass of men" who lead lives of quiet desperation. Unhappily married to the shrewish Rosalind Ivan, laboring at his position with little personal gratification, Robinson's Cross returns from having been honored for years of service, only to come upon a young woman (Bennett) being attacked by a flashy, ill-tempered lout (Duryea). Robinson's sense of chivalry (and use of a handy umbrella) enables Cross to get the better of this well-dressed hooligan. This is somewhat reminiscent of Robinson's meeting with Bennett in the earlier film, only this time the lady is far from a damsel. She's Kitty, streetwise, and madly in love with Johnny, a louse who just happens to be the dandy in question. Joan Bennett would later comment that on the several occasions Duryea was to hit her that "he looked like he meant it . . . we had several scraps and I wound up a bedraggled substitute for a woman." Lang, a perfectionist, would shoot such scenes as often as six times. In another unfortunate incident, Lang wanted Duryea to break a glass in a certain way. While demonstrating how he wanted it to be done, Lang wound up injuring his own hand, later lamenting "that's probably not the way to do it."

The movie's twisted narrative has Johnny persuading Kitty to encourage Cross's attentions, since they perceive him to be a man of means (something not discouraged by Cross)—and especially after Johnny discovers that Cross's passion for painting reveals him to be a talented artist. Johnny's actions, particularly with regard to encouraging the denizens of the art world to believe that it's Kitty who is the actual painter, and pimping Kitty in order to hold on to Cross, lead not only to potentially ruinous consequences within the film but also to the makers themselves.

Once the Production Code got a look at the finished product in the spring of 1945, it would be a long time before the board would allow it to be released. Many of their objections centered on details of the relationship between Bennett's Kitty and Duryea's Johnny. There were countless notes from Joseph Breen regarding Bennett's dress—or, rather, her state of *undress*. Any shots including or implying lingerie had to be eliminated. There were some scenes where Johnny is seen sleeping in Kitty's apartment; these, too, had to be cut. Several of Johnny's and Kitty's more suggestive lines had to go, such as Kitty telling Johnny, "I don't know why I'm so crazy about you," and Johnny's reply, "Oh, *yes* you do." Another eliminated exchange was this one between Kitty and Johnny:

KITTY: Can't you do any better than *that*?
JOHNNY: That's *all* you think about, Lazy Legs.
KITTY: What else *is* there to think about?

Finally, Cross's fury when Kitty treats him like a laughingstock results in his stabbing Kitty in bed several times with an icepick. The Production Code prevailed upon Lang to cut it to one stab; the release as we now know it has around four quick stabs through the sheets. Clearly, Lang and Breen had been able to reach a compromise.

When one views *Scarlet Street* today, particularly in a restored print (for years the film had been languishing in the public domain in murky, jerky, occasionally unwatchable versions), one sees a seminal work, not only of Lang's and Duryea's but of film noir in general. Robinson is the archetypal dupe, albeit an occasionally crafty one, as when he maneuvers a meeting between his wife and her long-presumed-dead spouse—a meeting in which he frees himself of his shrill harpy of a wife (Rosalind Ivan, no shrinking violet, she). But he is no match for the machinations of Bennett's Kitty and Duryea's sublimely repellent Johnny. Bennett is perfection as Kitty, whose occasional flickers of conscience have no chance when measured against her fatal attraction to the supremely salacious Johnny. In this formidable company, one might argue that Duryea steals the movie from his more experienced costars. Duryea's Johnny is vicious and exploitative, yet he also displays enough sheer magnetism to convey what attracts Kitty to him. Their heated exchanges (in more ways than one) are usually just foreplay to their eventual embraces, followed by Kitty's breathy "Jeepers, I love you Johnny"—even after he threatens to hit her. Duryea's Johnny also possesses a degree of cunning (animal and otherwise) and smugness, which enable him to emerge relatively unscathed in his unsavory business dealings. Watch how he effortlessly deceives the art critics into thinking Kitty is the real painter or how he later criticizes Robinson's work by saying, "You have a little trouble with perspective," to which Robinson knowingly replies, "That's something

I never could master." This is a character and actor supremely self-confident, aided and abetted by dialogue (which Duryea superbly delivers) brimming with dark, ironic humor, enhancing the Duryea persona of the overly smug, lecherous piece of slime. In one such example, he reads a movie magazine and remarks how these actors "get big money for acting tough and pushing girls in the face. What do they do that I can't do?" He encourages Kitty to get her claws into Cross; "write him, date him up . . . get big-hearted Lazy Legs" (his oft-repeated pet name for Kitty).

Kitty's murder at the hands of the betrayed Cross and the subsequent plot developments were one last hurdle to overcome on the way to the film's release. In the film, after Kitty, the so-called artist, is murdered, all fingers are pointed at Johnny, who has done nothing to dispel these accusations, particularly since he clears out her jewelry immediately after discovering her corpse. When Johnny is forced to stand trial for Kitty's murder, several witnesses testify as to how Johnny manhandled her. When Cross is brought in, he is discredited as the true painter by his vindictive wife—an action that both preserves Cross's freedom while denying him any credit for the painting or blame for her death. In these courtroom scenes, Duryea is suitably frantic, and after he is pronounced guilty, he goes to his death shouting, "Somebody give me a break!" Where this section proved to be advantageous to Duryea's career, as well as potentially troubling with regard to the film's release, has to do with the Code itself, which had long decreed that murderers should not get away with their actions. In terms of Cross's freedom, Lang argued—as it turns out, successfully—that Cross would be forever haunted by what he has done, reduced to alcoholism and poverty, while always hearing the refrains of "La-a-a-zy Legs . . . *Jeepers*, I love you Johnny." Ironically, preview audiences were not particularly perturbed that Duryea's Johnny was executed; as Lang remembers it, many thought Duryea's character deserved his fate. Despite the fact that he had not really committed any capital offense, Duryea's Johnny was so rivetingly despicable that audiences both loved to hate him and were happy to see him in the chair. The only other adjustment that was made to the final release concerned a scene in which Cross ascends a pole, so as to detect the electricity at the hour of Johnny's execution. Censors seemed to feel this was a trifle too macabre, so the scene was eventually dropped.

Even before the movie's release in December 1945, throughout its myriad previews and run-ins with the Production Code, *Scarlet Street* gained plenty of attention for its frank subject matter, as well as for the reunion of Lang and his three stars. While Robinson and Bennett received their fair share of laudatory notices for their finely honed performances, it was Duryea who garnered the most praise for his charismatically sleazy portrayal. John Maynard spoke for many critics when he called Duryea "the best purveyor since the young Cagney of a chillingly unrecognizable pathological type of hoodlum. I would rather hate Duryea's characterizations to pieces than any characterization I know." The *Hollywood Review* said: "Duryea creates a priceless portrait of an absolute scoundrel. There is variety and infinite color to his work. . . . there is much to admire in his sharp sketching of this most unadmirable character." Bosley Crowther was one of the dissenters, calling the film tame and monotonous (a term Robinson would later invoke when describing his own work on the movie), but even Crowther would praise Duryea for his creation of "a vicious, serpentine creature out of a chiseling tinhorn." Finally, Ruth Waterbury of the *Hollywood Examiner* said Duryea "holds your attention masterfully as would a rattlesnake coiled up in the center of a bridal bouquet . . . when he dies in the electric chair for a murder he did not commit, even that red-hot ending seems too good for him."

Seventy years later, one cannot help but be impressed by how well both *Scarlet Street* and Duryea's portrayal hold up. The reviewers seem to have caught the essence of Duryea's appeal: he is a villain who could be charming and reprehensible within an instant, clever and clueless, innately vulgar but with an aura of feigned sophistication, and he is possessed with an excess of self-confidence that will cause him to be trapped with his own machinations, thus hurrying him to his eventual demise. If the critics loved to hate Duryea, so did audiences. In the wake of the tremendous box-office success of *Scarlet Street*, Duryea's fan mail suddenly skyrocketed to an average of 6,000 letters per week.

This overwhelmingly positive response was pleasing to Duryea and served as a vindication of his singular talents. He thought it "fun to get yourself collectively hated . . . when you hear an audience exult 'Good Riddance' as the villain is polished off, you know you've succeeded in turning out a real heel." In addition, Duryea was fast becoming a reliable interview, a quotable fella who was more than happy to invite reporters to his home on Mulholland. Why shouldn't he? Duryea was proud of being a happily married man living in the Hollywood Hills, and quite a presence in the community apart from his chosen profession. Even though Duryea was 4F during the war on account of his heart condition, he remained busy on the home front. He was active as an air-raid warden and also was among the more successful actors at raising money in his community through the sale of war bonds. In addition, Duryea would frequently visit bedridden servicemen in the hospitals. He was visibly moved by their morale in the hospital, but offered this concern: "I wonder how they'll be back home. They don't want to be pitied or babied or stared at."

Duryea himself was pretty self-sufficient—as self-sufficient as anyone with a big salary in Hollywood could be, meaning he took an active role managing his own financial affairs. While he did have an agent, he did without a business manager. When asked why, Duryea explained there was no need, since "one night a week I go over my bills . . . any actor who can't handle his own money better quit." This newfound financial stability meant that he and the family could fly East and visit White Plains. It was the first time Duryea had been home to visit his parents in five years, and he would make it a point of not letting so much time lapse again.

Hollywood was certainly providing Duryea with opportunities to cement his standing and even broaden it. For instance, in 1945, around the time Duryea was filming *Scarlet Street*, RKO announced it would be using Duryea as a romantic lead—as a bandit—in a proposed Eddie Cantor/ Joan Davis movie called *Come On Along*. As intriguing as the result might have been, these plans were derailed when Cantor decided to take a trip East himself, which delayed the start of filming. As Universal had several projects in mind for Duryea (1945 and 1946 would be extremely busy years), Duryea asked for his release, which RKO granted.

Duryea's next picture, *Black Angel*, would be one of his best, and certainly one that would consolidate his standing within the Hollywood community, as well as exemplify why Duryea and film noir were pretty much made for each other. The source material was a book by the noir icon Cornell Woolrich, whose dark excursions into ill-fated romance and murder contributed to his books being adapted frequently in the mid-1940s. Novels such as *Phantom Lady*, *Deadline at Dawn*, and *The Black Path of Fear* (filmed as *The Chase*, with Robert Cummings and Peter Lorre) present protagonists either being pursued by, or pursuing, some mysterious killer who might be someone they know. *Black Angel* was no different in that the book's female protagonist is seeking a murderer while acquiring the occasional helpful hand from various shady, haunted characters, among them Marty Blair (whom Duryea would portray) and the haunted Ladd Mason. Universal had picked up the option for the 1943 novel, and Roy William Neill, late of the *Sherlock Holmes* series, and one who was known to have a talent for sustaining both mood and pacing, was given the directorial reins.

As adapted by Roy Chanslor, the film *Black Angel* is fairly faithful to the spirit (despairing as it is) of Woolrich's novel, while taking several liberties with the plot. In the movie, Cathy (June Vincent), a former singer, is desperately searching for the real murderer of chanteuse Mavis Marlowe, a femme fatale who had ensnared Cathy's husband Kirk into a tawdry affair and is later found murdered. Since Kirk happened upon the body, he winds up being arrested for her murder—and soon after (as can only happen in the movies), Kirk is sentenced to death, all the while claiming there was another man there. Duryea's character, Marty Blair, an alcoholic piano player (and the ex-husband of Mavis) is really an amalgam of two characters from the book: Martin and the afore-mentioned Ladd Mason. It was a fortuitous change for Duryea, since in the novel, a forlorn Martin Blair commits suicide early on. Duryea's Marty is just as melancholy; when the film begins, he attempts to visit his estranged wife, Mavis, but is refused entry. Nevertheless, the spurned Marty sends her a gift of a small heart brooch. Marty also sees why he has been denied, as Mavis is about to welcome yet another male admirer up to her lair—who may indeed be the one who was also in Mavis's apartment and made off with Mavis's brooch (as Kirk had later claimed). After embarking on a prolonged drunken spree, he is prevailed upon by Cathy (who has since discovered he was both Mavis's husband and col-laborator—and was outside her apartment that night) to admit to killing her. After Marty turns out to have a pretty solid alibi, since he was both passed out and generally confined to his room, Cathy asks him to help find this mysterious man, who turns out to be shady nightclub owner Marco, played by fellow noir icon Peter Lorre in good form. Cathy and Marty contrive to audition for a gig at Marco's club with the idea of gain-ing access to Marco's safe, which presumably holds the elusive brooch—even if it means having Cathy feign a romantic interest in Marco.

In the course of assisting Cathy, it becomes clear to the viewer (al-though not to Cathy) that Marty is falling hopelessly in love with her. Duryea does a fine job of conveying Marty's furtive longing, as well as his growing sense of protectiveness toward Cathy. He also managed, through some intensive training, to master the songs that are in the picture, as there was no doubling of his hands for the piano sequences. As a result of his attention to verisimilitude, Duryea effortlessly projects the fragile state of an artist—in this case, a pianist and composer—trying desperate-ly to overcome his inner demons and repair his professional and personal life. One sees that while Duryea's Marty would like to help Cathy, he realizes that if her husband were really the murderer, it might clear the way towards winning someone he recognizes as a kindred spirit. However, after a confrontation with Marco proves to be fruitless—especially since the police have already established Marco's innocence—Marty's disclosure of his feelings leads Cathy to gently affirm her devotion to her husband, simultaneously discounting any possibility of romantic entanglement with Marty.

This development leads to another drunken spree for Marty, and a revelation that fully immerses Duryea's Blair in the noir universe, for it is the doomed romantic Marty who (unbeknownst to himself) is the real murderer. His binge leads to a nightmarish sequence where the viewer sees that in spite of Marty's friend's (an affable, low-key turn by Wallace Ford) best efforts, Marty was able to sneak out of his room, confront Mavis, and forcibly put an end to her predatory ways by strangling the life out of her. Later, his pleas to be released from a "drunk tank" so that he can confess and save the condemned husband (who is inching closer to the electric chair by the minute) are played with just the right mixture of desperation and urgency. Finally, his admission of guilt (helped by his recovery of the all-elusive brooch) seals his fate—while arousing mixed feelings from audiences. If Duryea's rivetingly detestable turn in *Scarlet Street* caused audiences to root for his demise (again ignoring the fact he had done nothing of a capital nature to warrant it), viewers and critics alike wanted Duryea's achingly romantic Marty to evade the gallows. Such was the power of Duryea's playing that he could not help but acquire even more encomiums for what the *New York Times* considered to be his "versatile performance in the central role." The *Hollywood Reporter* said: "Duryea has won the right to stardom and attains it with *Black Angel*." The *Los Angeles Examiner* reviewer would consider this film a validation of his own feelings about the actor, citing the actor's star quality and ability to transcend the material: "We said for a long time that Duryea was star material, a romantic figure and now he proves it . . . he turns a mediocre picture into something darned interesting to watch."

Under the firm, atmospheric direction by Roy William Neill (this was his final film, as he died in 1946), *Black Angel* would later be recognized as one of the benchmarks of 1940s noir. This wasn't only because of the strength of all the performers (especially Duryea, Lorre, and Vincent) but because the film precisely conveyed the integrity and fatalism of the book (though it was changed) and of the author himself. Francis Nevins, in his definitive biography of Cornell Woolrich, *First You Dream, Then*

You Die, opined that "if a single Woolrich feature could be preserved for future generations, and all the rest had to be destroyed, *Black Angel* is the one I would opt to keep."

For its part, Universal sought to enhance Duryea's star power and romantic aura by casting him as kind of a likable Dapper Dan in a romantic comedy, albeit one with some criminal undertones. The film would be *White Tie and Tails*, directed by Charles Barton, who had some renown as Abbott and Costello's favorite director in such madcap outings as *Buck Privates* and *The Time of their Lives*. Duryea was cast as a trusted, erudite, supremely elegant head butler for the wealthy Latimer family, who decides to live the life of a gentleman while the Latimers are away on vacation—part of which involves going out on the town in "white tie and tails." He offers his assistance to a socialite/damsel in distress (Ella Raines) by helping to bail out her younger sister's gambling debts at the hands of a ruthless Damon Runyon-esque mobster (William Bendix). Complications ensue when Bendix reveals that the presumed debt is not in the hundreds, but more akin to $100,000—and escalate even further when Bendix visits the "gentleman" Duryea and relieves him of two of the Latimers' valuable paintings as collateral for Duryea's check.

Duryea was very enthusiastic about his new role, since it allowed him to be romantic, sophisticated, and benevolent, qualities he possessed in real-life. However, he did admit concern over taking a role both comedic and benign: "What will people think? Will they stand for the switch? Will they like me?" For his part, Duryea was doing plenty to counteract the public's tendency to confuse the actor with the star. (Duryea was not alone in this; during Humphrey Bogart's career, countless individuals would come up to him at bars and restaurants, challenging him to act tough, like the on-screen Bogart.) He gave interviews discussing his love for the outdoors and the fact that he serves as an honorary Big Brother to many of the neighborhood children. He also made reference to his passion for horticulture, while pointing out he was perhaps the only screen villain raising ice plants. Universal was also doing all it could to help promote Duryea in the romance department, especially by illustrating, via publicity photos and press releases, how Duryea is *kissing* his leading lady instead of slapping her.

Upon its release in November 1946, reviewers at the time treated *White Tie and Tails* respectfully but still could not conceal an air of disappointment. Otis Guernsey of the *Herald Tribune* was more complimentary than most when he called it a "flimsy but diverting screen comedy." The *World Telegram*'s Alton Cook said Duryea was "an ingratiating comedian but he had better make his fun more substantial or he will roll up a new reputation as a well-intentioned but aimlessly shambling entertainer." Bosley Crowther of the *New York Times* echoed the thoughts of many when he wrote that "although Duryea speaks with assurance and speaks his lines airily, he does not have the polish for upstairs high comedy."

Perhaps because it hasn't been widely seen in many years, *White Tie and Tails* has acquired a degree of infamy as being one of the low points in Duryea's career, especially because of his atypical role and perceived unease in the genre of sophisticated comedy. However, looking at it recently, *White Tie and Tails* passes the time agreeably enough, and there are indeed some things to recommend it, especially William Bendix as an art-loving gangster who takes a liking to Duryea and Raines. As for Duryea himself, while the genre isn't an ideal fit, he acquits himself rather well in the early scenes, in which his butler resolves all the family's "pressing" issues with effortless grace and aplomb. He is suitably chivalrous with the comely Raines, even in the midst of some improbable plot devices. In the end, while Duryea is certainly capable, there is nothing really distinctive about his playing (aside from the aforementioned early sections). He is good enough but there is little sparkle; one feels any number of Universal contract players could have handled the part as well. When the film didn't perform well at the box office, Universal decided to pull it and subsequently rerelease it under a new title, *The Swindlers*, in the hope that this new, rougher title would draw in those who liked Duryea in crime mode. But audiences didn't respond to this title either, and *White Tie and Tails* (aka *The Swindlers*) has subsequently languished in near-oblivion, with its somewhat undeserved cinematic standing intact. Duryea himself would contribute to the perception of the film as a complete fiasco, never failing to take advantage of an opportunity to point out how miscast he was, at least in the eyes of the audience.

Despite the lackluster critical and audience response, Universal nevertheless continued to be impressed with Duryea's talents, as well as his standing with audiences, exhibitors, and critics. In 1946, Duryea was in the top ten list of "Stars of Tomorrow" as decided by the nation's motion-picture exhibitors. While Duryea was #8 with exhibitors in the area of personality impact, he was #2 with critics, with regard to his acting talent. It was therefore no surprise when it was announced, in December 1946, that Universal had signed Duryea to a seven-year exclusive contract. While his previous contract had been for two pictures a year, with the opportunity for outside deals, Duryea's new one would be for three pictures a year. Any pictures Duryea made away from Universal would be on loan-out (meaning the studio could keep the difference between his salary and what the other studio would pay Duryea). Duryea's first movie was to have been an adaptation of the Dorothy Hughes novel *Ride the Pink Horse*, with Ben Hecht and Charles Lederer working on the scenario. His role, however, would be claimed by Robert Montgomery, once Montgomery signed on as both actor and director.

Before he would begin his first film under the new contact, Duryea explored the possibilities of radio. At this time, it wasn't unusual for movie stars to retain a foothold in radio, usually by appearing on an entertainer's show or in a dramatization of a popular film. In 1944, Duryea had appeared on the *Lux Radio Show* for a radio version of *The Woman in the Window*, in which he, along with fellow stars Edward G. Robinson and Joan Bennett, reunited for a well-received adaptation. Duryea decided to take an option on a radio drama called *The Man from Nowhere*. It was about a soldier who has amassed a fortune as a crooked gambler but who has a change of heart and wants to return the money. It was a project that might have capitalized on Duryea's heel/hero persona, but never made it to the airwaves. Duryea would later have his own radio show, as well as appear on others, but for now, a series would have to wait.

Although there would be no new Duryea films released in 1947, under his new contract he would make a slew of pictures that would see the lights of cinema screens the following year. In April 1947, Duryea, Yvonne De Carlo, and Edmund O'Brien were announced as the lead players in Universal-International's production of *Black Bart*. The story had been hanging around Universal for a while, but not until Universal and International merged, in late 1946, did the project get the green light. *Black Bart* was loosely based on the real-life outlaw Charles E. Boles, a refined, poetic type who would carry an unloaded gun and leave verses at the scene of each robbery—usually of Wells Fargo stagecoaches. Black Bart's outlaw endeavors ended quite by chance, as he had lost a shirt cuff at the scene of a holdup and was later traced through laundry marks, eventually being arrested and sentenced to prison in 1882.

Quite often in Hollywood, what is originally announced is not what finally occurs, and this proved to be the case with *Black Bart*, beginning with the film's leading players. Before Duryea had been cast, Charles Korvin (then a fixture of Universal films but now known to many *Honeymooners* fans as Carlos, the mambo instructor) had been penciled in as Bart. In addition, O'Brien would not take part in *Black Bart*, instead signing for *Imagination*, which would be ultimately released as *A Double Life*, earning Ronald Colman his only Best Actor Oscar. O'Brien's role would be taken over by Jeffrey Lynn, a former second lead at Warner Bros. This was an important assignment for Lynn, as it would be his first freelance film following a stint in the army.

Since his lead in *Black Bart* would be rather gracious despite his ventures into outlawry, Duryea took the opportunity to prime his prospective audiences for it, especially after the overwhelmingly negative response to *White Tie and Tails*. Duryea maintained in interviews (such as with Hollywood columnist Sheilah Graham) that his character would be still a heavy, but a heavy with a twist, in that he actually has a fighting chance to get the girl. This was probably in response to letters from unhappy female moviegoers who felt let down whenever he became "likable," or when reality collided with the illusion brought forth by the seductive allure of the screen. One lady wrote: "When I read about you on a tractor digging up the dirt, it spoils my dream of you." In essence, Duryea and Universal were trying to have it both ways: maintain Duryea's appeal as a "tough guy" while slipping in Duryea's off-screen gentleman status under the door, in hopes that audiences would respond.

Black Bart was a relatively lavish affair by Universal (and Duryea) standards, with a budget of $854,000 ($90,000 to Duryea for the six-week shoot); it also marked Duryea's first appearance in sumptuous color. It is a fairly entertaining romp, though any resemblance to the facts is purely coincidental. The movie preserves the real Bart's courtliness and love of poetry, inserting him into a fictional tale of two genial outlaws (Duryea and Jeffrey Lynn) who decide to go their separate ways after nearly being hanged—though not before trying to relieve each other of their ill-gotten gains. Duryea's travels take him to that boom town Sacramento and a new career as a stagecoach robber, complete with mask and new identity (the notorious Black Bart) while maintaining a well-developed cover as a respectable, prosperous rancher. This peaceful existence is interrupted by the arrival of some passengers on a fateful stagecoach (that Duryea's Bart just happens to be robbing). One is his ever-larcenous ex-partner Lynn, and the other is the world-famous entertainer Lola Montez (Yvonne De Carlo), who is intrigued by the gentleman in the black mask. For his own part, Lynn is also drawn to the mysterious marauder, particularly since that masked man sounds like his old partner. It is at this point that the film both stretches credulity while simultaneously shedding any adherence to the facts. For one thing, the real Lola Montez died in 1861—or sixteen years before Bart's first holdup. And, given the distinctive nature of Duryea's voice, that any character (not to mention his partner Lynn) could take even as much as a minute to figure out who the masked man really is doesn't bode well for our appreciation of the characters' intelligence. It is difficult to take any of the antics seriously, as entertaining as they may be.

When Duryea, De Carlo, and Lynn converge in Sacramento, things proceed as one might guess: Duryea becomes smitten with De Carlo (who gets to do a few numbers), Lynn and Duryea engage in some verbal one-upmanship while planning to outdo the other on both the De Carlo front and the larceny front (Duryea plans to stop robbing stages, while Lynn wants his share of the takings), and finally De Carlo becomes quite fond of Duryea, whom she knows to be Bart—and has even persuaded to hang up his mask. As lighthearted as this is, however, this is a Western with plenty of lawbreaking, which could not escape punishment as per the censors, and the fiery climax has our heroes perishing in a blaze of glory, but not before expressing some regret and reaffirming their friendship.

Black Bart would never be mistaken for a major Duryea achievement but it is a solidly entertaining, slightly tongue-in-cheek affair. The exchanges, especially those between Lynn and Duryea, are sharp and well-played; in particular, Lynn is a big and welcome surprise. In his Warner Bros. films, Lynn projected what one might call a colorless sincerity; opposite Duryea, he is relaxed and charmingly larcenous. De Carlo is fine as Lola, although a trifle more demure than the plot demands, but she and Duryea share some lovely scenes as they become more sincerely enamored of each other. This was the first of three films in which they costarred, but it would be the closest Duryea and De Carlo would come to achieving romantic bliss (they would be "connected" in their other films, but happiness doesn't even make a fleeting appearance in them). Duryea is engaging throughout, whether wisecracking as he is about to be hanged or amorously pursuing an initially reluctant De Carlo while fending off Lynn (as well as Duryea's new, covertly villainous partner, John McIntire).

Although *Black Bart* impressed preview audiences, with many responses praising the work of Duryea and Lynn, critics and paying audiences weren't as welcoming when the film was released in February 1948. The *New York World Telegram*'s Alton Cook, a longtime Duryea supporter, wrote that "Duryea smirks and swaggers through the title role." The *New York Daily Mirror* thought *Black Bart* to be "above average, with bright comedy dialogue, but Duryea seems miscast as the rootin' tootin' bandit." Some critics appreciated its tongue-in-cheek humor, but it didn't improve the box office; others thought perhaps a change of title might help, something like *Fabulous Lola*.

Soon after completing *Black Bart*, Duryea found himself back in wolf's clothing for another lush Technicolor epic opposite Yvonne De Carlo, this one called *River Lady*, granted an even larger budget of $968,000. Duryea would again receive $90,000 for six weeks' work. He would also have to sport a moustache that he had scant time to grow, since production would commence only a few days after *Black Bart* wrapped (Duryea would need a little help from the make-up department so that this moustache would register on camera). Rod Cameron would take the third lead alongside De Carlo and Duryea, with Helena Carter and John McIntire in other major supporting roles. George Sherman, who put Duryea and De Carlo through their entertaining paces in *Black Bart*, was engaged to direct the pair again, with a script provided by D. D. Beauchamp and William Bowers.

It's a pity that the final result represents a comedown for all involved—and a definite step back for Duryea. Set in the 1850s among the lumber camps nestled on the Mississippi River, *River Lady* stars Duryea and De Carlo as partners in a plan to buy up the smaller lumber companies, resorting to violent methods when the small business owners are not too amenable. Enter Rod Cameron as a struggling lumber man, whom De Carlo takes a fancy to. The fed-up Cameron leads the smaller companies in a rebellion against this syndicate (after first being tempted by the wiles of De Carlo). Toss in a few fistfights, a climactic brawl, and an explosion or two . . . and one realizes why it all went wrong. In the first place, the script is by the numbers, with nary a surprise present. The dialogue exchanges are limp, and the actors find themselves placed uneasily among far-fetched plot developments.

Duryea himself seems to be going through the motions. He adopts his lower register for a main character trait as the screenplay has Duryea evolve (rather rapidly and implausibly) from a soft-spoken, cagey businessman to a ruthless, murderous syndicate chieftain. His quasi-romantic banter with De Carlo (who is not "The River Lady" of the title, as that sobriquet belongs to a riverboat, supposedly the same one used in the 1936 *Show Boat*) is tame and without spark. The only scenes in which Duryea seems engaged are the ones where he is rallying the disgruntled loggers into joining his own company. But by then, all we're waiting for are the climactic fireworks, wherein Duryea plans to blow Rod Cameron to hell and back—mainly because the script tells him to. Duryea is thoroughly professional, but it's clear that his heart isn't in this one—perhaps he knew all too well that his talents were being squandered on inferior material. Preview audiences seemed to agree, as they said on countless response cards that they had seen hundreds of films similar to *River Lady*. One said that "Monogram Pictures produces movies with more realistic acting than this one." *New York Times* referred to it as "routine and second-rate stuff."

River Lady, though set in mining camps along the Mississippi, was not shot on location; instead, it was filmed on the vast expanse of the Universal backlot. Duryea, while harboring no great affection for soundstages, professed even less love for location shooting. He would be given ample opportunities to discover how difficult location filming could be, admitting to some residual displeasure with the "good old days." In a later interview, he recalled: "Soundstages were either freezing or like ovens . . . if we were on location, things were even worse. Our food was slapped together, served in paper boxes, always cold. There weren't luxurious motels all over the landscape . . . we were put up in rundown hostelries with creaking beds, ancient plumbing and peeling wall paper." In that same interview, he would also reflect on his frustrations with the limitations imposed under the studio system, particularly as it affected him as an actor: "They may have made stars, but it also made for frustrations, for stultification not only of the players, but of the whole industry. If someone wanted to try something new, he was always nearly licked before he started."

When Duryea was away from the studio, he would occasionally find the opportunity to express his feelings about civic affairs, including those pertaining to Hollywood. He could be a prolific letter writer once he found a worthwhile cause. For instance, as a parent he was becoming dismayed over the lack of true family films produced by Hollywood. As an actor, of course, he was hardly blameless, since his output included some of the meanest vermin yet exhibited on-screen (with worse yet to come). However, he put his money where his byline was; in a series of letters to columnists, Duryea implored them to urge movie producers to make more films that were suitable for children.

Duryea was also among the first to see movies not only as an art form, but as a craft that warranted the creation of schools dedicated to mastering the craft of filmmaking. He was among the earliest supporters of separate schools devoted to the art and craft of motion pictures. In an interview with columnist Lowell Hedelings, Duryea stressed the need for these kinds of institutions, stating, "The industry has become extremely specialized . . . and it requires a specialized knowledge to become successful in the various parts of filmmaking. There are a few institutions that include courses but they barely scratch the surface. There should be courses in film photography, sound engineering, production, art and other crafts." This would be emblematic about how Duryea felt about his chosen profession: that it was an art form that one should not go into lightly, and that it was a form of entertainment that was worthy of respect.

Duryea's next film role would also go a long way to recapturing some respect, as well as some former glory. Lillian Hellman, who provided Duryea with his breakout role as Leo in *The Little Foxes*, had decided to go back in time to further explore the Hubbard clan—this time, including not only Regina, Ben, and Oscar, but also their parents—to see the exact points when these serpents acquired their sting. The resulting play, *Another Part of the Forest*, was a Broadway success, and the property was subsequently acquired by Universal. Fredric March and his wife (and occasional screen partner) Florence Eldridge were engaged to play the parents of this unholy trio, while Ann Blyth, recently *Mildred Pierce's* venal daughter, Veda, was given the role of a young Regina. Interestingly enough, Duryea was first cast as the young Ben Hubbard, while Edmund O'Brien was assigned the role of a young Oscar. Before shooting, however, Universal decided the roles should be switched, with O'Brien cast as the ever-scheming Ben, leaving Duryea to play Oscar, the father of his own indelible creation, the perpetually sniveling Leo.

The publicity people at Universal decided to make much of Duryea returning to the Hubbard family, coming up with all kinds of ideas to enhance Duryea's standing as a screen villain and to show the contrast between the real-life Duryea and the on-screen Duryea. This was something Duryea completely supported, since he privately admitted disappointment about how often his villainous screen persona would negate his off-screen standing as one of Hollywood's most devoted family men. Duryea wasn't the first actor who tried to distance himself from the roles he played. Famed movie hoodlum James Cagney was a modest country gentleman who loved farming and writing poetry, and he was married to the same woman all his life, spending much of his off-screen time in Martha's Vineyard. Edward G. Robinson might have achieved stardom as *Little Caesar*, but away from the studios, he never failed to remind reporters that he was a cultured art collector who took pride in his expanding collection.

Besides making use of Universal's publicity machine, Duryea himself contributed an article while making *Another Part of the Forest* in which he addressed the problems of raising children when one is always cast as a reprobate. He would later admit that, when it came to discipline, he would usually leave matters to Helen: "She had a favorite gold slipper that she used, but when Peter and Richard were older, we usually deprived them of something if they got out of line."

Helen and Dan made it a practice to keep as "normal" a life as they could. As Helen said, "In private life, we don't see a great deal of the movie crowd. We think it better to cultivate our neighbors." When Dan wasn't on set, he could probably be found, as Helen put it, "working about the place," tending to his roses, or plowing the land of his hilltop home astride his tractor. "That machine," Helen said, "next to his family, I think he loves it most. You see, he has terraced the whole hillside."

Throughout the childhoods of Richard and Peter, Duryea was as present as possible, especially when he was nearby shooting at the studio. Friday nights were movie nights; Duryea bought a projector and invited neighborhood kids (and families) to watch prints of recent movies (though generally not his own). This was a practice that would continue until the early 1950s (when televisions would become more prevalent in households). Duryea was also an active member of the PTA and could be seen selling hotdogs at the Carpenter School carnival; he and Helen also contributed their time as scoutmasters. He was a proud father during the shooting of *Another Part of the Forest*, bringing Richard and his recently won swimming trophy to the set in order to "show off." Later in the filming, Richard's tonsils were removed, so Duryea arranged for an extra bed so he could spend the night at the hospital with his son.

Another Part of the Forest, this return trip to whence the Hubbard clan began, does an efficient job of establishing the dynamics that informed its predecessor. Set in 1880 Alabama, fifteen years after the Civil War, the Hubbards are prosperous businessmen but social pariahs, since it is no secret that patriarch Marcus Hubbard (Fredric March) was a war profiteer, inflating the prices for much-needed supplies, such as salt. In addition, Marcus treats his sons Ben and Oscar as mere clerks with a vague promise they'll inherit everything after he dies, and callously dismisses his patient wife, Lavinia (Eldridge)—particularly her desire to start a local hospital for the poor. Daughter Regina wants to run off with a dashing returning war veteran, while Oscar wants to make enough money to marry his dance-hall girlfriend, Laurette. Add to this a young Horace Giddens, whom Regina is being maneuvered into marrying, as well as plenty of machinations courtesy of the outwardly genial but inwardly seething Ben, and one can see how and why these "foxes" would become the symbols for all titans of industry who would ravage the country for their own selfish aims.

If the finished product doesn't quite measure up to *The Little Foxes*, it wasn't for lack of effort from Universal, which spared no expense in bringing Hellman's malevolent creatures back to the screen, with a budget of $1,400,000 ($60,000 for Duryea, as opposed to March's $100,000 and O'Brien's $34,000). The casting is sound for the most part. March does a fine job of communicating intransigence, as well as a feigned air of graciousness when Ben delivers the death blow in the form of blackmail over his past cowardice and treachery. Ann Blyth does well as Regina, her character's charm not altogether hiding her innate cunning, while Florence Eldridge manages to make her good and long-suffering character as interesting as the dastards who surround her. As for the two brothers, it might have been interesting to see what Duryea would have done with Ben, but O'Brien does well by the role, masking Ben's malevolence with an outward air of conviviality.

Oddly enough, the one weak link—especially given his connection to the material—is Duryea himself. This is for a number of reasons, only some of which have to do with Duryea. For one thing, while it isn't essential to know *The Little Foxes* in order to appreciate the movie, it certainly does help. Conversely, if one knows *The Little Foxes*, and has seen Carl Benton Reid's Oscar, one can't help but think that this younger, callow Oscar—as depicted in *Another Part of the Forest*—bears little resemblance to the older Reid's stern, uptight, heartless Oscar. Duryea's Oscar, as written and portrayed, is frantic, nasty, and cowardly—more like the younger, more energetic Leo (minus Leo's occasional wit) than the man who would age into Oscar. Perhaps Oscar in this version was too much an amalgam of Duryea's previous characterizations for it to have been played by anyone in the cast other than Duryea. Yet it's our very identification—not only with Leo and Oscar, but with the original material itself—that works against Duryea's interpretation. In the end, one is always thinking this young 'un could not possibly "mature" into Hellman's Oscar of *The Little Foxes*. Perhaps the only way to really appreciate Duryea's Oscar is not to have seen his predecessor at all.

Maybe that is what Universal was thinking when it released *Another Part of the Forest* in July 1948. The studio decided to downplay *The Little Foxes* in its ad campaign, preferring instead to highlight March's recent Oscar (for *The Best Years of our Lives*), the cachet of adapting a Broadway hit, the star power of its cast, and the shock value of the drama itself. The *San Francisco Chronicle* and the *Los Angeles Examiner* both thought the film "brilliant," while the *New York Daily News* felt that "after an hour in the Hubbards' company, they and their devilries begin to pall." Duryea managed to recapture some of the good favor that he had lost with *River Lady*; Archer Winsten of the *New York Post* called him "slyness and cowardice incarnate," while the *San Francisco Examiner*'s Hortense Morton would add that "Duryea creates a screen personality long to be remembered."

In spite of *Another Part of the Forest*'s shortcomings, especially when compared with *The Little Foxes*, there was an aura of prestige about the venture; this aura was nowhere to be found in Duryea's next picture, an extremely ordinary little crime drama called, unimaginatively enough, *Larceny*. This was to be Duryea's third film under the direction of George Sherman, and would be noteworthy for other reasons, too. It would be the first (and least) of three films he made with John Payne, as well as with Shelley Winters. It would also be costar Joan Caulfield's first film since leaving Paramount and the fond embrace of Bing Crosby in *Blue Skies* and *Welcome Stranger*.

Larceny had three screenwriters (Herbert Margolis, Louis Monheim, and William Bowers) and a relatively thin, predictable story to show for their efforts. Payne and Duryea are con artists (Duryea's moniker is Silky Randall), Shelley Winters is Duryea's occasional girlfriend, and Joan Caulfield is their hopelessly sincere mark, a recent war widow. Payne encourages the mourning Caulfield to raise money for a war memorial building in her late husband's honor—all the while planning to split the funds with his cohorts. You can probably write the movie from here: Payne slowly falls for Caulfield, and Duryea becomes suspicious of Payne, not only with regard to his intentions towards Caulfield but as to Winters's obvious attraction to Payne. The story plays out exactly as one would expect, as there is too little tension in the narrative and not enough suspense in its eventual outcome. It's all so lackluster that Duryea isn't even afforded a distinctive death scene; rather, he is apprehended in a perfunctory manner, mutters a supposedly tart last line, and then it's off to prison . . . and cue the final credits.

Surprisingly, *Larceny* did receive its share of respectful reviews, with the *Motion Picture Herald* going so far as to label it a "tiptop melodrama." Duryea was noted in various reviews for being his usual menacing self, while Payne, in his first stab at film noir (or in this case film noir *light*), received a measure of opprobrium for being rather sullen and less interesting than the characters he interacts with. (Payne would eventually meet with greater noir success under the sure hands of directors Phil Karlson and Allan Dwan.) Any praise would go mainly to Shelley

Winters, flying high after her turn in *A Double Life*. The *Chicago News* called her "Jean Harlow with Dynamite."

It had been eight years since *The Little Foxes*, and while Duryea had gained a great deal of success, there would be some changes. His Universal contract was revised by the studio; instead of three films a year, he would now be contracted for one picture a year for four years, while being allowed to take on outside assignments of his own choosing. Another change occurred because of the dynamic nature of the move business itself. In 1948, as part of a publicity stunt, Duryea would participate in the test for a new alarm—a silent bulletproof camera called "the pictograph." As part of the test, Duryea was in Hollywood at the Owl Rexall drugstore on Beverly and La Cienega Boulevard, where he poked his prop gun over the cosmetics counter. As soon as the camera starts rolling, it buzzes the local police station. It was all part of a day's work, as Duryea tried to keep himself visible to the public outside the confines of the motion picture screen. Not so oddly enough, a customer there thought he was Richard Widmark. Widmark had made a splash the previous year for 20th Century Fox as the sadistic Tommy Udo in *Kiss of Death*. Now, Widmark was the new gleeful, sadistic villain on the block, but unlike Duryea, Widmark didn't have to wait to ensure his stardom, as Fox wined him, dined him, and signed him for both villainous roles and heroic parts in films like *The Street With No Name* and *Down to the Sea in Ships*. If Duryea was bothered by this, he didn't let on; that was not his style. But Duryea couldn't help but notice how important a studio could be to a rising actor's career—and if it fell short in that department, then the actor would have to take a more active role in securing his own future.

CHAPTER 6

Happy in Hollywood, Happier Away

DURYEA'S RESTRUCTURED CONTRACT WITH UNIVERSAL ALLOWED HIM the option of doing freelance assignments; this afforded him the opportunity to augment his Universal work (and films that might seem all too universal) with some intriguing endeavors at Paramount and United Artists. 1949 and 1950 were prime Duryea years for a number of reasons. Privately, he had been toying with the idea of moving away from Hollywood, at least for part of the year. Duryea was determined that his sons have as regular an upbringing as possible, considering that he was a rising star by Hollywood's standards. Professionally, Duryea's choice of film roles would give audiences the opportunity to see Duryea in whatever shade they wanted. One could conceivably see the smiling, slimy Duryea villain; the confident, cocky know-it-all who is undone by his own cleverness; the self-centered, hard-bitten cynic who manages to find the altruism buried within; the ruthless, vengeful Duryea in pursuit of lost money . . . and lost amour; and, finally, the weak opportunist undone by unrequited lust (we dare not call it love) which remains unquenched despite the solace of the bottle.

The first few of the bunch are pretty much the least and both done under the auspices of Universal. *Johnny Stool Pigeon* was another in a series of *Johnny* movies that proved to be in fashion during the 1940s. Many of these were popular and quite a few of them were interchangeable. Whether it was called *Johnny Stool Pigeon, Johnny Allegro, Johnny O'Clock, Johnny Apollo,* or *Johnny Eager,* all these *Johnnies* had something in common: a hard-bitten protagonist with a desire for revenge and a streak of integrity (in some cases, a very thin streak) that resulted in some form of redemption by movie's end.

The director of *Johnny Stool Pigeon* was William Castle, who was by now a veteran of lower-tier crime drama, having overseen a number of installments in the Warner Baxter *Crime Doctor* series, Warren William's *Lone Wolf* series, and some compelling noir entries such as *When Strangers Marry*. Here, Castle keeps everything moving at a pretty fast clip; ultimately, however, this tends to gloss over some of the potentially intriguing and ultimately unrealized elements of Robert Richards and Henry Jordan's screenplay.

Howard Duff is top-billed as a grimly determined FBI man out to smash a heroin ring. The opening sequence depicts a botched operation (film buffs should note the presence of a very young Tony Curtis as a sinister, swarthy, and very silent assassin) which results in one dead operative and the need for Duff to find some other way to dismantle this nefarious drug cartel. Duff's idea is to persuade a gangster he had imprisoned (Duryea) to be released for the purpose of using his underworld connections to infiltrate the organization and stop the trafficking of heroin into our United States; it's a tall order, no doubt, but a relatively new one for American films. Duryea has a little baggage of his own: he hasn't forgotten that Duff was the one who put him in the big house, and if that isn't enough, Duryea's wife died of a heroin overdose while Duryea was languishing in prison. Duryea grudgingly decides to be a "rat" and help Duff, but we're supposed to be uncertain if Duryea has other ideas in mind. The stage is set for a battle of wills.

This is where the movie proves to be a letdown. In this battle of "equals," Duff is the clear loser, playing a one-note character as precisely that. He is all grim determination, nothing more, nothing less. This may fit Duff's FBI man (other characters point out Duff's single-mindedness as a grievous character flaw) but it doesn't sustain audience interest. In addition, after the first thirty minutes (in a movie that runs barely seventy-five minutes), there is never any doubt about Duryea's motives; the movie takes pains to present him as a conflicted, misunderstood, but basically decent person. Duryea's ongoing banter with Shelley Winters, who plays a lost soul with a hankering for the generally unresponsive Duff, provides Duryea with a few opportunities to reveal his own character's tarnished hide, while his confrontations with Duff give Duryea a chance to wax eloquently about the need for both of them (especially Duff) to connect with others. Conversely, the drug-smashing aspect of the plot is too predictable; you know the kingpin as soon as you see his overly genial exterior, and the action-packed finale is a little rushed, even by Universal standards. There is one welcome sight since it's one of the few movies in which Duryea was allowed to walk off with his female costar (in this case, Shelley Winters), while the disappointed but grimly determined Duff looks on.

One Way Street, also for Universal, under the direction of Hugo Fregonese, gave Duryea a chance to work opposite James Mason. At this point in his career, Mason had come to Hollywood from Britain; he had been making noirs like *The Reckless Moment* and *Caught*, films that he would speak disdainfully of in later years. (Mason contributed some barbed reflections for his own entry in Citadel Books' *The Films of . . .* series. One might think Mason suffered immensely while making the vast majority of his movies.) *One Way Street* would be no exception, although it isn't half-bad, especially the sections with Duryea. The setup is promising. Duryea is a wanted gang leader and he's holed up in a dingy hotel suite, after his gang has just pulled off a huge robbery. He's got the patented moll (the alluring Marta Toren), troubleshooting (literally) second-in-command William Conrad, and mob doctor James Mason, who has been furtively carrying on with Toren. Unluckily for Duryea, Doc Mason sees the stolen money as an opportunity to start a new life with Toren, so he slips Duryea some poison and threatens to withhold the antidote unless he is able to get away. An untimely appearance by late hood Jack Elam almost thwarts those efforts, but the not-so-good doctor is able to make his escape.

It's a terrific opening section. There is a palpable tension between Mason and Duryea even before Mason slips him the "drug." The feeling of claustrophobia is reinforced by the nighttime setting and the cramped room, while the prolonged wait for one of the henchmen exacerbates the feeling of unease. Mason's quiet dissatisfaction in plying his dubious trade for his belittling employer, and his desire for both Toren and the good things in life, reveal heretofore untapped reserves of cleverness and courage. Needless to say, these developments cause Duryea to proclaim to Mason that there is nowhere in the world where he can hide. Clearly, it's not just the money (though it helps)—it's that lowly Doc Mason has made off with the real prize, as in the lovely Toren.

After this opening sequence, rife with simmering unease, resentment, and bursts of violence, as well as a sense of fatalism, the stage is set for classic noir that might incorporate a classic manhunt, clashes laden with mordant wit, and perhaps a doomed romance. Well, you get *one* out of three. Mason and Toren end up in a small village in Mexico, where, under the spiritual guidance of Father Moreno (Basil Ruysdael), Doc Mason uses his medical skills to help cure the villagers and become the village's most revered figure. Along the way, Mason realizes he and Toren can never really be happy (although it appears otherwise) unless he returns his ill-gotten gains to Duryea, who has ill-gotten them in the first place. These scenes among the peasants might provide Mason with a degree of serenity, but they are entirely too peaceful and lacking any sense of danger (except for a Mexican bandit who is quickly disposed of).

A big reason for that is a screenplay that confines his pursuers Duryea and Conrad to that cramped, crummy hotel room. One might think that with Duryea's connections and stature, he would find a way to make good on his "stop at nothing" threat. Instead, the movie periodically cuts back to the hotel room, where Duryea and Conrad comment on where they know Mason to be, yet they never leave their hotel to pursue him.

It all makes for a largely tranquil noir, one that only picks up steam at the end when Mason returns to the big city for a final rain-soaked reckoning. Though Duryea's footage is limited, he makes the most of it. Duryea and Mason square off early on, and Conrad makes a good foil for Duryea in their tense hotel scenes as they await word on the elusive Doc Mason. Amazingly enough, Duryea's discarded gang leader is able to elicit a degree of viewer sympathy toward the end, as his street proves to be just as one-way as Mason's.

Paramount Pictures provided Duryea with the lead role (you wouldn't know it from the third billing) in 1949's *Manhandled*, in which Dorothy Lamour was the nominal star. Lamour was pregnant at the time; she resented being relegated to what she felt was a lesser feature. The cast included Sterling Hayden, Art Smith, and Alan Napier (known mainly as Alfred to Adam West's Batman, but a respected character actor since the 1940s). Lewis Foster directed and cowrote the screenplay, along with William Chambers, based on H. R. Goldsmith's story, "The Man Who Stole a Dream." The film's premise has plenty of potential. An unsavory private eye (Duryea) uses a psychiatrist's assistant (Lamour) to supply (unwittingly) information about his patients, namely, a wealthy author (Napier) who has recurring dreams of murdering his faithless wife. When the wife is indeed murdered—and her jewels stolen—the police, along with intrepid insurance investigators (Art Smith and Sterling Hayden) have their hands full trying to figure out which parties are guilty of what.

Manhandled has a striking opening, wherein Napier's husband savagely wrings his wife's neck, in a sequence that is soon revealed to be a recurring nightmare. Enter Duryea's cocky, swaggering ex-cop-turned-private-eye, being the "good neighbor" and dropping in on ostensible love interest Lamour. It's quintessential Duryea on display: the slicked-back look, the blatant desire for both sex and money, the seemingly attentive demeanor shielding a serpent's nest of unsavory motives (at least he masks them from the all-too-naïve Lamour—savvy moviegoers know better). He tries to take her to a movie, "trusts" her with $1,000 to deposit in her bank account, and offers to take her back to her job when duty calls—all the while, he's looking to fence stolen jewels that he may or may not have murdered to acquire.

Had *Manhandled* focused entirely on Duryea and his machinations concerning Lamour, the police, and the psychiatrist (who has a backstory of his own), it could have been a classic noir. Duryea is certainly in prime form as "a congenital wise guy" who winds up outsmarting himself: the way he smoothly handles Lamour; the ease with which he seems to placate the police; the menace he elects to use with the devious psychiatrist. One can't help but admire how he seems to be the smartest guy in the room, albeit one not above resorting to murder. Toward the end, after having framed Lamour for robbery and murder, he attempts to ensure her silence by killing her and making it look like suicide. Duryea would comment to Kenneth Turan of the *New York Herald Tribune*: "It's not enough I twice punch the leading lady in the jaw and want to throw her off the roof. I run along the edge looking for a straight drop to make sure there is no fire escape or other obstruction to break her fall. And I had to go to Cornell to learn this sort of thing."

While Duryea said this publicly, the truth is that behind the scenes, he was very complicit in these developments. While *Manhandled* was being filmed, *Black Bart* was released, with the public unhappy with Duryea's gentleman bandit. Duryea was aware of this, particularly when his fan mail plummeted (as it had following *White Tie and Tails*). While he did yearn for those leading roles, Duryea also knew that the public liked him best when he was slapping his leading ladies around. In the wake of *Black Bart* and his courtly bandit, the public would slap him down once again. He had even spoken to a psychiatrist about the phenomenon and the psychiatrist said these women received a vicarious thrill from seeing one of their sex mishandled—especially when Duryea was doing the mishandling.

The public might have been saying: "Courtly, you say? Leave that to Errol Flynn. We've heard you're a loving husband and family man in real life—but don't you dare shatter the indelible illusion of nastiness that you've created." The Hollywood columnists, and there were many, fueled that sentiment. Duryea had his yearnings but he was also an immensely practical man. Consequently, there was a conscious effort on the part of the writer, director, and actor to make Duryea's character as nasty and morally repugnant as possible, to counteract the damage done by the poetry-spouting *Black Bart*. Setting aside these disingenuous lamentations to the press, Duryea creates a vivid portrait of cheerful malevolence in a film with some skillfully intricate plotting.

Where *Manhandled* falls apart is with the inclusion of some gratuitous comic relief involving the police (headed by Art Smith) and to some extent the insurance investigator (a lighter than usual Sterling Hayden). There are a number of unfunny gags depicting various levels of incompetence, so that their ultimate ability to crack the cases seems far-fetched, to say the least. In addition, a running gag about a police car and defective breaks culminates in a cringe-inducing payoff (immediately before the final credits) guaranteed to please no one.

While Duryea was racking up the notices and the fan mail reinforcing his slimy scoundrel image, his off-screen life was taking him somewhere else entirely. He was doing quite well financially, what with his lucrative Universal contract and scrupulous attention to such matters. Duryea was looking for a retreat away from Hollywood, where he could spend his off-hours raising his sons and indulging his interests in gardening and sailing. Duryea gave Helen two choices around the time of their anniversary: a new mink coat or a second house (he privately hoped she would choose the latter). When her choice wisely proved to be the house, they quickly found a retreat in Lake Arrowhead, ninety miles north of Los Angeles. He nicknamed their new residence "Minkote" in honor of the mink coat Helen sacrificed.

The Duryeas would have many happy years there. Most winters, the family would spend their weekends in Arrowhead, especially if Dan was filming at the studio. They would stay practically every summer at "Minkote," and Duryea made a concerted effort to film as little as possible in July and August; he would certainly try to avoid location work during that time. It was at Lake Arrowhead that Duryea and his sons, Peter and Richard, not only built sailboats in a woodshop that Duryea had constructed, but actively raced them. The elder Duryea had brought Dan up to pursue hobbies, and Dan imparted this philosophy to his children.

Here in Arrowhead, Duryea was just one of the residents, albeit a respected and fondly remembered one. Sharon McDaniel, Duryea's next-door neighbor in Arrowhead from the early 1950s, recalls that Duryea, unlike his screen roles, demonstrated "a great moral sense that he presented to us . . . he expected people to behave in a certain way." As he did on Mulholland Drive, Duryea downplayed his fame most of the time, except on the rare occasion when he brought his family, and perhaps some friends, to the movies. To McDaniel, as well as to many of his neighbors, Duryea was "a bigger than life personality who loved his family; his work was incidental—he didn't play it up when he was at Arrowhead." If Duryea was humble about Hollywood, he was not as yielding about sailboat racing. On most weekends, Duryea would be content to support the boys as they raced; however, each year brought the special "Father's Race." McDaniel recalls Duryea having a competitive streak; he had a special sail made "in order to get the edge" in those yearly races.

Duryea's distinctive laugh and impish nature left an imprint on his fellow Arrowhead residents. Mary Bernard, Duryea's next-door neighbor from the mid-1950s (and who counts Duryea's son Richard as her first boyfriend), fondly remembers Sunday mornings in Arrowhead: "Mr. Duryea would be out in the driveway with a hose cleaning his car, and he'd laugh that laugh of his as we were going to church. And every Sunday my mother would say 'I'll pray for him.'" Those who knew Duryea would say that he never seemed as happy as when he was at Arrowhead with his family.

But he still had to earn his keep, and he was back in Hollywood for his next film, *Criss Cross*, a Universal release, costarring with Burt Lancaster and Yvonne De Carlo. In events typical of Hollywood at the time, some key individuals didn't want to do the film, including Lancaster. Mark Hellinger, the original producer, had recently died of a heart attack, and Lancaster, who had already played the all-American sucker in a few films, including his debut, *The Killers*, was begging Universal to be loaned out to Fox (for *Down to the Sea in Ships*). Finally, he was convinced (by restauranteur Toots Shor, no less) to reunite with his *Killers* director Robert Siodmak to make what would later be recognized as one of the exemplars of film noir. Aided by Siodmak's masterful direction, Daniel Fuchs's adaptation of Dan Tracy's novel presents a compelling mosaic which artfully entraps its doomed protagonists. The movie begins outside of a nightclub with an eternal Brazilian beat as Lancaster's Steve Thompson and Duryea's Slim Dundee get into an argument that might have been staged for a concerned detective, Ramirez (Stephen McNally). In the shadows, Steve and Slim's wife, Anna (the sultry De Carlo), share a bit of passion and some hopes for a better tomorrow. The next day, Steve reports to his job as guard for an armored-car company—and we get an extended flashback wherein Lancaster recounts, in archetypal noir voice-over, how he became the inside man for an armored-car robbery. Lancaster is superb as one of the premier fall guys in noir, assuring the viewer and himself how far he's trying to avoid his first love, Anna, even as he puts himself in places and situations that ensure anything but.

As good as Lancaster is as the fatalistic Steve, Duryea matches him scene for scene as one of the most indelible villains in film noir. Duryea's Slim Dundee is a well-known, charismatic criminal who nevertheless the police cannot arrest. He has some surface charm, money, and, most of all, to Lancaster's consternation, Anna as his prized possession. Not that Anna loves Slim, for once Lancaster's Steve re-enters the picture, no matter how much those crazy kids try to deny it, they are drawn to each other like moths to a flame. The renewed relationship of Steve and Anna causes them to take some unnecessary chances, which result in some suspicion from Dundee, as well as some stern lectures from concerned cop Ramirez. Not even Anna's marriage to Dundee can diminish the throes of passion that exist between her and Steve, which leads to a rather inopportune meeting with Slim and the boys at Steve's house— and a classic Duryea moment. When pressed as to why he is with Anna, Steve improvises that it's really master criminal Slim Dundee he wants to see. Duryea calmly takes this all in, after saying with considerable understatement, "This don't look right, you can't tell me it looks right," and asking Lancaster, "*Me*? You wanted to see *me*? What *possible* business could you have with me, Stevie?" Lancaster's response—that he wants Dundee's assistance in pulling off an armored-car robbery with Lancaster as the inside man—is his way of getting out of this predicament and ensuring a future with the materialistic Anna. In reality, however, this only solidifies his own unfortunate destiny.

The robbery sequence, complete with pulsating music by Miklos Rozsa, is a masterpiece of controlled mayhem. Gas bombs explode, creating an otherworldly atmosphere of fog and smoke, out of which emerges Duryea, still recognizable despite the gas mask, coldly killing one of the guards and consigning all participants to a place in Hell. After the resultant fireworks, the hapless, wounded Steve is spirited out of the hospital by one of Dundee's henchmen, leading to a final confrontation which reveals to Lancaster once and for all Anna's true nature. When Anna chastises him for being a hopeless romantic, Lancaster's line, "I'll know better next time," is infused with all the irony and despair at the actor's disposal. Not to be outdone, Duryea's final entrance out of the darkness, with a limp and a gun, seals everyone's fate. Duryea is able to create a sliver of sympathy for Dundee, even as he is about to pull the trigger on the star-crossed couple. His understated, resigned delivery of the line, "You see Stevie . . . I loved her too," humanizes the monster, adding another layer to the complex, powerful creation that is *Criss Cross*.

1949's *Too Late for Tears*, directed by Byron Haskin, contains another classic Duryea character, only this time he turns out to be the eventual fall guy at the mercy of heartless murderess Lizabeth Scott. Roy Huggins, who would later find greater fame with the TV series *The Fugitive*, penned this tale which starts out with a young couple (Arthur Kennedy and Lizabeth Scott) driving down life's dark highway, where, as fate would decree, a satchel full of money is tossed in their car. The righteous Alan (Kennedy) wants to give the $60,000 to the police while his materialistic wife, Jane (who has a pretty dark past), desperately wants to keep it, intimating that the marriage won't be any good without the money. Alan relents, and checks the bag at the local bus station, keeping the all-important claim check in the lining of his coat. The fact that Jane doesn't physically have the money doesn't prevent her from spending it, adding another layer of friction to an already fraying marriage. Enter Duryea, as Danny Fuller, all confidence and charm, with an undercurrent of menace. In what seems to be a virtual reprise of his role in *The Woman in the Window*, he strolls in, insists on searching the place, finds what he needs (boxes of expensive presents), and ascertains that Jane and her husband indeed have his money. He wants it returned soon—or there'll be trouble.

This is where the similarities to *The Woman in the Window* end, because unlike the more malleable Joan Bennett, Liz Scott's Jane is intractable and ever-resourceful in her desire to keep the money, and Duryea's wary but pliable Harry can't keep up. . . . plus the fact that, despite his better judgment, Harry winds up falling for her doesn't help matters. Jane entices Harry into meeting her at the lake, where having just disposed of her hubby point-blank in a boat, she persuades Danny to impersonate her now submerged spouse in order to cover her tracks. Duryea's reaction as he discovers that she knows no moral bounds, a mixture of admiration and disgust (both with her and himself), shows Duryea at his best. Harry's involvement in her subsequent machinations, such as buying poison on her behalf, coupled with his growing attraction to Jane, in spite of his misgivings about her, lead to his taking refuge in the bottle.

By movie's end, Duryea's Harry is as thoroughly played as Lancaster's Steve in *Criss Cross*. With the money in hand, a dissipated Harry deludes himself into thinking his future lies with Jane and all his problems are over; he even allows Jane to fix him a celebratory drink—laced with the very poison he has purchased. Jane herself flees over the border, where fate and a persistent pursuer in Don De Fore lead to her taking a header off a luxury hotel.

Too Late for Tears is another Duryea film that has grown in stature over the years. Dismissed at the time as a tawdry melodrama, the film has much to recommend. Lizabeth Scott's Jane proves to be one of noir's supreme femme fatales. Like Barbara Stanwyck's Phyllis in *Double Indemnity*, she is aware that she's no good. Unlike Phyllis, she warns people about her predatory and duplicitous nature, but most of the men in this film either underestimate her or allow themselves to be sucked into her vortex. Arthur Kennedy makes the most of his limited footage as the ill-fated husband, and Don De Fore, long before *Hazel*, does a good job as the mysterious stranger who is also after Scott, for reasons of his own. The ill-fated Harry is a quintessential Duryea creation, incorporating many elements of the Duryea persona: the patented Duryea blend of charm, confidence, and avarice, supplemented by pangs of unrequited desire, vulnerability, and self-loathing. It's a gripping portrayal in a film that had slipped through the cracks and yet ultimately was widely seen, thanks to public domain.

A change of setting was about to come Duryea's way at Universal, courtesy of Anthony Mann and James Stewart, with the influential, powerful 1950 Western, *Winchester '73*. The postwar James Stewart was looking to deepen and darken his folksy, all-American image; he found a willing collaborator in Anthony Mann, who had forged a career in dark crime dramas for both MGM and Eagle-Lion. Robert Richards and Borden Chase collaborated on what would be considered one of the key Westerns which helped move the genre into adult territory. Additionally, it would be both financially and critically rewarding for Stewart (via a hefty share of the profits), launch Mann and Stewart on a creative partnership that included five critically acclaimed Westerns, and provide Duryea with a scene-stealing, career-defining role.

The plot of *Winchester '73* revolves around Stewart's Lin McAdam and his desire to reclaim his prized rifle, the Winchester '73, after it has been stolen from him by the unsavory outlaw Dutch Henry Brown (Stephen McNally). McAdam follows the trail of the gun (which, in the screenplay, becomes a character itself), as it changes hands from Dutch Henry to a wily trader, encountering a wagon train (containing costar Shelley Winters's Lola and Charles Drake as her fiancé, Steve) about to be attacked by Indians. After Stewart and the besieged travelers defeat the marauders, the gun finds its way into Drake's hands, en route to a fateful rendezvous with the much-wanted outlaw Waco Johnny Dean, a magnificent creation by Duryea.

Duryea's involvement in *Winchester '73* reflects the fact that he was rarely concerned with the size of his parts. On more than one occasion, he has said that all he needed were a couple of good scenes, and he could make a movie his. Waco doesn't even appear until the last half-hour of *Winchester '73*, but once he arrives, the movie belongs to Duryea. He rides in guns-a-blazin' with his gang, the posse at his heels, and takes over the house (amidst much gunfire) where Lola and Steve have been waiting. Waco takes a look at Steve's Winchester and decides he *must* have that gun; the way Duryea plays it, the gun is like a woman that Duryea simply has to own. When Steve proves unwisely resistant to a sale, Waco begins the process of humiliating Steve, forcing him to make coffee and wear an apron (!), eventually goading him into a showdown, thus ridding the movie of a superfluous fiancé (Winters's Lola and Stewart's Lin have by now made a connection) and gaining possession of the prized rifle—for a time.

After Waco and Lola successfully flee Waco's pursuers, courtesy of Waco cheerfully sacrificing his own henchmen, they meet Dutch Henry, who reclaims the Winchester. Even though McNally's Dutch is doing some heavy emoting, one can't help but watch Duryea: how his eyes size up the situation, calmly placating Dutch Henry, all the while planning to get the rifle back at some future date ("The way I got it back from Steve," he confides to Lola). Waco and Dutch Henry plan to rob a bank in Tascosa (a town that has been robbed in so many Westerns over the years, it's a wonder there is any money remaining), and Duryea's Waco is supposed to help cover their escape.

The saloon in Tascosa where Waco and Lola are biding their time waiting for the robbery provides a scene featuring several classic moments for both Duryea and Stewart aficionados. Duryea's Waco is so conceited, so certain of his power over women that he tries to romance Winters's Lola, even as she's still grieving over her dead fiancé. When Stewart's Lin walks into the saloon, Lola warns him about Waco (whom he knows is traveling with Dutch Henry) and his stealthy left-handed draw. In a moment that redefined Stewart's career, he slowly walks up to Waco, asking him the whereabouts of Dutch Henry. Duryea sizes Stewart up, tries to go for his gun, wherein Stewart slams Duryea's head against the bar, savagely twisting Duryea's arm until he relents. It's a powerful moment, one in which the viewer feels Stewart's fury and Duryea's intense agony. Waco's subsequent, flamboyant death at the hands of Stewart's

Lin—following his ill-fated attempt to simultaneously wrestle away another man's gun and draw on the forewarned Stewart—puts an exclamation point on Duryea's dazzling turn.

It's a measure of the movie's power that it still has ten minutes left and yet manages to survive Duryea's exit. Lin chases Dutch Henry into the rocky hills for a fateful gunfight (the viewer learns that they're really brothers, and that Dutch Henry killed their father). In Mann's hands, aided by the forceful playing of Stewart and McNally, there's real danger in them there hills. We're not given mindless shooting from actors who know the guns are firing blanks; Mann shows you the terror, the maneuvering, the ricochets that can kill a man as much as a well-aimed shot. It's a tense, riveting conclusion to a Western that drew heaps of praise, not only for Mann's powerful direction, but for Stewart and Duryea in what would prove to be archetypal roles. Their on-screen antagonism notwithstanding, *Winchester '73* would provide Duryea the opportunity to form a lifelong friendship with Stewart. Many of Duryea's friends came from outside the Hollywood circle, but Stewart and Duryea really bonded during the location shoot. Their friendship, marked by genuine affection and a mutual love of storytelling and practical jokes, would also see them through three more films, the last of which was the 1966 all-star epic *Flight of the Phoenix*.

With two years of roles that contained at least hints of villainy, it would have been surprising to see Dan Duryea star in a 1950 United Artists release called *The Underworld Story* and think he'd be cast as anything but a criminal. Yet this little, unheralded film is full of surprises. Originally called *The Whip* or *The Whipped*, Duryea's role was, as first devised, a conventional one, fairly altruistic and far from the villainous types he usually portrayed. One would think that Duryea would have jumped at the chance to play this kind of part, given his desire to branch out into heroic roles. But Duryea compelled the writers (story by Craig Rice, adaptation by Henry Blankfort and the director, Cy Endfield) to make him more of a heel, at least in the early going, reasoning that his eventual turnabout would carry an element of surprise with audiences. Duryea's instincts were very sound in this regard, and *The Underworld Story*, as it was eventually released, would provide a strong showcase for his talents. It's a shame he couldn't do more about that title. Yes, there is an underworld figure in it (avuncular but deadly Howard Da Silva) but it's mainly a film about greed, corruption, ignorance, prejudice, and mob-rule mentality, with a dash of redemption thrown in for good measure.

Duryea is cast as Mike Reese, one of those tabloid reporters you see plenty of in the movies: strong on confidence, light on ethics. He's working for a big-time newspaper in the big city, but his world falls apart when his article leads to the murder of a government witness, as well as the wounding of the district attorney (Michael O'Shea) about to testify against an underworld kingpin. His boss fires him (after disclaiming any role in the article's publication), and soon Mike finds himself a leper, eased out of town by current and former associates. One friend gives Mike the brush-off by reminding him they were roommates ("Funny, I was going to say that to you," Mike responds). A newspaper ad is brought to his attention: the opportunity to buy a half-interest in a small-town paper (still within reach of the city). It's the chance to be his own boss, but he's a little low on ready cash. Reese capitalizes on the generosity of that underworld figure (who should be grateful to the author of the article revealing the witness's whereabouts, Reese figures) and manages to walk away with $5,000. He's still a little short, but Reese thinks his experience and confidence will carry the day.

Reese's arrival, bearing money and a wealth of experience, initially lands him in the good graces of the beleaguered but very attractive publisher (Gale Storm) and her crusty pressman, but that doesn't last. In short order, Reese conveys his disdain for the "strawberry picking" stories that are the hometown paper's stock in trade, hinting that the paper would be more profitable if it were turned into a vehicle with which to blackmail residents caught in compromising situations. When he is on the verge of being thrown out, some headline-worthy local news breaks out: the daughter-in-law of publisher Herbert Marshall, who owns all those papers in the big city, has been found murdered in the woods near the offices.

Reese, sensing he's in on a very lucrative scoop, gets on the phone with various newspapers. It's a virtuoso scene for Duryea, captured mostly in one take, as he handles both the phone and Storm, pitting publisher against publisher to get the biggest price for an exclusive. It's also a revealing scene for the character because, throughout the movie, as much as Reese thinks he's in control of things, we see how in the dark he really is. The promised payoff for the exclusive never comes through because the police chief reneges on a promise to give Reese time to file the story. We also learn that while the deceased woman's black maid is the chief suspect, the real murderer is Marshall's son, who wastes no time in admitting his guilt—and persuading his reluctant father to help cover it up.

When the accused Molly shows up on the newspaper's doorstep (she's friends with Storm), proclaiming her innocence, Reese sees this as an opportunity for him and the paper to claim the $25,000 reward offered by grieving father-in-law Herbert Marshall. Reese is thwarted by the DA—who gets the woman to admit that she came in of her own accord—and Storm, who along with the accused doesn't hold with Duryea's attempt to sell people for filthy lucre. Undeterred, Reese resorts to another scheme: getting concerned prominent citizens to come to Molly's aid with a "defense fund," money to go in part to a high-priced lawyer, and in part to Reese. Reese still believes Molly is guilty, but as he says to Storm, "Why question the motivation?" One of the distinctive aspects of the film is its depiction of the inherent conformity of small-town life, as well as its latent prejudices. The town is quick to support Molly, at least for a while, and some of its most prominent citizens lend their time and money to the cause. And then the townspeople, having been poisoned by Marshall and his murderer-son with insinuations about the girl (and Reese's unsavory background), quickly withdraw their support, venting their wrath upon Duryea and Storm, as well as their printing press.

What makes the film percolate is that one still doesn't know which way Duryea's Reese will turn. Up until now, he's been doing a good job taking big defeats and turning them into fleeting victories. Money and prestige still seem to be his main motivating factors. Then, amidst dwindling funds in the defense fund, the high-priced lawyer tries to get Molly to cop a plea to manslaughter. Something about Molly's willingness to preserve her dignity and her innocence moves Reese. In a touching moment, Reese offers to give up his own share of the funds to defend Molly; with this gesture, Duryea confirms that Reese is now on the side of the angels. After this pivotal moment, complications do ensue: Marshall and son ask Da Silva to lean on Duryea, who's still unaware of "who's pulling the strings"; a witness materializes who can prove Molly's innocence; Reese finally figures things out and tries to pull off a grand play concerning some presumed hush money and a well-timed arrival by the still seething DA—but it doesn't come off exactly as planned. There'll still be a happy ending, but the characters, especially Reese, have to endure a number of hardships to earn it.

Why *The Underworld Story* isn't better known is a bit of a mystery. Certainly the reviews could have been more encouraging. Some critics, like Bosley Crowther of the *New York Times*, spent more time condemning how the movie pilloried the press than on the film's actual merits or thematic elements: "An alarmingly low opinion of publishers and newspaper men . . . poorly made, haphazard . . . Duryea acts in his customary, loudmouthed way." And, because of its generic title, the film was written off as just another underworld saga, especially by those who hadn't bothered to see it.

Another possibility is the fact that its director and writer—the film's two main creative forces—would be blacklisted within two years of its release. Henry Blankfort, who wrote the screenplay with Endfield would be blacklisted by the early 1950s. Endfield, meanwhile, would soon flee America rather than go before the House Un-American Activities Committee (HUAC). He would complete another savage indictment of mob rule, *Try and Get Me,* and later in Europe, following his blacklisting, *Hell Drivers* and *Zulu. The Underworld Story* conveys the imprimaturs of much of Endfield's 1950s output: vivid atmosphere, incisive characterizations, and powerful depictions of social injustice. The film is a courageous work, although it pulls its punches a little: Mary Anderson, a very talented actress, touchingly plays Molly, but there is no disguising the fact that she's a white actress playing a part that called for a black actress. This wasn't an unusual practice at the time, and Endfield has gone on record that he would have preferred to cast a black woman but was under studio pressure not to.

Duryea's work is an integral part of the film's power; his Reese is a vivid characterization in a film that capitalizes on Duryea's persona only to turn it on its head. Reese's own surprise at his subsequent heroism mirrors the heroine's as well as our own. As good as Duryea is, he's not alone. Gale Storm (pre-*Little Margie*) provides strong support as his new-found partner who is reluctant (with very good reason) to succumb to Duryea's brazen manner. Howard Da Silva, soon to be blacklisted himself after refusing to name names, is exceptional as the jovial yet deadly underworld boss who envisions himself as a social climber. Herbert Marshall also contributes a fine performance of a powerful man saddled with a dangerous, weakling son, torn between doing the right thing and doing whatever he can to protect the family's good name. Marshall's agonizing dilemma, coupled with Duryea's crisis of conscience, ultimately provide the moral foundations of what remains a strong, vastly underrated film that still retains its power—and perhaps rings even truer today.

This two-year period was among the most productive and personally satisfying of Duryea's life. He had successfully tested the waters in terms of freelancing, enhanced his standing at home studio Universal, and enjoyed no small degree of happiness at his summer home in Lake Arrowhead, somewhat beyond the reach of Hollywood. While all was "milk and honey" now, the next year or so would find him making some hard choices about his career—especially if he wanted to continue it.

CHAPTER 7

Career Crisis, Then Television Calls
with *China Smith*

AFTER HIS GOOD-GUY/BAD-GUY ROLE IN *THE UNDERWORLD STORY*, Duryea would next venture to Columbia Studios and into the West for his next role, which would be another take on a real-life outlaw, this time *Al Jennings of Oklahoma*. Ray Nazarro would direct from a script by George Bricker. Like the scribes on *Black Bart*, Bricker didn't let facts get in the way of this purported biography. While the real Al Jennings specialized in mail-train heists, the movie's Jennings robs both trains and stagecoaches with equal abandon. Dick Foran would play Al's brother Frank (and eventual partner in crime), while Gale Storm, who winningly costarred with Duryea in *The Underworld Story*, would again be Duryea's attractive, initially reluctant love interest.

In this fictionalized version of Al Jennings's life, he is a brash, hot-tempered young man from Coldwater, Kansas, who plans to practice law with his older brothers and father. He and his brother Frank ride to Oklahoma to join brothers John and Ed, encountering along the way both a genial outlaw, Fred (Guinn "Big Boy" Williams), and a runaway carriage bearing the fetching Margo (Gale Storm) whom Al is immediately smitten with. Not surprisingly, the Jennings' successful (though unorthodox) practice of law in the gunplay-prone Wild West leads to Al's brother Ed being gunned down. Al impulsively decides to take the law into his own hands, first by trying to force a confession out of Ed's killer, then by being a little faster on the trigger after Ed's killer draws first. In the absence of witnesses, however, Al's actions—and subsequent flight—make him an outlaw, and he and his loyal brother Frank live up to their billing by joining Fred's gang of ruffians. With the sheriff on their trail and a bounty on their heads, the brothers hightail it to Louisiana, where they nudge themselves toward respectability by becoming cotton merchants. In these new surroundings, Al encounters the fair Margo again and vows to stay on the right side of the law. Yet the posse will not rest; between the machinations of the law and the duplicity of Al's partners, Al eventually finds himself back in court.

Al Jennings of Oklahoma is no classic by any means, but it is another opportunity to see Duryea—in Technicolor—as a congenial good/bad man, and a romantic lead to boot. He is gracious with Storm, while building a lively sense of camaraderie with both Foran and Williams as his affable cronies (the true villains in the piece are those on the side of the law who twist it according to their purposes—and Williams's wife, who betrays Al in a futile attempt to get her own husband out of the outlaw trade). Duryea also manages to be persuasively passionate and tough-minded as the initially righteous yet quick-tempered fledgling lawyer. But the movie feels oddly rushed as the final indignity for Al (a lengthy prison term imposed by a crafty judge) is accompanied by a voice-over declaring that this miscarriage of justice would eventually be redressed by none other than President Theodore Roosevelt. Moreover, this stentorian narrator informs us, Jennings and Margo would live and love happily ever after. All of this occurs within a span of two minutes, and decidedly to the film's detriment.

The movie did receive some good notices, with the *Daily Variety* calling it a "nifty package of western entertainment." However, *Al Jennings* made headlines of another kind when the real Al Jennings, then a spry eighty-six (and really pardoned by President Roosevelt in 1900), threatened to sue because he felt the film had maligned him. He also claimed he had not been paid for his autobiography. In an interview with Aline Mosby of the *Los Angeles News*, Jennings declared "that movie's someone else's life—not mine . . . they even have Dan Dur-y-ea or whatever they call him robbing a stagecoach . . . I stuck to trains. They also made me too tough. I was really too soft to be a successful bandit."

Around the time of his latest foray into the West, Duryea's name was mentioned in connection with several potential film projects. One possibility was RKO's *Cry Copper*; a more intriguing option was *The Kaldens Story*, about a returned GI who embarks on an eighteen-month crime and murder spree, was subsequently confined to a mental institution, and then was released and found work at the post office. There was also the prospect of traveling to Mexico for *The Big Catch* and *The Golden Promise*, to be produced by William Rowland with scripts by John Bright. These never came to fruition nor did a long-proposed project for producer-director William Castle (from *Johnny Stool Pigeon*) called *Models Inc.*, in which he would reportedly play his meanest, nastiest character yet: that of a phony agent who lures beautiful, naïve girls into a life of crime.

Opportunity literally came knocking, however, with a project that did indeed materialize. It was a script by John Reinhardt and Milton Carter in which Duryea would play an embattled father facing various difficulties while desperately trying to discover the fate of his injured little girl. The movie would be a micro-budget affair and while the part was exceptional, the money was minimal—a small salary and 30 percent of the profits. Duryea held off, since he did not wish to make the film on a deferment, but the producer Peter Berneis and its director, Reinhardt, sought him out at his Lake Arrowhead retreat. There, Duryea looked over the script again, made some suggestions, and papers were signed. And since the deal was consummated at his getaway in Arrowhead, the production company would be called Arrowhead Pictures.

Duryea would become extremely enthusiastic about the film, which was eventually released as *Chicago Calling*. It provided him a rare opportunity to play a humane role as a parent and ordinary working fellow—albeit a flawed one, prone to alcoholic excess and bouts of despair. As he would tell the columnist Erskine Johnson: "I'm out to prove I can do straight parts and character leads. This is the kind of part I never get. Nobody would think of giving it to me." As a coproducer, Duryea managed to get some exceptional talent despite the budgetary constrictions, not the least of whom is Mary Anderson, so good in *The Underworld Story*, as his long-suffering wife, as well as Gordon Gebert, a child actor who had already proven himself in films such as *Holiday Affair*, *The Flame and the Arrow*, and *House on Telegraph Hill*.

Gebert recently recalled that while some interiors were shot on a soundstage, the majority of the filming was done on location in downtown Los Angeles. Said Gebert, who would later become a professor of architecture: "This was mesmerizing for me, shooting near Angels Flight, to know LA had that sort of thing . . . it helped shape my view of urban life." To Gebert, it was clear even at his young age that "this was an independent production. The number of crew members was minimal . . . no time was wasted. Every shot counted." Duryea, as both producer and actor, was "sympathetic and helpful. I could see he was a caring father. He did everything to keep me engaged." Gebert observed that as a producer, Duryea was content to let the director run the show, as opposed to someone like Burt Lancaster (Gebert played his son in *The Flame and the Arrow*) who couldn't help but exert his weight on the set. One incident that stood out for Gebert involved having to chase Duryea up a flight of stairs while hurriedly speaking some dialogue: "I kept screwing up my lines. The director told me that Duryea had a heart condition so you have to get it right. I thought the director was making that up." As a footnote, when I apprised him of Duryea's health issues, Gebert was indeed relieved of some lingering skepticism toward the director.

The premise of *Chicago Calling* is pretty straightforward, and fairly devastating at that. Duryea is Bill Cannon, an unemployed photographer in Los Angeles who has squandered the good will of his family and many of his friends because of his drinking and inability to hold down a job. After his latest all-night binge, his wife, Mary (Mary Anderson), regretfully leaves him, taking their young daughter, Nancy (Melinda Plowman), with her. In a quietly affecting scene, a remorseful Bill tries to convince Mary to stay, but given his empty promises of the past, he realizes that her leaving may be best for Mary and his daughter. After his subsequent two-day bender, Bill returns home to find his telephone being disconnected for nonpayment of a $53 bill—and a telegram from Mary saying that Nancy has been seriously hurt in a car accident outside Chicago, and that she'll call him the next day after the operation. He persuades the diligent phone line worker to at least leave the phone in service for another day. Thus begins a desperate journey to scrounge up $50 by almost any means possible, so he can receive that all-important phone call.

The scenes that follow, depicting Bill's odyssey through the lower depths of Los Angeles, are masterfully captured by the cinematographer Robert de Grasse—they are gritty, pointed, and heartrending. The phone company points to the notices Bill has neglected, and while banks and loan companies are outwardly pleasant, they are resistant to lending him the money since he lacks any kind of collateral; even the one company willing to give him the funds would make him wait a few days to get it. His friends are no help, either, since they have their own money troubles—and Bill has been a bad risk in the past. Not all is unremitting despair however; in one scene, Bill comes upon Peggy (a lovely turn by Marsha Jones), a compassionate food truck worker in whom he can confide—and a radio producer, who sees in him a hard-luck story that will be embraced by his listeners. Bill is reluctant to accept this "charity," but the issue becomes moot since the promised windfall would not arrive in time to assuage his current situation. While Peggy is moved by his difficulties, she sadly tells him she doesn't have the $53 for him—but, in an unexpected act of kindness, she gives him $5, purportedly from the radio producer but really out of her own pocket.

The turning point comes when Bill meets Bobby (Gordon Gebert), a little boy who accidentally hits Bill's dog with his bike. Bobby has his own problems, since he is living with his callous older sister who plans to abandon him just as soon as she gets married to Art, her live-in fiancé. However, Bobby offers to give him the money out of his own savings; when that proves impossible (older sis has kept the money "for his own good"), Bobby "borrows" the money from Art's wallet and practically forces it on Bill, who reluctantly accepts it and dashes off to the phone company—only to find the phone company closed.

Bill finds himself bonding more with Bobby, who sees in Bill the father he never really had. After urging Bobby to go home, Bill relents and takes his newfound charge to a baseball game. The scene at the stadium represents one of the strengths of the film: its ability to take the viewer on a veritable emotional roller coaster without resorting to pathos. Bill and Bobby enjoy the game and each other's company—notably, the ability each has to make the other forget his own troubles. Then Bobby realizes he has lost the money somewhere in the stadium, and after some frantic retracing of their steps, they report the loss to the lost-and-found, whereupon the money is quite unexpectedly returned, with the clerk commenting that Bill must be doing something right to deserve the break. In order to live up to that—as well as to prove a moral example to Bobby—Bill decides to return the money to Art and take his chances. This sequence is sincerely played by all involved, exhibiting the movie's quality of sprinkling a degree of hope, understated and sans histrionics, amidst all the despair.

After some last-minute complications, and some unexpectedly kind gestures from a few other parties, Duryea is able to receive his call. Without divulging every detail (especially since this formerly hard-to-find film can now be acquired through Warner Archive), if anything is a little difficult to accept about *Chicago Calling*, it's the rushed nature of the conclusion. Duryea and his surrogate son become even closer after the call, but this viewer would have liked to see Duryea's on-screen wife incorporated into the denouement, since there remains plenty of unfinished business between the two.

Duryea was quite proud of his work in *Chicago Calling*, calling it his favorite role. It's not hard to see why he would single this film out. No doubt playing a husband and loving father appealed to Duryea, since being a family man was such an integral part of his life. Rarely was Duryea given the opportunity to play a humane, warmhearted role and allowed to dominate the proceedings, as he does here. Duryea's Bill is heartbreaking without becoming maudlin, from his resigned acceptance of the end of the marriage, to his sorrow at seeing his daughter leave, to his unerringly mounted reactions, both to the indignities he is forced to suffer and to the unsolicited kindnesses that crop up along the way. Bill's scene with Bobby, in which Bill gently but forcefully advocates for living a moral life no matter the cost, shows Duryea at his sincere, understated best.

Heartened by the word-of-mouth at previews, Duryea decided not to sell his financial interest in the film, preferring instead to take his chances with the moviegoing public. Unfortunately, the love shown at the previews for *Chicago Calling* did not translate into box-office revenue—or a substantial amount of critical praise. The film was released as a second feature in January 1952 (first on the bill was Paul Henreid in *For Men Only*). *Variety* called it "downbeat and depressing although Duryea is quite good." The *Hollywood Reporter* said: "Duryea works valiantly to make the character believable but rarely succeeds." However, the *Los Angeles Herald Express* said *Chicago Calling* featured one of Duryea's best performances, while *Photoplay* called it "a little gem that will hit you where you live." In the end, this *"American Bicycle Thief,"* as its producers would refer to it, would pedal its way to box-office oblivion. The anticipated profits would never materialize, and Duryea was disappointed that the public would not accept him in this offbeat role. The only solace Duryea would have was knowledge of a job well done—and the fact that his wife wept throughout the screening, saying it was her favorite movie of his.

But this comfort wasn't enough to keep one household running, let alone two. Personally favorable notices notwithstanding, the studios weren't coming through with offers—at least on films that had actual production dates. Duryea did go to London to perform in Newcastle's Royal Film Performance. It was a stage show where he sent up his tough-guy/lover image in two different sketches. Duryea would appear with British star Googie Withers and newcomer Peter Reynolds in a sketch in which he won Withers from a rather bemused Reynolds; another sketch would have him trading quips with a future costar, Jane Russell. As rewarding as the experience was—complete with wife, Helen, accompanying him on what would essentially be an all-expenses-paid working vacation—Duryea was still looking for some form of consistent employment.

For the past few years, Duryea would occasionally lend his vocal talents to radio drama—namely, the popular series *Suspense*. The series, dubbed "radio's outstanding theater of thrills," ran from 1942 to 1952, attracting actors such as Cary Grant, John Garfield, Edward G. Robinson, Gene Kelly, and Judy Garland for half-hour dramas that can be regarded as precursors to such popular television dramas as *Alfred Hitchcock Presents*. In fact, *Suspense* would utilize many of the same writers; Duryea would star in three of these half-hour dramas. In his first, "The Will to Power," broadcast in January 1947, Duryea is a secretary who covets his boss's wife and money (though not in that order), so he murders his boss and marries the wife. Soon after, Duryea frames her for the husband's murder, enabling himself to live happily ever after. That is, until a blackmailer enters the scene. It's a well-crafted episode, and it's interesting to hear Duryea as the intended victim of a blackmailer, for a change.

Duryea's other *Suspense* roles would build on the actor's contentious on-screen relationship with the opposite sex. For "The Man Who Could Not Lose," from December 1947, Duryea was a gambler on a losing streak who treats his wife rather badly but still needs her money. When she refuses, he kills her to get it. Afterwards, he finds himself on an incredible winning streak, but since this is *Suspense*, there is bound to be a twist in his good fortune. His last role for the series was 1952's "Remember Me," in which Duryea was a hoodlum who robs a store, killing its owner. However, after having hidden the body, he is interrupted by a woman who is a former classmate. Now he is torn, because though the woman isn't yet cognizant of his role in robbery and murder, she could still identify him—a prospect that leaves Duryea with few options.

Since movie studios still weren't calling, Duryea found himself on the radio again, this time as a crime-fighter. *The Man from Homicide* was a dramatic detective series, a genre that was popular on the airwaves, and one that Duryea thought had a good chance at success. He was to play Lew Dana, a station-house detective, on a show that would supposedly deal with legitimate police work. Movie tough-guy Charles McGraw originally had played Dana in the pilot for NBC, but the network passed. By the time ABC picked up the series as a summer replacement, McGraw was no longer available, so the producers (among them former *Son of Kong* actress Helen Mack) selected Duryea to play hardboiled Lew Dana. Duryea's Dana is an uncompromising, hard-bitten detective, especially after years of dealing with the underbelly of society: "If I'm tough, it's because guys like you have made me tough." On nearly every episode, Dana would boast (in what would be his signature line), "I don't like killers."

Besides Duryea, there were other distinguished talents behind the microphone. Willis Bouchey was Inspector Sherman, Dana's crusty but avuncular (is there any other kind?) sidekick, while Tom Tully, Jim Backus (soon to achieve fame as the voice of Mr. Magoo), and Arthur Q. Bryan (better known as the inimitable voice of Elmer Fudd) were among the regular crop of supporting players. The initial installments of *The Man from Homicide* received favorable notices, but the program itself had only middling ratings after it premiered in June 1951. The show was canceled after two months, then brought back temporarily after a spurt of high ratings, eventually ending its run in October 1951. After this, Duryea's radio appearances would be sporadic—generally to publicize a film or upcoming personal appearance.

Television, however, was another matter. He had already made a live television appearance on *The Kate Smith Evening Hour* in January 1952. At that time, variety shows offered something resembling true variety; on any of the variety shows of the early fifties, one might find a comic, a singer, a dancer, or even an actor in a short dramatic sketch. Such was the case of Duryea appearing on Kate Smith's show, performing a short drama called "Land's End." It's a serviceable but not particularly well-developed work, as it is more of a vignette about a doomed ex-con (we know he's not long for this world because of the occasional cough and the constant references to his own mortality) at a little tavern called Land's End. It is here that Duryea awaits the arrival of the new mayor—whom he had worked for when they were both racketeers, and whom he blames for being unjustly sent to prison. For the most part, it's a fairly well-acted two-hander, though weighed down with obvious symbolism and a camera that gets a little too cozy with the actors who are trying to balance stage technique and the intimacy of the small screen. This experience left Duryea open to doing more television—just not *live* TV, which he found a little too nerve-racking.

But he liked *filmed* TV. In the early 1950s, many major film studios were cutting production and personnel, forcing stars to look elsewhere to practice their craft. On the comedy front, stars like Lucille Ball and Ann Sothern would gain newfound and enduring popularity, while others, like Ralph Bellamy, would headline crime dramas. Still others, like Robert Montgomery and Douglas Fairbanks, Jr., would host weekly dramas. Duryea himself deflected offers of roles that he felt were trite, along the lines of a detective, railroad agent, or newspaperman. After appearing as a raffish adventurer on *Schlitz Playhouse's* drama "The Souvenir of Singapore," producer Bernard Tabakin came along with a half-hour show called *The Affairs of China Smith* and, to hear Duryea tell it, "I knew this was the series I was looking for."

Duryea was enthusiastic about the opportunity for several reasons. The first was the steady employment that television would provide (although the long hours would be a drawback). Another was the chance to play what he saw as a "virile sort of character" who manages to stay on the right side of the law even if his dealings bring him into conflict with the local police. China Smith is an enigmatic American soldier of fortune in the Orient. As Duryea would put it: "Although you don't know much about his past, you get the impression he has some degree of education and breeding . . . he's attached to his beat-up Panama hat and whose linen suit looks as though he has slept in it . . . he's sexy too." Even so, many of the early episodes would not give Duryea much chance to display those masculine charms. Duryea made it clear that he wasn't looking to escape from the nasty roles that had been his bread and butter; he only hoped that television would afford him the chance to broaden the public's perception of him and to reacquaint studio heads with his skill and versatility.

Duryea committed to fifty-two episodes of what was first to be called *The Affairs of China Smith*, then *The Adventures of China Smith*, which would be produced by Bernard Tabakin under the aegis of Edward Lewis Productions. During the initial run of twenty-six episodes, Duryea's Smith would be in a Hollywood-recreated Singapore facing adversaries such as Communists or those who were bigger crooks than he was. He would also be assisted by a local madam played by Myrna Dell, and alternately helped or hindered by the chief of police (Douglas Dumbrille). To say the series was on a tight schedule would be putting it mildly; the first thirteen episodes were shot in twenty-one days, according to Robert Dennis, one of the head writers. After being granted six weeks to come up with another twelve episodes, this next batch was done a little more leisurely—two days per episode. The series itself provided opportunities to some fledgling directors, notably Robert Aldrich, to hone their craft; it also utilized established writers like Geoffrey Homes (best known for that seminal noir *Build My Gallows High*, aka *Out of the Past*).

Viewing the series more than sixty years after its initial run, *The Adventures of China Smith* is a mixed bag; while there are no outright clunkers in the series, some work better than others. Several episodes are flawed by the necessity of wrapping things up in twenty-six minutes. The series tries hard to offset its budgetary limitations with pacing, occasional action, ersatz Oriental settings, and flavorful dialogue. Many of the early episodes would begin with Duryea's voice-over narration introducing his character—usually seen on foot, stalking the Singapore streets—while acquainting us with his new investigation, which quite often he is in the middle of. One such episode is "The Bamboo Jungle," with a very young Rita Moreno guest-starring as a damsel in distress, as Smith tries to sort out threats involving local bandits. In this episode, Duryea's Smith admits to enjoying gambling (and more often losing) and to not being above using women to get what he's after.

Two of Duryea's early *China Smith* episodes were directed by Robert Aldrich; this would be an association that would later prove beneficial to both Duryea and Aldrich away from the television screens. In "Straight Settlement," China Smith is in a load of trouble and must prove his innocence after a serum disappears—and he's accused of stealing it. He has to comb the Singapore underworld while trying to pacify the possibly doomed victim's daughter; it's a tight, well-paced episode that makes good use of Duryea's crafty tough-guy persona, while allowing him some tender (not romantic) moments with the daughter. The other episode, "The Shanghai Clipper," has China Smith investigating a mysterious death wherein a passenger took a header off the titular plane, while searching for the map the victim had been killed for. In this episode, Duryea sports an Irish brogue at first (as might befit someone from Ireland who is wanted for treason), an affectation that he'll use throughout the run of the series when trying to show he's not full of blarney. Thankfully, he soon dispenses with it here; accents would never be Duryea's strong suit, but that didn't stop him from trying.

In addition to Aldrich's assured handling, the two defining points of "The Shanghai Clipper" have to do with the China Smith character's relations with the police—and with the opposite sex. This episode would be typical in establishing his mutually respectful relationship with Douglas Dumbrille's chief, who is aware of Smith's shady past but manages to help him apprehend the bad guys on cue. He even allows Smith to maintain his crooked standing within the Singapore community, all the better to deceive the bad guys who might confide in Smith. The second defining point concerned Smith's dealing with women. In this instance, he is akin to a noir hero, in that Duryea's Smith, clever as he is with regard to his fellow criminals, is at a distinct disadvantage when it comes to the ladies. Sparring with the talented Marian Carr (with whom he'd reteam later under Aldrich's direction) and searching for a map while dealing with counterfeits, Duryea's Smith is a little too trusting and too willing to think his natural charm will reap positive results with the ladies; his efforts often result in disillusionment.

When *China Smith* finally began airing, it garnered mixed notices from the critical community. Several reviewers gently admonished Duryea for his occasional side trips to Barry Fitzgerald-land (courtesy of that regrettable brogue), while publications such as *Variety* wrote that "the writing seems to have cribbed every action cliché from every third-rate whodunit on 'The Late, Late Show.'" Despite the notices, the ratings were quite positive and the show proved to be very profitable; though his own salary was marginal, Duryea was shrewd enough to acquire a substantial ownership stake tied to repeated showings. Since *China Smith* was syndicated, these twenty-six initial episodes found themselves playing all over the country on a frequent basis throughout the 1950s. There would be more episodes to come, but these would not be filmed right away, as the Screen Actors Guild challenged the producers on some of their past practices. In the interest of thrift, the producers had gone to Mexico to film the first six episodes. Because of this, the producers claimed they didn't have to make residual payments as required by the guild. Because of this somewhat unpleasant situation, Duryea decided not to do any more episodes until the matter was resolved.

In the interim, Duryea was overwhelmed by the new attention, especially from kids who would say to him, "We know you're China Smith—what's your real name?" Duryea and Helen would go to parties, where the conversation would be about incidents in the show and what the guests liked—sentiments that Duryea would rarely hear for his screen roles. He said to interviewers: "I believe TV assists an actor's career—it brings him closer to the public." Given the ease with which actors now move back and forth from movies to television, Duryea's words were fairly astute. Granted, there were still those who preferred to see Duryea slapping damsels rather than helping them, but the show's overall popularity helped enable movie producers to rediscover him, and the first to come through with an offer would be none other than his old studio Universal.

In addition to adapting to the breakneck pace of *China Smith*, Duryea also appeared on the *Lux Video Theater*, one of many anthology series that proved popular in the 1950s, as many actors could land a high-profile engagement while on a hiatus from the movies. Duryea would have starring roles on several different anthologies in the 1950s and '60s. This particular episode was "The Brooch," costarring Mildred Natwick.

Based on a William Faulkner short story, "The Brooch" was about a matriarch, her powerful hold over her son, and a certain family brooch. It was a dark tale, since in the original story, the son is married to someone who might charitably be called a tramp—and he eventually kills himself. In this adaptation, Duryea (as the son) stands up to his mother, and the finale sees the mother giving the family brooch to her misunderstood daughter-in-law. The actors received good reviews, but Faulkner's screenplay drew some criticism for bowdlerizing the original story. Regardless of the reviews, widely seen shows like *China Smith* and *Lux Video Theater* kept Duryea in front of audiences.

Hedda Hopper was the first to break the story that Duryea's television sojourn got him a job as one of the leads (reputably that of a so-called heavy) in *Thunder Bay*, costarring with James Stewart and Joanne Dru. Besides the television exposure, there may have been other factors at play. First, the film's director, Anthony Mann, made no secret of the fact that he wanted to work with Duryea again. Additionally, Stewart and Duryea had become pretty good friends after *Winchester '73*, so when a strong actor was needed to play Stewart's fast-talking, happy-go-lucky pal (nothing "heavy" about the part), Stewart suggested that Duryea would be the perfect choice. In the end, no one would have any reason to be displeased by Duryea's casting, and *Thunder Bay* would mark Duryea's heartening return to the big screen.

With a budget of a little over $1,000,000, *Thunder Bay* commenced shooting on location in Morgan City, Louisiana, from a script by Borden Chase, who had written, among other films, the earlier, well-received Stewart/Mann collaboration *Bend of the River*. It would also be the first Universal picture shot in widescreen (although the 1.85:1 ratio would not be as wide as CinemaScope's 2.35:1 ratio). Set in 1946, *Thunder Bay* stars Stewart and Duryea as partners who have staked their last dollar (as well as that of some investors, led by Jay C. Flippen) on a scheme to drill for oil off the coast of Louisiana. Stewart is the more obsessed partner, not unlike his traditional Mann Western hero, while Duryea's Gamby is more laid-back, accustomed to enjoying all aspects of the local scenery. The partners' desire to drill in the Gulf brooks some opposition from the local fishermen (led by Gilbert Roland), while Duryea's romancing of a local gal arouses the ire of her fisherman papa and embittered sister (Joanne Dru).

The filming would prove to be both gratifying and eventful for Duryea. He relished being back on a movie set, even though it meant being away from his family. The residents of Morgan City (renamed Port Felicity for the movie) proved to be gracious hosts, embracing the cast and crew, and involving them in local activities. In his spare time, Duryea helped judge a local beauty pageant and participated in an oyster-eating contest. Duryea impressed those in Morgan City for being the antithesis of his screen persona, and by the time the film company departed in November 1952, he was made an honorary policeman.

The location shoot was not without its bumps—literally. In October, Duryea suffered a broken rib, along with contusions and bruises, when he fell from a roof of a tugboat. He had slipped on a cabin roof while filming a scene and fell seven feet to the boat's deck. The fall knocked him unconscious, and the resulting injuries forced him to miss a couple of days of work.

As for the film itself, if you can get past the fact that much of *Thunder Bay* resembles a feature-length advertisement for the oil industry (which Stewart strongly supported), there is plenty to enjoy. In an early scene, when faced with the probability of winning over an unwilling populace, Duryea asks Stewart if he has any entertainment skills. Stewart replies, "I can do a swell imitation of that tall, drawling movie star," to which Duryea replies, "*That* guy? Never mind!" Stewart is perpetually confrontational with the opposing fishermen, especially in a scene that plays right out of a Mann Western, as a dynamite-wielding Stewart faces down a veritable lynch mob of local business owners. Duryea's romancing of Marcia Henderson (playing Joanne Dru's sister, the daughter of a venerable fisherman who represents the opposition) affords him the chance to exhibit his gift for well-timed banter; it also adds spark to the strained relations between the oilmen and the fishermen.

Perhaps Duryea's best scene comes in his climactic confrontation with Stewart. In what has become a typical situation in any Mann/Stewart collaboration, Stewart has driven his men past the breaking point, and after an ill-timed oil rig mishap (during which Duryea has been conspicuously absent, having tied the knot with Henderson), Stewart further depletes the men's good will by telling them they have to work "gratis" (big business funds having run dry), then berating them when they prove reluctant. Enter Duryea, who passionately informs Stewart about how he's "been riding the men too much—but you're not gonna ride me," immediately followed by some fisticuffs, in which Duryea (temporarily) emerges triumphant. However, Duryea's revelation that he is now married to Marcia leads Stewart to unceremoniously deck him—and fire the lot. Upon being told that Stewart at one time offered them a bonus if they had stayed on, Duryea tells the men, "You should have taken it," exhorting his fellow workers to give Stewart at least a little more time. Duryea's self-deprecating humor, ironic sensibility, and impassioned eloquence constitute not only a highlight of the film but of Duryea's career.

Thunder Bay turned out to be a substantial hit for Universal; the film was a personal success for Duryea as well. Although it had only been eighteen months since the underseen *Chicago Calling*, reviewers welcomed him back to the big screen, and many, such as the critic from *Variety*, remarked that Duryea had his best role in years. The *San Diego Sun* would echo what others may have felt when offering the following observation: "Duryea has his first likable part in a long line of villainy. But his history doesn't hurt him. It adds spice because you're never completely sure he'll stay good for the rest of *Thunder Bay*." This critic was quite perceptive as to what was so right about the casting of Duryea in this film, and what Duryea was aware of—should producers be wise enough to cast him in roles containing some ambivalence. His cinematic history preceded him, lending an aura of uncertainty and suspense to almost any film he was in, even routine endeavors—provided he wasn't cast as an out-and-out villain (as was too often the case).

With the renewed studio interest in Duryea's film career, it's difficult to see what drew Duryea to his next project, the low-budget *Thunder Jet Commandos*, later released as *Sky Commando* by Columbia Pictures. While the director was the fairly competent Fred Sears, what passed for a script was composed by no fewer than three writers. Samuel Newman received screenplay credit, and the story was credited to Newman, William Sackheim, and Arthur Orloff. The producer was none other than Sam Katzman, who was becoming well known in Hollywood circles as a man who had never met a cost he couldn't cut, and *Sky Commando* stands before you as representative of the Katzman touch—years before such howlers as *The Giant Claw*.

Duryea is a flight commander in Korea, reputed to be a heartless martinet. An early sequence shows the aftermath of a flying mission; naturally, some make it back, while others don't. A bitter pilot who saw his buddy go down flails away at an unresponsive Duryea, who sees death as coming with the territory. While the pilot is nursing his psychological wounds, Duryea's old friend drops in to tell this pilot a little story, consisting of a flashback to Duryea's World War II days that takes up the bulk of the film's sixty-eight-minute running time. It would appear that Duryea's methods as a flier (leading missions to photograph enemy targets) had come into question before; he came under fire for saving himself at the expense of his fellow fliers. Mike Connors (then billed as "Touch" Conners) is Duryea's copilot, and after a mission that shows Duryea justifiably making some difficult choices (like jettisoning his fallen comrades to lighten the plane's weight), the film insists on maintaining the conflict between Duryea and Connors—to the point where Connors insists on joining Duryea in Africa "to keep an eye on him." All issues get resolved when it is revealed to Connors that Duryea had saved his life, as well as those of the crew, in their latest mission, helping ensure their escape from enemy territory with the help of local partisans.

Sky Commando is perhaps the worst Duryea movie to feature Duryea in the lead role—although some might hold out for 1968's *The Bamboo Saucer*. A film with Sam Katzman's name affixed to it has a quality all its own, and *Sky Commando* carries the hallmarks of a true Katzman production. The poverty-row approach to filmmaking is apparent throughout, including in the "matching" of stock war footage with the film's action, which makes clear the paucity of both the screenplay and the budget (the planes in the film clearly don't match those in the borrowed footage). The screenplay itself conveys most of the information through its liberal use of voice-over narration; in fact, there is so much of it that *Sky Commando* begins to resemble an educational film from the 1950s. Key plot points are conveyed through voice-over, as in this passage in which a youthful partisan's off-screen death is relayed: "Poor Jorgy, their friendship was short-lived, as he took a bullet just yards away from the boat that would carry them to safety." This could have been a dramatic moment in the film . . . had it bothered to have been dramatized. Yet this sorry excuse for a script is what Duryea and his managers knowingly enlisted for. Worse still, casting Duryea as a rigid military man confines Duryea and hinders him from introducing nuances and shadings—especially since the script tends to favor the "Touch" Conners character throughout. Though Duryea must have welcomed the chance to play this heroic character, it would have been more advantageous had he held out for a stronger screenplay. As the final result clearly demonstrates, this *Sky Commando* should have been permanently grounded.

Duryea followed up this lackluster effort with a welcome trip to England. In the early 1950s, Hammer Films, before becoming exclusively a horror/science fiction mill, was providing steady employment to an array of American talent (mainly rising stars and fading stars). Actors such as George Brent, George Raft, and Dane Clark would lend their talents to films that could be termed "light noir," as they possessed some of American film noir's darker sensibilities without necessarily leading to a bleak conclusion. Duryea was recruited for a film that would be released in

England as *36 Hours*, but would find its way to America under the title *Terror Street*. There would be some pretty fair talent behind the camera: Montgomery Tully was directing, but Jimmy Sangster, soon to be one of Hammer's top horror directors, served as assistant director. The story and screenplay were by Steve Fisher, who had scripted *I Wake Up Screaming*, which starred Victor Mature, Betty Grable, and Laird Cregar in a prime example of early American film noir. In addition, the filming would be done at Bray Castle, which had since been converted to Exclusive Studios for the use of such entities as Lippert Productions.

One of the working titles of this British noir was *Goodbye to Katie*, which would have been a better and more evocative title than *Terror Street*. Duryea is an American flyer (his second one of the year—perhaps he was getting typecast!) in London who wangles an unauthorized thirty-six-hour leave to see his wife, Katie. When he arrives at her presumed flat, she is not there; after some legwork, he manages to find her new apartment and settles in, bottle in hand, to remember their first meeting. These early scenes, with Duryea silently surveying his surroundings and recalling (complete with voice-over) their courtship and eventual strained parting, have some of the feeling and atmosphere of American noir. He displays a tentative charm during the courtship scenes, while British actress Elsy Albin makes a worthy but ultimately ill-fated partner. Following Katie's return in the present, Duryea is clocked from behind by her male associate, Hart. Katie argues with Hart, who murders her because of some unnamed items. Hart then puts the gun in Duryea's hand; upon reviving, Duryea is then forced to come up with his wife's killer by the time his leave is up. His subsequent nighttime flight, followed by a furtive meeting with a charitable mission worker named Jenny, have an urgency and energy that dissipates as the film progresses. Duryea has ample opportunity for some fisticuffs and legwork, but for plot purposes, his character is maneuvered into some highly implausible situations, leading to a hopeful conclusion wherein the deceased Katie is revealed to have been not so "fatale" a female as Duryea was led to believe.

Terror Street makes fairly good use of the tender side of Duryea's Hollywood persona, and there is an amusing encounter with a charity worker who thinks Bill is too well fed to need a meal. In general, however, Fisher's mundane screenplay ultimately lets everyone down—even when it isn't self-consciously trying to replicate the hardboiled patois of American noir (as in when Hart says, "Goodbye, Katie, you shouldn't have tried to cross me," before plugging her). In spite of this, Duryea's Bill has several opportunities to portray the doomed romantic idealism of the noir hero, embodying the fatalism inherent in the genre. At the end, after being shown proof of Katie's good intentions, Bill offers that Katie "always told the truth"; Duryea utters the line with the proper blend of wistfulness and regret, as only he could deliver it.

When it was eventually released on both sides of the Atlantic in 1953, most reviewers called *Terror Street/36 Hours* a fairly routine programmer. The British Film Institute's *Monthly Bulletin* observed that "the rather commonplace murder story loses much of its interest simply because Dan Duryea has not the look of a sympathetic character," while *Today's Cinema* would provide an interesting example of the fleeting nature of fame when it gave its readers a pronunciation guide (Doo-re-ay) for the Hollywood veteran's name. The *Los Angeles Times* would be in the minority when it called the film a "better than average whodunit," but some reviewers did allow that Duryea was effective as the aggrieved husband. The film would be a one-shot British film appearance for Duryea, although he would return to England in the mid-1960s. Presently, however, he was about to make his way back to the Hollywood Orient, in a familiar guise, with a familiar director, in what would be one of his best roles.

CHAPTER 8

A Very Busy Year:
Audie, Aldrich, Payne, and a Pool

SINCE DURYEA'S *CHINA SMITH* BECAME A WELL-KNOWN COMMODITY on the syndication front, some of the people responsible for its success—namely, producer Bernard Tabakin and director Robert Aldrich—were hoping to produce a big-screen version of this raffish hero's exploits, with Duryea in the lead. However, after much discussion, Tabakin and Aldrich abandoned the idea of a straight adaptation of *China Smith*. Duryea concurred, surmising "people don't like paying what they can get for free at home."

Instead, Aldrich, Tabakin, and writer Lindsay Hardy (along with the blacklisted, uncredited screenwriter Hugo Butler) elected to produce a slightly darker, feature-length variation of the series, raising the ante for the hero to encompass not just his own personal stake but the world's as well. The film was to be called *World for Ransom*, starring Duryea in a trademark hat and tattered white suit. But he's not China Smith—he's adventurer Mike Callahan. In many ways, however, the film was reminiscent of the television series, especially in terms of atmosphere and budget. Like *China Smith*, *World for Ransom* was set in a perpetually nocturnal Hollywood-made Singapore; also like its predecessor, it was shot in a rather crisp manner. The film's budget was $120,000 and had a ten-day shooting schedule. Despite (and maybe because of) the hurried nature of the enterprise, Aldrich managed to create a fast-paced, evocative tale of intrigue, romance, and eventual betrayal—all with an assuredness that transcends genre and budgetary limitations. This also represented yet another occasion in which Duryea was willing to put his talent on the line, for very little remuneration, provided it was a project he believed in.

In *World for Ransom*, Duryea's Mike Callahan uneasily navigates his way through the busy Singapore streets alone. He is encouraged to "take a chance" by a local madam, and politely declines. Yet the whole film is all about the chances the still-idealistic Callahan takes in defense of love and friendship. His good friend and former partner, Julian March, is engaged in some dubious activities, one of which may concern the imminent kidnapping of an important nuclear scientist. In addition, Callahan carries a not-so-hidden torch for his former girlfriend Frennessey, who is now March's wife and who refuses to divulge any of March's dealings. However, she isn't above playing on their past relationship to get Callahan to promise to do whatever he can to protect March. Because of Callahan's association with March, and his own acquaintance with members of the Singapore underworld, he is hounded by the police after the scientist is indeed kidnapped, later finding himself caught between his loyalty to March (and especially Frennessey) and his own sense of honor.

Besides March, Callahan's closest friend is a photographer named Lee Wong, who has the misfortune of being present—and snapping a picture—as O'Conner the scientist is being kidnapped by March and an imposing thug named Guzik. After Callahan sees the picture, he alerts Frennessey to March's involvement; subsequently, Wong is murdered by Guzik, with March in attendance, and everything Callahan has assumed about loyalty and integrity is put into serious jeopardy. Even though the police (led by Douglas Dumbrille, providing another reminder of *China Smith*) believe Callahan to be involved, they allow him to escape, hoping he'll lead them to March and perhaps the scientist.

In the end, Callahan emerges triumphant after his journey through the jungle, but it comes with a cost. He forges a brief friendship with Major Bone (warmly played by Reginald Denny) who believes in Callahan's innocence and helps him to storm the kidnappers' compound; Bone is killed, and Callahan assumes the blame because, in his eyes, he failed to make sure one of the enemies is indeed dead. Upon finding Julian in league with the kidnappers, Callahan prevails upon Julian to turn on them and he agrees—up to the point when he decides to dispatch Callahan as well, whereupon Callahan blows him and his own illusions to kingdom come. If that's not enough betrayal for this tortured soul, Callahan's self-destructive streak gets a thorough going-over when he visits

Frennessey and admits that he killed his friend—her husband, Julian. Callahan's assertion that Julian was ultimately no good holds very little sway over a grieving Frennessey; instead, she turns on Callahan with a vengeance, bitterly dismissing his misbegotten attempt to console her while savagely informing Callahan that he'll never be the man March was. Frennessey's betrayal, abetted in no small measure by Callahan's idealization of her (she's not just on a pedestal, she had been placed far above it), solidifies Callahan's standing among the upper echelon of noir's wounded heroes who are left to muddle through the world alone, reluctant to again "take a chance."

Duryea's Callahan, aided by a smart script and Aldrich's firm direction, is more than just a spinoff of *China Smith* (although that had been the original intent). Callahan is a true antihero who, despite his own cynicism, has a code that he follows unwaveringly, along with a self-destructive streak that haunts him to the bitter end. It is a pitch-perfect realization of fallen idealism and doomed romanticism, laced with opportunities for self-deprecating humor, all with an ironic edge. Duryea has rarely been as affecting as in his early scene with Frennessey, where he pours out all of his yearnings to a seemingly receptive Frennessey. In Duryea's scenes with March (a capably duplicitous Patric Knowles,) Duryea astutely conveys Callahan's protectiveness and integrity, as well as a degree of jealousy that hovers over their purported friendship.

Duryea himself was pleased not only with his own work in *World for Ransom* but by another opportunity to be playing the hero, as he felt that "good villain roles don't come along too often and if you get typed as a heavy, you wind up playing fifty mediocre parts for one good part." Aldrich also confessed to his own affection for the film and for Duryea, whom he regarded as a consummate professional and a willing collaborator. As for the critics, they were perhaps a tad reserved in their response. The *Daily News* called it "a tight thriller that maintains suspense," while the *New York World Telegram*, noting the presence of such performers as Knowles, Denny, Arthur Shields, and Gene Lockhart, noted that "the supporting cast is almost a museum of old favorites." Bosley Crowther of the *New York Times* was singularly unimpressed: "Aldrich produced and directed. He was trying. Some day he may learn how." Its B-movie origins and tepid response notwithstanding, *World for Ransom* has gained stature over the years as a pivotal film in Aldrich's career, coming as it did before the explosive *Kiss Me Deadly*. The film was also another indication that Duryea could command the screen as a flawed hero, almost as much as he could as an out-and-out villain.

Duryea was still reluctant to take on the "heavy," especially in light of his recent, occasionally well-received forays into relatively virtuous roles. Yet three of his next films, all 1954 releases (it would be a very busy year for Duryea on-screen), would display his villainous side—though the first would allow Duryea to be as likable as the hero. He would return to Universal for *The Breckenridge Story* under the veteran Jesse Hibbs's direction. Eventually released as *Ride Clear of Diablo*, it would be the first of three pairings with Audie Murphy—and the most successful. Although decorated war hero turned Western star Murphy had his own share of personal demons, on-screen he displayed an understated, sincere demeanor that complemented the more flamboyant and outlandish Duryea.

Although Duryea was seen as a "returning hero" by the producers at Universal, these feelings didn't necessarily translate into a bigger budget (this one was slightly under $500,000, as opposed to, say, *River Lady*, with its nearly $3 million budget) or higher salary (being paid a not-so-princely total of $20,000 for four weeks of filming, as opposed to $15,000 per *week* for *River Lady*). If this diminished standing dismayed Duryea, he didn't let on; at forty-seven, he may have simply been content with the work and for the opportunity to put a fresh spin on his carefully cultivated bad-guy persona. In interviews at the time, Duryea professed to relish yet another opportunity to play the gleefully cackling outlaw: "I like to chuckle when I plunge a knife into his back . . . it always pays off with customers." He was aware of how much the audiences embraced his villainy, especially when accompanied by his jaunty swagger and distinctive laugh. In this particular outing, Duryea allegedly laughed himself sick. Two hours of filming of a laughing jag (that would prove to be a highlight of the film) also resulted in a throat condition brought on by the excessive laughing.

Looking at *Ride Clear of Diablo*, it's a wonder Duryea's throat condition didn't result in laryngitis, since his laugh is present throughout. Duryea is Whitey Kincaid, a somewhat legendary outlaw whom novice deputy Clay O' Mara (Audie Murphy) has been sent to apprehend on the pretext that Whitey is responsible for the deaths of Clay's brother and father. (In fact, he isn't—it's the corrupt sheriff and lawyer who have done the dirty deed, and they send Clay out hoping he'll be killed by this sharp-shooting varmint.) Far from being angered by his arrest, Whitey takes a liking to the sincere deputy, even advising him to keep an eye on certain characters. Whitey doesn't yet give up the people he knows to be guilty, since it would ruin his own pleasure in seeing how events play out. Nor does his sympathy toward Clay prevent the wily Whitey from scheming to smash Clay's head (always smilingly) with a loose rock.

Even though Murphy is the nominal star of the movie, Duryea seizes center stage about twenty minutes in and dominates throughout. The script affords him several scenes to establish a bond with Murphy, especially during their eventful ride back to town, where Murphy not only has to cope with Duryea's attempts to escape but with those who would try to rescue Duryea. Duryea's plausibly develops his character's growing fondness for Murphy, while not neglecting Whitey's perverse streak that causes him to withhold vital information from Murphy. Such is Whitey's reputation for balderdash that even when he reveals the identity of the bad guys, he is dismissed by the still naïve Clay. It takes the larcenous actions of a subsidiary henchman (Russell Johnson, a decade before he became the professor on *Gilligan's Island*) to finally bring Clay and Whitey together for a showdown against Sheriff Kenyon, lawyer Meredith, and a few gunmen—a brief but exciting gun battle in which a severely wounded Whitey sacrifices his life in order to give Clay the chance to save himself and finish off the real culprits.

Ride Clear of Diablo, as formulaic as it might be, given the hero's triumph and the good/bad man laying down his life, is still an essential entry in the Duryea filmography. Whitey is one of his most likable bad guys, and Duryea plays him as a smiling, swaggering, yet strangely softhearted force of nature. Given Duryea's presumed inclinations toward unbridled villainy, audiences might have figured he would eventually turn against the hero (which is yet another convention of this genre); instead he remains a loyal, if puckish ally. Whitey's actions are occasionally even a mystery to him, as he wants nothing more than to stir things up and be present to enjoy the fruits of his mischievous labors. One can't imagine anyone but Duryea playing Whitey, and he inspires Murphy to raise the level of his own work. The reviewers were favorable, with Duryea getting much of the praise for his "engaging heavy" (*Variety*), or, in the words of the *New York Motion Picture Herald*, "Duryea's unusual characterization of a good bad man who uses laughter as a weapon of sarcasm."

It's too bad that Duryea's next Western heavy, in the first of a two-film contract at Universal, was much more conventional. In *Fort Laramie*, Duryea would again be working with that reliable contract director Jesse Hibbs, only here he would be going up against the stalwart John Payne in another formulaic outing that had at least one unusual key plot element, involving the first female jurors in the history of United States law.

In *Rails into Laramie*, as it was released, Duryea is a saloonkeeper in 1869 Wyoming. Duryea's continued prosperity depends on impeding the progress of the railroad through Laramie, since its construction would mean that the workers would move on—and he would lose their extremely profitable patronage. Payne is Duryea's friend, an army sergeant who carries a torch for Duryea's very faithful wife (Joyce McKenzie) and who has taken on the formidable task of completing work on the railroad—even if it means taking on both the town and the increasingly Machiavellian Duryea. Payne's devotion to duty predictably causes friction between the two former friends, as corruption, bribery, and physical violence fail to deter Payne from accomplishing his goal.

After repeated attempts to indict and convict Duryea prove to be fruitless—especially given how much sway Duryea has with the male contingent—Duryea's disillusioned partner and former paramour Mari Blanchard (who almost had the monopoly at Universal on tough-talking attractive saloon gals) suggests that Payne commission a female jury. Women had recently been allowed to serve as jurors (but had yet to actually do it). These females are more than a match for Duryea, delivering what Payne heretofore couldn't: a guilty verdict for the murderously smug Duryea.

In spite of some last-minute, rather busy developments (involving Duryea's wife using Payne's affections to gain access to the imprisoned Duryea and an ultimately unsuccessful attempt to use the train for a getaway), *Rails into Laramie* is no more than a fitfully entertaining little Western. Payne is more animated here with Duryea than in their previous collaboration, *Larceny*, and Duryea worked hard in order to make his character even more reprehensible than the script allowed. Toward the end, a fugitive Duryea takes a little time from fleeing to deliver a hoped for coup de grace in the form of a bullet fired at Mari Blanchard. After filming this scene, Duryea said: "I must be slipping; just shooting Mari in the back is a little tame for a dirty dog like myself." Duryea suggested that he shoot Mari again on her way down; Hibbs agreed and it remained in the finished film (though she does survive her injuries, earning the long-term affections of a grateful Payne at the conclusion).

As for Duryea's trademark cackle, it's in short supply here, even though Duryea said to a reporter during filming: "I discovered that folks hate me twice as much if I mix the dirty laughs in among the dirty things I do in the movies." It was as if Duryea didn't find much in the script or in the plot's protracted machinations to inspire such revelry. Perhaps he yearned for a less conventional role, one not defined solely by unrelenting avarice. Although Duryea received some good personal notices, there were several reviewers, like the *San Francisco Examiner* critic, who wondered "why don't they put the lad in more sophisticated roles."

Though his roles may not have been sophisticated, on- and off-set Duryea was not only sophisticated, but solicitous toward his fellow actors, too. Myron Healey, who appeared in *Rails into Laramie* and would act alongside Duryea in other films, would later tell author Gene Blottner how Duryea assumed the role of Cupid. It involved Healey's visiting girlfriend, and Healey's desire to secure lodgings for her out at the Wyoming location. Duryea suggested Healey stay with him in his luxurious suite, and that Healey offer his own room to the visiting girlfriend. Duryea would say to Healey, "Make yourself at home, we'll sip some scotch. And after we have a couple of drinks and everyone is settled in for the night, you can go and kiss your lady goodnight . . ."

As busy as Duryea was in 1954 (both acting and playing Cupid), he never lost sight of his obligations as a father and member of his community. As much as Duryea was concerned with his own sons not running with the wrong crowd, the rise in juvenile delinquency and lack of facilities for those not as privileged as his own children was something he felt compelled to act on. Duryea spoke at a community board meeting at Belmont High School on behalf of building a pool in Echo Park as a way of protecting the area against the growth of what he termed "nothing-to-do gangs." Duryea spoke at length about "recreation and what it means to our youth." He also stressed the value of the project in fighting juvenile delinquency: "Let our children be water rats and not rat packs." Since Duryea's sons were both in their teen years, he felt he had to do his share—and perhaps use some of his Hollywood cachet to help safeguard his family and provide a voice for others. Activities like this would contribute to Duryea being named as Father of the Year by the Independent Photographers Association. In a way, these forays into community affairs would also serve to counteract the bad-guy image which Duryea's screen appearances only further bolstered.

It was an image that would be reinforced with Duryea's next film. He was announced for RKO's Western *Four Desperate Men*, or as it was ultimately released, *Silver Lode*, with Duryea again playing opposite John Payne in what would be their third and final screen pairing. *Silver Lode* remains famous as one of the first pictures to make reference to the witch-hunts in Hollywood from the late 1940s to the 1950s. As directed by the veteran Allan Dwan from a script by Karen De Wolf, Duryea plays intractable Marshal McCarty (a not-so-veiled reference to Senator—and aspiring demagogue—Joseph McCarthy). Duryea's McCarty, accompanied by some deputies (including Harry Carey, Jr., and future *Gilligan's Island* Skipper Alan Hale, Jr.), arrives in the town of Silver Lode to arrest prominent citizen John Payne for murder. As it turns out, Payne is accused of murdering the vengeful McCarty's brother; furthermore, it's Payne's wedding day—he is to be married to the lovely Lizabeth Scott—and the town is justifiably angry with the crafty marshal's accusations directed at one of their most revered residents. To a man, they endorse Payne's integrity and oppose any efforts on McCarty's part to extradite him to California. That is, until it's revealed that Payne did indeed kill the marshal's brother (as Payne says, for good reason). Dormant suspicions are reignited among the good people of Silver Lode pertaining to Payne's arrival in town a few years back, with money in his pocket. Since the marshal's papers seem to be in order, and because McCarty has outwardly pledged to work with the town to "do what's right," the townspeople begin to slowly but irrevocably change their sympathies—much to Payne's distress, as he sees his friends succumb to McCarty's slanderous statements and unproven accusations.

This was very much akin to what was capturing the public's attention in the 1950s, when today's stars could become tomorrow's pariahs under a studio-sanctioned unofficial blacklist. Whether it was under the purportedly patriotically inclined House Un-American Activities Committee in the late forties or the McCarthy-led hearings of the fifties, the Hollywood blacklist was very much a part of the American cultural fabric. Duryea's son Richard remembers that his father was "downright terrified" after witnessing the damage done to friends and colleagues, such as Cy Endfield from *The Underworld Story*. Duryea himself avoided coming under the scrutiny of HUAC, even though he had worked closely with blacklist victims in the past. Maybe it was because Duryea kept his political beliefs to himself; Richard remembers when he would be asked whom he was voting for, his father would reply, "I vote for one person, your mother votes for the other, so we cancel each other out." The causes Duryea supported were ones that related to his community and family, far from the political causes and occasional "Communist fronts" that other celebrities contributed to. While there were indeed actual Communists working in Hollywood who integrated their philosophy into their films, others fell victim to accusations and insinuations, including actors like John Garfield, Larry Parks (star of *The Jolson Story*, whose career never recovered), and Edward G. Robinson, to name a few. It was also a time where people were given the all-too-distasteful choice between saying nothing, and perhaps irrevocably damning their own careers, or naming names, thereby saving their own skins at the expense of their self-respect and esteem in the industry.

In the film, the accusations against Payne lead to some drastic actions on his part. Upon learning that one of Duryea's deputies is willing to turn against Duryea (for a price) and reveal Duryea's bogus marshal status, Payne moves fast—but not fast enough—to stop McCarty from murdering both Payne's unlikely savior and the town sheriff who believed in him. McCarty pins both murders on the hapless Payne, who now faces the town's wrath as they shoot up Silver Lode in an effort to get their hands on their formerly respected leading citizen. It's only through the efforts of unwavering fiancée Scott and his former lover, dance-hall girl Dolores Moran, that Payne is exonerated (yet naturally embittered by his town's betrayal).

Silver Lode succeeds both as a tense, compact Western laced with bursts of well-choreographed mayhem amidst rapidly evolving relationships and conflicting character loyalties. Though De Wolf's script sometimes teeters over into melodrama, the fast pace and assured acting keep the events plausible. If the town's eventual hysteria seems to strain credibility, history shows us that events like those depicted here are distressingly not so far-fetched. Duryea's role does not lend itself to many shadings, especially since his real status is tipped early on, but he maintains the intensity throughout, leavening it occasionally with some sly humor. Duryea is at his best when confronting Payne one-on-one about what is required for his fraudulent lawman to leave Payne alone—that is, nothing short of Payne's entire holdings. After all, a dead brother may be a dead brother, but land—especially lots of it—would certainly provide a salve for McCarty's alleged emotional wounds.

Silver Lode, like many of Duryea's films, received mixed reviews at the time, although the *Daily Mirror* called it "no ordinary shoot-em-up saga," noting its elements of hysteria and mob violence that were central to the movie's themes. Duryea was also fond of the picture and his role—as well as the challenges that his villainous roles present: "These give myself and my family a comfortable life and a lot of fun, career wise. Few actors could be in a better spot. The parts I play might come under the classification of villain, but I try to make the parts I portray new and different in concept and performance."

As much as he believed that he was in "a better spot," Duryea thought he had just as much to offer in non-villainous roles. He would embrace opportunities to portray what he perceived to be relatively vulnerable characters. Such was the case when he accepted a return engagement to RKO for a color noirish soap opera released as *This Is My Love*. Filmed under the titles *Night Music* and *Night Without End*, Stuart Heisler would direct this twisted tale of jealousy, unrequited love, and almost all-consuming bitterness. The film starred Duryea, Linda Darnell, and Faith Domergue (an RKO fixture thanks to her modicum of talent and plenty of attention from Howard Hughes). The film begins on a rainswept night, with Darnell recounting, in a very fatalistic voice-over, the events of the last few weeks. Darnell and Domergue are Vida and Evelyn, two sisters who operate a diner owned by Evelyn's husband, Murray (Duryea), a wheelchair-bound former dancer who harbors no illusions over his diminished status as a man—or as a husband. Vida, who is currently engaged, had once dated Murray. Now, they all live in the same house, along with Murray and Evelyn's two kids, a domestic situation that lends itself to some fairly melodramatic complications. These arrive in the form of young, good-looking Glenn (played by handsome but stiff-as-oak Rick Jason), who manages to capture the attention of both sisters. After some foreplay with Vida, Glenn decides that Evelyn is the one—and vice versa. When Murray isn't dreamily ruminating about his long-lost agility, he is correctly deducing that Evelyn's late-night returns from work have nothing to do with the business of the diner. Meanwhile, Vida has to suffer with the attractive Evelyn once again stealing her man—as well as the possibility of being cast out entirely if Murray succeeds in selling the diner and moving to the seashore. Since this is borderline noir, there will be an untimely death—and some consequences.

Duryea was very enthusiastic about his role as the bitter Murray, seeing the role of the cuckolded paraplegic as "the most sympathetic, yet dramatic part I've played," spending the entire film in a wheelchair, except for a brief dream sequence with Linda Darnell. For this scene, Duryea was fitted with a special wire brace to hoist him into the air. Mobility restraints notwithstanding, Duryea was able to imbue Murray with a great deal of passion and rancor—perhaps a little too much at times. As written and performed, Murray is given to extensive, exhaustive, and exhausting rants—about his unjust fate and his wife's indiscretions. Rather than gain sympathy for the put-upon Murray, Duryea—evidently given free rein by Heisler—is beyond grating with his unrestrained tirades, making one wish that someone will put Murray out of his (and our) misery. Duryea's best scene in the film comes when he and Darnell have a bit of a heart to heart. Since they are both lovelorn losers (she pining for Glenn, he for Evelyn), Vida confides that she herself wanted

Glenn. After lending a charitable ear, Duryea unleashes that trademark laugh and lashes into her for "not being able to hold onto a man!" It's a piercing scene, and for once in the movie, Duryea's fury is pitched just right. It's a shame the rest of his portrayal is not at that same level.

Jerry Mathers (better known as the Beaver from *Leave it to Beaver*) was also in the film, as Duryea's son. It was one of his first films; Mathers recalls when he saw the production was looking for an actress to play his sister, he suggested his sister, Susie. Jerry remembers Duryea as being very kind and supportive to both him and Susie, who made her film debut on *This Is My Love*.

The notices for *This Is My Love* were not too loving. The *Los Angeles Times* saw Duryea as "poignantly sympathetic," but that was a minority view. More critics thought along the lines of the reviewer in the *St. Louis Post Dispatch*, who opined that "all concerned seemed to think this constitutes heavy drama; what it actually constitutes is heavy, indigestible ham." These reviews must have been a crushing disappointment for Duryea, but he only had himself to blame. He would have a tendency—especially with his so-called "sympathetic roles"—to go overboard for the more overtly emotional moments. This intensity, so well-utilized in the service of his villains, would produce a negative impact on Duryea's "good" men. It also didn't help that many of these characters were fundamentally weak, so any opportunity for the characters to assert themselves was seen by Duryea as a chance to histrionically seize the moment. And when the director was unwilling—or unable—to curb Duryea, the results could be unpleasant, especially for the viewer. Duryea was much better with such roles when he exercised a certain degree of restraint.

In any case, 1954 was a very busy and challenging year for Duryea. If his movies didn't provide the complete artistic satisfaction he sought, they did provide Duryea with some opportunities to stretch his talents to some degree, and to go beyond the garden variety bad-guy roles that had become his stock-in-trade. He would indeed be back in villain's garb in 1955, as well as his old white jacket, as the small screen would continue to present him with opportunities not readily available on the big screen.

CHAPTER 9

Snowbound with Cornel Wilde; Back to *China*; A Jape with Jack Benny

AFTER HAVING SPENT 1954 PRIMARILY ON SCREEN IN FILMS OF VARIABLE quality, the next few years would see Duryea increasingly alternating between the worlds of film and television. Television would not only prove to be fast-paced but also relatively rewarding, both financially and even artistically. The small screen would sometimes provide him with roles with more depth than he might find on the big screen. Take a half-hour drama from 1955 called "The Lie," made for the anthology series *The Star and the Story*. Each episode in the series would be introduced by that week's star, who would speak briefly about why he or she chose that particular story. Duryea's episode was based on a story by Kathleen Norris, and Duryea is relaxed and engaging during his scripted introduction.

"The Lie" itself is a crisp drama about a sanitarium inmate who had been convicted many years ago for murder, based on the testimony of a young girl (played as an adult by Beverly Garland). As the episode begins, Duryea is visited by Garland, who confesses that she lied, not actually having seen the crime in question, but regrets her actions and wants to make it up to Duryea—and expiate her own guilt—by inviting him to her spacious villa and helping him rebuild his life. He reluctantly accepts, but once out there, begins planting hints in neighbors' minds about Garland's stability, and it becomes abundantly clear that he's setting Garland up for a very untimely demise disguised as suicide. The tale has a few twists and turns, as well as delicately rendered portrayals from Garland and Duryea as two lost souls (for different reasons) who find a second chance in each other. It's understated, sincere, and relatively free of melodrama—qualities unusual for TV at the time.

It wasn't unusual for a star to make the rounds of anthology series at the time, but Duryea was quickly becoming a steady and eminently reliable presence. He appeared on a similar anthology series called *Star Stage* in an episode called "The Marshal and the Mob." Here, he's an easygoing marshal who has to deal with an unhappy girlfriend, a dangerous situation regarding an outlaw, and a town that has become accustomed to second-guessing both the marshal's motives and his courage. For *Jane Wyman Presents The Fireside Theatre*, Duryea starred in "Nailed Down." Here, Duryea plays a doctor who turns to outlawing and later helps the owner of a ranch (and a reformed gang member) whose wife is going to have a baby. After some difficulties, ex-doc Duryea delivers the baby and later dies while trying to rescue remnants of the gang. For *Schlitz Playhouse*, he had appeared in various dramas through 1956, including a well-received effort called "Kinsman." Here, he plays a man released from prison who tries to locate the son (Richard Eyer) he hasn't seen in ten years, only to find he has been placed in a mission.

Besides his appearances on these anthologies, Duryea was able to don his tattered white suit and finally revive *China Smith* for another twenty-six episodes. These episodes went under the moniker *The New Adventures of China Smith*. This time, the show's producers chose to recreate the Orient in San Francisco. The hectic filming pace was slowed somewhat, although the episodes were still shot swiftly as to make today's shooting schedules seem leisurely by comparison. While he was pleased with the shows in general (as well as his own share of the syndication rights), Duryea was more than a little regretful that the speed and relative low budget prevented *China Smith* from being truly quality fare.

Occasionally, Duryea would get to exhibit his lighter side, usually by sending up his celebrity or on-screen persona. For instance, in 1955, Duryea played himself on Spring Byington's comedy series, *December Bride*. In the episode "High Sierras," directed by movie veteran Jerry Thorpe, Duryea is trying to enjoy his vacation in the mountains with his film director friend (Douglas Fowley, known as the harried director from *Singin' in the Rain*). This presumably peaceful sojourn is interrupted by the arrival of Byington and her friend Verna Felton, both of whom are pursuing an interview. Duryea has a lot of fun pretending to be his screen gangster image, even performing an exaggerated, very funny death scene. Later, in an attempt to assuage Byington, he gives her the "facts" about his life—but these facts really belong on Richard Widmark's bio, as he later confesses. It's a very amusing episode with some good moments from the entire cast.

It's also illuminating in terms of the Dan Duryea-Richard Widmark connection. First thought of as a worthy successor to the cackling villainy personified by Duryea, Widmark was able to transcend his initial impact as Tommy Udo to carve out a career in leading-man roles in films such as *Panic in the Streets*—although ultimately he, too, felt stifled in supporting-villain roles during the tail end of his initial Fox tenure. While he was rarely as memorable in good-guy roles (he could sometimes seem stodgy and even uncomfortable as the stalwart hero), Widmark nonetheless was able to cross over and travel freely between lead roles as hero or villain. Furthermore, Duryea—who considered Widmark to be one of his few Hollywood friends—was now being regularly confused with Widmark, so much so that Duryea began handing out autograph cards which read: "Thanks a lot, but I'm not Richard Widmark." There were also some reports at this time of Duryea and Widmark teaming for a film called *Friendly Enemies*, but the project never came to fruition. For all his making light of the Widmark/Duryea connection/confusion, it still must have bothered Duryea that he wasn't able to shed his bad-guy persona as thoroughly as Widmark was supposed to have done. (In later years, though, Widmark, by then having been in the business for forty years, would note that the first question interviewers would ask is: "How's Tommy Udo?")

Another classic television appearance came courtesy of *The Jack Benny Show* in an episode called "The Lunch Counter Murders." In a spoof of noir with a knowing nod to Duryea, Benny (aided by his amusing deadpan voice-over) plays a lunch counter proprietor, complete with a pay-it-yourself cash register that is all too quick to snap off customers' hands. Benny is ready to call it a night when likely killer Dan Duryea walks in with his two sidekicks (one of whom is the erstwhile Dennis Day, imitating a younger Duryea, among others). As in *December Bride*, Duryea hilariously lampoons his tough-guy image, threatening Benny and letting loose with his infectious cackle, indulging in a tango with Dennis Day, and going through another protracted (yet very funny) series of death throes. It has since become a favorite episode among both Jack Benny and Dan Duryea fans.

Lest one worry that Duryea was turning all his attention to comedy (though he would have welcomed the shift to lighter fare), the creative forces behind *General Electric Theater* cast Duryea in the drama "The Road That Led Afar." Piper Laurie starred alongside Duryea in this evocative drama about a backwoods girl who marries a widower with four kids. As Laurie recalls: "This was the first quality part I had ever had, and the first job away from the studio . . . my recollection was of a polite and serious actor who seemed as focused off-camera as I was. I think we both understood that open friendliness might have hurt our work in such a fragile piece." Their work did not go unnoticed, as its director Herschel Daugherty received an Emmy nomination for Direction of a Half-Hour Program (losing to Sheldon Leonard).

Duryea's movies around this time weren't especially artistically rewarding, although each had its merits. For example, take his first release of 1955, made at MGM, his first film there in over ten years: a relatively small-scale Western saddled with the somewhat generic title *The Marauders*. I was pleasantly surprised with the lean screenplay by Jack Leonard and Earl Fenton, the taut direction from Gerald Mayer, and some forceful acting, especially from Duryea and Keenan Wynn. Set in 1875, deep in the Arizona desert, *The Marauders* presents Jeff Richards (MGM was grooming him to be a star but the public didn't respond in kind) as Corey Everett, a homesteader who holds his ground against big ranch interests trying to drive him out—mainly by convincing his attackers, through some well-placed rifles, that the land is well-fortified (instead of protected by one lone gun). When a wagon rides up carrying a couple and their child, the defenders number four. Meanwhile, head rancher Rutherford and his mild-mannered, very tubercular bookkeeper Avery (Duryea) go on the offensive—in spite of Rutherford's son's request to leave the squatter alone. An attack on the homestead goes badly for both the ranchers and the mercenaries they've hired to do their dirty work, leaving both Rutherford and his son badly wounded.

And here is where the film starts to get interesting. A fatally wounded Rutherford has a change of heart regarding the squatter—but Avery won't hear of it. Instead, Avery calmly informs Rutherford that because of his weakened condition, Avery himself will assume command, sporting his dead brother's Confederate uniform. After Rutherford expires in a futile attempt to stagger to his men, Avery forcibly takes over, surprising the "troops" with his gun prowess—and his decisive tactic of shooting out the water barrels so that their only option is to lay siege to the squatter's fortress, the only place in sight with access to water. Duryea perfectly modulates Avery's ascendancy, and is authoritative as the mild man who becomes a formidable opponent, not just to the squatter but to his own men, who would like nothing more than to jump Avery or kill him.

Because of the severe circumstances and the nature of his coup, Duryea's Avery is more than a little paranoid—and absolutely certain he's in the right. Avery won't even acknowledge the possibility that the "enemy force" is small, leading him to execute the father when he maintains there are only a few defenders. Avery's megalomania and madness lead to constant interjections of "I don't like whispering" whenever anyone is within earshot. Many of Duryea's scenes are with Keenan Wynn as his reluctant second-in-command aptly named Hook (you'll see why), and their scenes together crackle with tension. Their best moment comes when Wynn's Hook reluctantly swears "loyalty" after Avery kills a deadly rattlesnake closing in on Hook. Later, Hook (who's really not the most honorable of men) enlists a visiting artist to position Avery for assassination by placing him in a specific spot to be sketched—a scheme that goes deadly awry in a suspenseful highlight.

In the meantime, Richard's homesteader (still deemed a squatter by the ranchers, despite Arizona's rights-of-possession statute) clings to his land, aided by a widow (who had wounded him earlier but is now receptive to him and his cause) who sees how unhinged Avery has become. Demented though he may be, Avery leads his men on a final attack, employing the use of a reconstructed wagon set on fire to burn 'em out—but is stopped dead in its tracks by some well-aimed dynamite. Duryea's dying scene is another memorable moment, as he insists that the enemy forces present themselves. Still incredulous when informed the defenders consist of just a man, a woman, and a child, Avery finally expires.

The Marauders was not an overwhelming performer at the box office, but Duryea received some good notices as the delusional would-be leader of men. Though *The Marauders* is not among the more well known or easily accessible Duryea films, it is a tightly wound, forceful little Western that deserves to be rediscovered.

Even though *The Marauders* was shot mainly on location, as were a number of Duryea's films made at this time, he still had the better part of the year to spend with his family, whether it was on Mulholland or in Arrowhead. Duryea would say in interviews that he was so busy that "my family complains they never see me without a script in hand." But again, the reality was somewhat different. For one thing, Duryea was still engaged in taking an active stance in his community, as he had done the year before when he was leading his fellow residents in constructing a public pool. Now, Duryea was a leading opponent to a plan to turn Mulholland Drive to a "superhighway." City engineer Lloyd Aldrich had come up with a proposal to convert Mulholland Drive into a four-lane highway that would run through certain homes. Duryea and many other residents favored a compromise plan, which amounted to a two-lane roadway from Cahuenga to Laurel Canyon Boulevard. Duryea's active stance against this superhighway was one of several factors that prevented it from being constructed.

Duryea managed to spend many weekends in Arrowhead when he wasn't on location—and, occasionally, even when he was. Rich Baughman, a childhood friend of Richard (who would be best man at Baughman's wedding), would recall that Duryea "was always there, like a second parent—at Arrowhead or on Mulholland." Mary Bernard was a former neighbor, as her parents bought the house next door to the Duryeas'. She recalls that Richard was her first boyfriend, and though she knew the name "Duryea," she doesn't recall being particularly starstruck, especially since Duryea downplayed his celebrity while in Arrowhead, rarely attending the "yacht parties" that were fashionable among certain high-profile residents.

There were things Duryea didn't downplay, however, such as his passion for building and racing sailboats. Richard recalls that one of the ongoing pleasures of spending summers at Arrowhead was the weekly races. Every Saturday and Sunday at 2 p.m., Duryea and the kids would race their friends and neighbors, with Duryea guiding his initially not-so-eager charges, advising them to check the equipment before each race— while Mrs. Duryea, not an avid sailor herself, was content to cheer them on. Sharon McDaniel, another neighbor (and youthful contemporary of Richard and Peter), recalls how competitive he could be. For the annual Father's Race, aimed at the fathers who would man their specially designed sailboats and set sail, Duryea had a special sail made in order to get the edge. According to McDaniel, he "was something to behold." In his woodshop, Duryea, with the aid of his sons, constructed what amounted to a small fleet: three sailboats, including an eighteen-foot centerboard called *Flattie*, a twenty-one-foot Chris Craft, and an outboard motorboat called *Little Mink*.

Duryea's next 1955 release saw him again in Arizona, shooting during the summer in 110-degree heat. He was back with Universal, as a freelance player in the romantic melodrama *Foxfire*. Duryea would later say that Aaron Rosenberg, the film's producer, liked to cast him occasionally in roles that might surprise the audience: "When Aaron Rosenberg was casting *Thunder Bay*, he wanted me for the heavy . . . who turns out to be a decent fellow after all. Rosy said, 'Get Dan and we'll have a surprise ending. Who would expect him to be a nice guy.' Much as it hurt my ego, I had to admit he was right. When he asked for me again for *Foxfire*, it was just understood that I would play the drunk, not a solid citizen." In actuality, Duryea simplified his own involvement in the film, since he is really cast as both the drunk and a solid citizen, as a doctor and friend to the leading man Jeff Chandler.

Aside from the intense heat, the filming of *Foxfire* didn't proceed entirely without incident—for various reasons. One positive occurrence was that two of the supporting players, Barton MacLane (a mainstay of 1930s and 1940s Warner Bros. dramas) and Charlotte Wynters, who had been married since 1939, were able to work together for the first time on *Foxfire*. The citizens of Oakman were also grateful for the filmmakers' presence; the town was virtually a ghost town after having been a booming mining town, and many of the remaining residents were happily employed by Universal as extras or in other capacities. On a less happy note, Chandler and costar Jane Russell narrowly escaped serious injury when a car they were in blew a tire and went into a ditch.

Foxfire—complete with theme song composed by Henry Mancini and performed by Chandler over the opening credits—stars Jane Russell as a wealthy young woman merely passing through Arizona; she falls for Jeff Chandler, a troubled mining engineer who is also a widower. She's a little taken aback when Chandler reveals that his mother is a Mescalero Apache, especially since she has said earlier that Indians "give her the creeps." After that misstep, they find themselves fiercely attracted to each other, which leads to a sudden wedding—but not exactly "happy ever after." For one thing, Chandler is really married to his mine, and certain traditions that go along with it, such as the Indian tradition that women are bad luck at a mine. Another is the clash of cultures, in which Russell's growing curiosity about Chandler's heritage is misunderstood by an increasingly moody and withdrawn Chandler. Though *Foxfire* doesn't offer anything really new on the topic of interracial marriage, it still was slightly daring for its time—especially a scene in which Russell visits Chandler's Indian mother (Celia Lovsky) in an attempt to understand her husband.

As for Duryea's presence, he remained enthusiastic during shooting about his drunken but relatively kindhearted character, joking that the part amounted to "the first doctor I played who doesn't poison someone." In addition, he was encouraged to collaborate with the writers D. D. Beauchamp and William Bowers on his conception of the role. In *Foxfire*, Duryea's doctor runs the town's clinic, when he isn't having a few drinks on the side. It might be tempting to say that he drinks because of his unrequited love for Russell—especially after she marries his buddy Chandler—yet his fondness for alcohol is established early on. When Chandler and a slightly sodden Duryea rescue Russell following a highway breakdown, it's clear he's fond of the bottle long before the appearance of the temptress who would threaten his friendship with Chandler. Throughout most of the movie, Duryea's character lingers on the sidelines, tossing a few longing glances in Russell's direction while neglecting the attentions of his very attractive nurse (Mara Corday), who is quite willing to have him—his Russell obsession notwithstanding. Though Duryea's role is essentially good-natured and even forbearing, it wasn't especially challenging; in essence, it's the Ralph Bellamy role if Bellamy's love-struck characters had been made over for a 1950s melodrama.

Foxfire wound up doing well at the box office and earned a number of favorable reviews. The *Saturday Review* praised the script and how "it probes unusually deep in analyzing the position of women in an Apache tribe." As for Duryea, the critics were respectful, although many echoed the sentiments of the preview audiences who felt "why does Duryea always have to be a drunkard or mealy-mouthed smart aleck . . . sure he could handle a more uplifting role if given the chance."

That may have been true, but it certainly wasn't the case with his next feature, *Storm Fear*, which marked a return to noir for Duryea. The movie, with script by Horton Foote, marked Cornel Wilde's first effort as a producer-director; Wilde had starred in melodramas and period pieces (*Leave it to Heaven* and *A Song to Remember*, among others) and, like several actors at the time, he yearned to be taken a little more seriously than his occasionally one-dimensional roles would allow. Wilde fortified the movie with a solid cast, including New York actors Lee Grant and Steven Hill, as well as Duryea, a master of noir who was taking on an atypical role within the genre.

Filmed on location and in sequence in Sun Valley, Idaho (doubling for a wintry new England), *Storm Fear* casts Duryea as Fred, a struggling writer living in New England with his wife, Elizabeth (Wilde's real-life wife Jean Wallace), and son, David. Fred is a little concerned about his difficulties in getting published (he had that one published novel, years ago), as well as the isolation he has imposed on his family. In addition, there's the hired hand (Dennis Weaver) who's more than a little attentive to Fred's wife. For a while, we might think we have been placed deep in Eugene O'Neill country—and this feeling isn't altogether dispelled with the arrival of Fred's younger, good-looking brother, Charlie (Cornel Wilde), who arrives both wounded and seeking shelter after robbing a bank, along with his confederates Hill and Grant.

It's not long before all are caught in a tangled web of emotions while trapped on this snowy, remote farm. Elizabeth was in love with Charlie—and still is. Charlie still loves Elizabeth but now wants to get close to her son David—who, we figure out (it's not exactly a well-kept secret), is really *his* son. Fred resents himself for his own weaknesses and Charlie for reintroducing himself into Elizabeth's life. At the same time, Hill and Grant linger on the sidelines, as Hill's psychopathic second-in-command is worried that Charlie is becoming soft, while Grant attempts to alleviate the tension with an outwardly easygoing manner and some well-timed comments.

Storm Fear is not great noir but it does manage to set and sustain the mood. Though it tends to be a tad talky (after all, the characters are snowbound in that cramped, loveless cabin for most of the movie), the script and direction offer opportunities for some cast members to make solid impressions—particularly the roles that call for some restraint. Wilde, Wallace, and Weaver do quite well, as does Grant in an early role reminiscent of her character in *Detective Story*. Wilde is less successful in corralling other actors—namely, Hill and, sad to say, Duryea himself. Wilde allows Hill to take his character into a never-never land for psychopathic henchmen—a clever fellow like Charlie, even in his weakened condition, would have figured out Hill's intentions long before the climactic confrontation on a snowy landscape.

As for Duryea, his Fred is one of his poorest characterizations, and another example of what could happen to him in the hands of a well-intentioned but overly indulgent director. In the occasional understated moment—as when he quietly expresses some affection toward his son or when he reflects on his wasted past and bleak future—Duryea is rather effective and even touching. Too often, however, Duryea registers Fred's frustrations by careening between grating and hysterical, whether he is confronting Wallace over her affections toward Wilde (and perhaps Weaver) or challenging both Wilde and Hill, and getting pummeled for it. There is little middle ground in Duryea's handling of Fred, and the net result is to take his ill-tempered yet passive character and dismiss him as an excessively whiny weakling who fully deserves his frozen fate. In *Storm Fear*, Duryea falls into the same trap as he had in *This Was My Love*; it's as if he seized on these parts for the histrionics they offered, as well as the chance to be seen working in a different vein, without realizing that by placing these characters at such a high emotional pitch, he ran the risk of alienating the viewers he was hoping to capture.

There were many good reviews for *Storm Fear* when it was released in the winter of 1956, with many critics praising both Wilde's direction and Foote's screenplay. Duryea himself received some surprisingly good notices. The *Daily Mirror* called him "smooth and polished as the weakling brother," while the *Daily News* observed that Duryea, "in a change of pace role does well as a man of many frustrations." On the other hand, *Variety* reckoned that "Duryea is given little to do besides register ill-tempered petulance." This was not exactly the kind of notice that would enable Duryea to continue his quest to be seen as the "good guy," although a few interesting roles were about to come his way, including a rare leading role in a gentle, heartwarming comedy.

CHAPTER 10

Still Smiling . . . and Yearning to Be More than a Villain

WHEN ONE THINKS OF THE CRUSTY YET AVUNCULAR SIDEKICK TO THE leading man—not to mention ostensible comic relief—the name "Dan Duryea" doesn't immediately spring to mind. Nonetheless, he was cast alongside the stalwart, heroic Rock Hudson in the 1957 war drama *Battle Hymn* at Universal. The film was based on the life of Dean Hess, a Protestant minister turned World War II fighter pilot, who accidentally bombed an orphanage during that war. During the Korean War, he returned to active duty, providing food and shelter to hundreds of orphans, later airlifting them to an orphanage on Cheju Island. The veteran Douglas Sirk would direct, continuing his career resurgence with successful 1950s melodramas such as *The Magnificent Obsession* and *All That Heaven Allows,* and Sirk's frequent star/collaborator Hudson was cast as the guilt-ridden Hess. Hess had been initially considered to play himself, but instead he was engaged as the film's technical director; he also flew during some of the film's combat scenes.

Since the role of the likable and fairly devoted sergeant is a character that one doesn't normally associate with Duryea (the more likely Keenan Wynn had been considered), he was quick to tell the press how excited he was to land the part: "The cigar-smoking sergeant is the best role I've had in a long time, comic and sympathetic for a change . . . they say my movies don't make money unless I'm a menace to society but I'll bet on *Battle Hymn* being a box-office winner." If you look at many of the quotes attributed to Duryea during this period, just about any role that offered a degree of compassion or complexity during this period encouraged him to deem the role "one of the best in a long time." Yet Duryea could be very realistic about where he stood in the Hollywood pecking order. In an article with his byline, Duryea laments that "again and again since I've come to Hollywood, I've tried to break the pattern. I'd like to win the girl for a change. I'd like to play the sterling hero. I really would. But nothing—yet. The other day I ran into a director who always corners me at Hollywood parties with the damning question: 'When are you going to do another picture like *Scarlet Street?*'"

Sometimes his screen persona would create some complications in his off-screen life. On location in Nogales, Arizona (doubling for Korea), for the filming of *Battle Hymn*, Duryea, having just phoned Helen long-distance, decided to put in an appearance at a cocktail party for the cast and crew. As Duryea later recounted: "There was a cute girl at the party. I had met her earlier, so I went over and talked with her for a while. In a moment, I felt eyes boring into my back and saw her boyfriend glaring at me. 'Stay away from my girl!' 'Hey fella, you have me wrong, I'm only a heavy in the movies.' He wasn't convinced and quickly scuttled his girlfriend into a corner." (As a number of actresses would later say, Duryea could be very charming—even a bit of a flirt—with the ladies.)

Apart from fending off jealous swains, Duryea was very popular among the twenty-five Korean youngsters who were flown to Nogales from the institution Hess helped found for orphans on Cheju Island; Duryea's relationship with the children off-screen was not far from their mutual affection on-screen. Nogales proved to be a welcome location for the visiting film company, as Duryea, along with the orphans and cast members, received honorary citizenship in Arizona. In addition to being fairly brave on-screen, Duryea displayed some on-the-set bravery when a bull that refused to be realigned for an upcoming scene decided to move in the direction of some children; Duryea held the bull until it could be wrangled, saving the children from possible injury. Other potentially severe mishaps occurred; Sirk broke his ankle on location while directing an evacuation scene, forcing him to make the rest of the movie from his wheelchair.

Hess and Universal were quite pleased with *Battle Hymn* when it was released in March 1957. There were many reasons for this, not the least of which was the opening scene in which the real-life General Earle Partridge praises Hess's courage and sacrifice, which was seen as "affirming the human spirit." Early on, Hess is haunted by his experiences during World War II (during which he earned the unfortunate nickname "Killer"), particularly an unfortunate incident in which his bomb was stuck and eventually fell, hitting a German church and killing children in the attached orphanage. Believing he has been failing his congregation back home in Ohio, Hess applies to be recalled to service during the Korean War, becoming a flight instructor. In Korea, while Hess is generally successful in instilling discipline among his troops, the situation becomes complicated by the presence of both civilians (seen as possible spies) and orphans. In addition, Hess struggles to reconcile his beliefs with the realities of war, coming into occasional conflict with his old war buddy Skidmore (Don DeFore), who now thinks Hess is too soft, especially with regard to retaliating against the enemy and his growing devotion to the orphans, manifested in his efforts to find them new quarters. As the Chinese advance toward his position, Hess, motivated both by his concern for the children as well as the affection of the children's Korean protector En Soon (the lovely Anna Kashfi), mobilizes his men to move the children toward an airstrip and eventual safety, though at some personal cost.

Duryea's Sergeant Herman is Hess's loyal sidekick, the happy-go-lucky but thoroughly committed second-in-command who gets the job done, whether it's procuring difficult-to-obtain supplies, entertaining the children, or even providing a sounding board to the occasionally conflicted Hess. Duryea is very engaging, and much of the film's publicity centered around Duryea's nice-guy role. Duryea himself was pleased with the results, especially since he had to win over the producers in order to be cast in the part. Yet, as gratifying as the role was for Duryea, it wasn't particularly challenging. Duryea might have benefited more had he pushed the producers (who were ultimately responsive to his desire to stretch as an actor) for the other heroic male role in the film, besides Hudson's. This would be Don DeFore's part as Hess's old friend who is blindsided by Hess's newfound faith. The character also has a surprisingly moving death scene in which he accepts the prayers of Hess, his friend and spiritual guide. *That* should have been the role Duryea lobbied for; DeFore is good, but Duryea might have done wonders with the role's shadings. Nonetheless, the film was a huge success, Universal's highest grossing release of the year, with praise heaped on everyone, including Duryea. The *Hollywood Reporter* wrote that Duryea provided "welcome comedy relief in an excellent portrayal as the wisecracking sergeant," while Wanda Hale of the *Daily News* said, "As far as I'm concerned, any picture is better with Dan Duryea in it, whether he is a meanie or not."

That would prove to be the case with Duryea's next release, *The Burglar*, though it was actually filmed a few years earlier. *The Burglar*, like *Chicago Calling*, was another example of Duryea putting his faith and talent into a very low-budget production, mainly because he believed in the strength of the material. In the case of *The Burglar*, the production originated in Philadelphia early in 1955, as Louis Kellman, the head of an industrial film company, decided to branch out into features. He enlisted fellow Philadelphian Paul Wendkos to make his directorial debut, and employed David Goodis, yet another Philadelphian, to adapt his own work for the screen. Kellman and Wendkos set up Samson Productions, with Goods as a coproducer for their initial venture. With Goodis's script in hand, they went to Hollywood and managed to sign both Duryea and Martha Vickers (an underrated actress who had come close to stealing *The Big Sleep* from Bogie and Bacall). Kellman was also able to acquire the services of Jayne Mansfield, on loan from Warner Bros., for the female lead, following her well-received appearance in Jack Webb's *Pete Kelly's Blues*. All of the filming would be done in either Philadelphia or in Atlantic City on a budget of around $250,000.

Before the start of shooting in 1955, Duryea had received some bad news; his mother, Mabel, had passed away. Throughout his years in Hollywood, Duryea would make regular trips out east, not only for publicity purposes. The occasion might be a Cornell reunion, since Duryea stayed in touch with many of his classmates, but more often than not, he would make the journey to see his folks. Three years earlier, Dan and the whole family had come out to White Plains for a party thrown by his brother Hewlett in celebration of their parents' fiftieth anniversary. After the death of his mother, Dan persuaded his father to move to California, where he would spend his remaining years until he, too, passed away in 1961.

Shooting in Philadelphia for *The Burglar* amounted to somewhat of a homecoming for Duryea, since he hadn't been to that city since his long-ago advertising days. He visited his former agency, and was jokingly greeted with: "Never mind the small talk, did you get the account?" While the filming in Philadelphia proceeded smoothly if rapidly, shooting in Atlantic City was delayed by the onset of a hurricane that caused Duryea to seek shelter in a basement throughout its duration. Later, Duryea would donate much of his pay (which was admittedly not much to begin with) to the relief fund for the victims of Hurricane Connie. Between the low budget and Duryea's largesse, Duryea's son Richard would say that "all my father got out of the movie was a couple of suits."

Those familiar with Goodis's work know that most of his novels involve hard-luck individuals of various kinds, whether they've been framed for murder (*Dark Passage*) or caught up in the murderous machinations of the underworld (*Shoot the Piano Player* and *The Street of No Return*). *The Burglar* is a little bit of both, as career burglar Nat Harbin and his gang set their eyes on a priceless string of emeralds. Nat enlists the help of his protégé, Gladden, to ingratiate herself with the owner, then he and the gang steal the emeralds in a tense sequence marked by the inopportune arrival of some policemen. Nat manages to allay the officers' suspicions by passing himself off as a traveling salesman—or so he thinks. It turns out the jewels are hotter than hot, which compels the foursome (along with Duryea and Mansfield, the other thieves are played by Mickey Shaughnessy and Peter Capell) to hide out together until they can find a fence.

These forced, cramped quarters bring out the worst in everyone: Shaughnessy's Dohmer would like to get his hands on Gladden; Capell's Baylock wants to get rid of the necklace and secure his retirement; while Nat fights his own feelings for Gladden. In a shadowy, stylized flashback, we see young, orphaned Nat being raised and taught his trade by Gladden's father, Gerald, who makes Nat promise to always take care of Gladden. After Gerald is killed during a robbery (due to Nat's error), the guilt-ridden Nat keeps his promise, but has since struggled to contain his own feelings for Gladden—failing to recognize Gladden's own tortured feelings. Their mutual frustrations lead Nat to encourage Gladden to strike out on her own, for Atlantic City, where she is met and romanced by Charlie (a very sweaty Stewart Bradley), the same policeman who had spoken to Nat at the crime scene. Meanwhile, Nat has met an attractive but somewhat jaded socialite named Della (Martha Vickers) and they develop a mutual attraction—until Nat overhears her talking to Gerald. Nat quickly realizes Gladden is in danger, prompting the gang to relocate to Atlantic City; the location shooting manages to capture the city in all its seedy, pre-revitalized splendor. In true Goodis fashion, events unfold so that Nat is indeed able to fulfill his promise to protect Gladden, by sacrificing his own life.

The Burglar is yet another Duryea picture that was quickly forgotten after its release but has since been rediscovered in the last decade. The movie finished shooting in 1955, but Kellman resolutely held onto the film until *after* Mansfield had attracted attention, with 20th Century Fox's publicity machine in full swing, as the next blonde bombshell in such pictures as *The Girl Can't Help It*. Columbia Pictures purchased *The*

Burglar and released it in 1957. The movie received some respectful reviews, with the *Hollywood Reporter* weighing in that "Duryea is excellent as the group leader." *The Burglar* then proceeded to languish in a state of semi-obscurity, until some critics and noir writers belatedly extolled the film's virtues. Showings in revival houses helped the movie to achieve a degree of cult status.

Besides the obvious—and not-so-obvious—assets of Mansfield, there are many reasons to appreciate *The Burglar* (now available in a pristine transfer on DVD): the atmospheric cinematography, especially in the final chase sequence through the funhouse; Goodis's intelligent, subtle script; Wendkos's stylish direction (though some deemed it pretentious at the time); and with one glaring exception (the increasingly overwrought Stewart Bradley as the corrupt, murderous Charlie), the major players, who convey the right blend of resignation and desperation. Mansfield herself is touching as the conflicted Gladden, frustrated with Nat's presumed indifference to her silent suffering, while Martha Vickers registers strongly as an attractive, sophisticated femme fatale who finds herself drawn to Nat, even if it means losing out on the necklace.

But *The Burglar* belongs to Duryea—though at forty-six, he looks a little too old for the thirty-five-year-old Nat. The filmmakers were quite aware of Duryea's value, and certainly tailored aspects of the film to capitalize on his strengths and recognition-factor among audiences. For example, the opening (singled out for praise by many reviewers, and perhaps owing a slight debt to Orson Welles) depicts a newsreel of the time with the necklace's owner on display, after which the camera gradually zooms out to reveal the darkened movie theater, with Duryea rising into a full close-up as the music swells and the credits begin to roll. It's an impressive opening, and the film maintains the momentum through the tense robbery sequence, wherein Duryea persuasively portrays Nat as a master burglar: he has an attention to precise detail coupled with an ability to improvise (while his comrades seem to fall apart at the slightest provocation). The film flags a little during the prolonged section when they're trapped in their hideout, wrangling about what do with the very hot necklace. Even here, though, Duryea excels by showing the right blend of intensity and restraint, whether he is admonishing his unstable gang members, or regretfully urging Gladden to leave, both to protect her and to insulate himself from his own unexpressed feelings.

The movie accelerates once Nat gets wind of Della and Charlie's scheme, and the action shifts to Atlantic City, as Nat tries one last time to protect an unsuspecting Gladden. Simultaneously, the police manhunt is building, with the net slowly closing on both the gang and Gerald (whose leave-taking in order to romance Gladden makes his superiors more than a little suspicious). Duryea's scene with Della and Gerald, in which he calmly stares down the barrel of Gerald's gun while trying to negotiate a deal, followed by his challenge to a gun-wielding Della as he walks out, is a highlight of the film, as his nuanced work here is among his finest pieces of acting. The following scene at the pier, in which Nat and Gladden reunite and finally acknowledge their long-suppressed feelings, is also well-acted by both Duryea and Mansfield, as the manic Gerald's pursuit leads to a foot chase through the funhouse, reminiscent of the dazed Orson Welles's flight in *The Lady from Shanghai*. Nat finally offers Gerald the jewels in order to spare Gladden's life; as the resigned but still noble Nat dangles the bounty ("You wanna *buy* a necklace, Charlie?"), the viewer sees that Nat knows he's a dead man. Nat gently tells Gladden he'll see her later, but they both know it's not to be. *The Burglar* would later be given a makeover in 1971 as a jaunty caper film called *The Burglars*, filmed in a very sunny and scenic Greece with Jean-Paul Belmondo as the daring thief and Omar Sharif as the suave but lethal policeman. That film is very enjoyable, but quite different in tone and denouement—it's lovely to look at though.

Like *World for Ransom*, *The Burglar* showcases Duryea in the best of his tarnished-hero roles; and he would have liked more roles along those lines, but he knew—in spite of the positive notices that he earned—that audiences and producers preferred him as the villain. When interviewed, Duryea would reiterate that he didn't mind portraying these blackguards, since "they've helped me and my family. When you have a family, it takes money—you have to keep that insurance policy going, boy—!" In fact, his next film would be a big-budget Western for Universal, in which he would be cast as another "laughing killer."

That movie was *Night Passage*, in which he was third-billed under James Stewart and Audie Murphy, in a cast including Brandon De Wilde, Elaine Stewart, and Dianne Foster. (The contract negotiations regarding place in billing and the size of billing could fill a book, as an examination of Universal's papers shows how precise the actor's place in the credits had to be). While the film marked Duryea's reunion with both these stars, much of the publicity would concentrate on how *Night Passage* was the first teaming of Stewart and Murphy. There were also some interesting behind-the-scenes elements as well, primarily surrounding the final choice of director. Originally Anthony Mann was to direct, since he and Stewart had completed a series of hard-bitten, adult Westerns such as *Winchester '73* and, most recently, 1955's *The Man from Laramie*. But Mann had reservations about what he considered a weak script, as well as the casting of Audie Murphy as Stewart's younger brother. (It's a "plot twist" that you can see a mile away—no reason to withhold it here.) Stewart and Mann would eventually part ways, and there would be no further collaborations between the two men, although Mann would play down their estrangement by saying that the films he was doing didn't have roles suitable for Stewart. Stewart recommended hiring the television director James Neilson, who would presumably be more amenable to the inclusion of several song interludes from Stewart and his trusty accordion.

Night Passage would be filmed on location in the Rocky Mountains above Durango, Colorado, shot in the very widescreen process of Technirama; the movie is markedly different if one is unlucky enough to view it in pan-and-scan format—sometimes one hears Duryea's laugh without even seeing him. Altitude troubles would plague the picture at the beginning, particularly with the leading ladies. Even though Duryea was pleased to be working with Stewart, whom he considered one of his best friends in Hollywood, there still wasn't too much to do when they weren't shooting. It reached a point where Duryea, Stewart, and Murphy would sit on a street corner (bottle in hand) and place bets as to which direction the next car would be going. Dianne Foster, costarring as someone whom both Stewart and Murphy care for, told interviewer Bob Larkins the following story about Duryea on the set: "Duryea had almost a leprechaun sense of humor, always saying something funny to keep the spirit going on the film set . . . a big storm came and there was a horrendous ride back. We were slipping and sliding down this big road. Dan was a nervous wreck. I mean, *everybody* was frightened, but it was funny to see this brave villain cringing."

In spite of the off-screen machinations and location incidents, *Night Passage* is a pretty enjoyable Western. The plot, such as it is, involves Stewart as a disgraced former railroad man who is given the opportunity to transport the payroll money for Jay D. Flippen's beleaguered railroad boss (who just happens to be married to Stewart's former love, Elaine Stewart). He's given the job because the payroll has been robbed a number of times (by Murphy and Duryea's persistent gang). The down-and-out Stewart, now earning a living playing the accordion, seems to be the least likely person to carry a $10,000 payroll. Enter Brandon De Wilde (not as adorable as he was five years earlier in *Shane*), whom Stewart rescues from a none-too-likable member of the gang (Robert Wilke) and from the Murphy/Duryea gang itself, which is beset by internal friction—not the least of which is their mutual suspicion and Duryea's generally unstable nature. There's more than enough drama and action to go around.

When viewing *Night Passage* in glorious Technirama, one can see why Mann accepted the film in spite of his reservations—and why he quickly departed. Mann certainly was fond of working with both Stewart and Duryea, and he may well have been attracted to the brother vs. brother dynamic—but the finished script doesn't develop it enough. Murphy and Stewart, while entertaining, both separately and together, are an unlikely pair of brothers (although they're hardly the most mismatched pair of cinematic siblings from the 1950s—that dubious honor goes to white-haired, craggy Spencer Tracy and callow Robert Wagner in *The Mountain*—if you can accept that pairing, you can accept *anything*). In addition, the frequency of the Stewart accordion interludes might make viewers think they were watching a musical Western, instead of a tough Western drama. Yet *Night Passage* proceeds swiftly and is beautifully photographed; there are also some exciting moments, especially the final shootout at a deserted mine shaft.

Duryea and Murphy get to share much of their screen time together in their second teaming, but the results are far less felicitous than *Ride Clear of Diablo*. As would occasionally happen when working with an inexperienced or indulgent director, Duryea went way over the top. His outlaw leader Whitey Harbin ("Whitey" was a popular name for Duryea's outlaws in 1950s Universal Westerns) is prone to either cackling, overstating his lines, or even outright declaiming, whether the occasion calls for it or not. Duryea's overblown line readings give credibility to De Wilde's claim that Whitey's mean and crazy, but they hardly make for a plausible characterization. Regardless of whether Neilson tried to curb Duryea or not, the on-screen results are not exactly flattering. By comparison, Duryea's grinning Waco Kid (from *Winchester '73*) looks like a model of restraint. Mann might have been able to make an impact on Duryea's characterization, but even this is uncertain since Mann usually trusted Duryea's instincts. In spite of this, there are some scenes where Duryea and Murphy entertainingly tangle, as Murphy is especially good as the wry, patient outlaw brother who takes pleasure in needling Whitey. Overall, however, *Night Passage* is decidedly not a high point in Duryea's career.

In spite of its relative lightweight status in the Stewart Western oeuvre, *Night Passage* did win some praise for the Technirama process and the breathtaking scenery. Murphy's growing assuredness was noted as well, while Stewart's acting (if not his accordion interludes) received some good notices. As for Duryea, a number of critics enjoyed his exuberance; Harry MacArthur of the *Evening Star* wrote that "Duryea makes his comedy portrait of a desperado stand out," while *Variety* gushed that "Duryea is immense as the outlaw chief."

Respectful notices notwithstanding, an increasing number of Duryea's more challenging roles during this period were coming from television, mainly from anthology series. For *Cavalcade of America*, Duryea starred as "The Frightened Witness," a half-hour tour de force in which his character witnesses a crime, and out of fear for himself and his family, decides to rescind his identification of the murderer. This decision, and the subsequent pressure from his family, the police, and ultimately from within gnaws at his conscience until the end, when he finally decides to stop being the "frightened witness." Duryea's growing hysteria is balanced by both a sense of guilt and civic awareness, making his wavering title character both vulnerable and eventually heroic.

Duryea accepted a more challenging role when he took on the lead role as a head doctor in "Four Hours in White" on the anthology series *Climax*. He played a beleaguered doctor, ready to leave for a restful weekend, who is faced with a multitude of problems, including the fate of twins (both played by an early Steve McQueen) injured in a motorcycle accident. In addition, for the first time (barring that ten-minute appearance on *The Kate Smith Show*), Duryea would be performing "live." He had resisted several such offers over the past few years, but was so enthusiastic about the role, and the opportunity it gave him to personify "grace under pressure," that he finally acquiesced. Duryea's capable playing, ably supported by an impressive McQueen, succeeded in enhancing what might otherwise have been a predictable medical drama.

An even more effective part was Duryea's career criminal on the anthology series *Suspicion*. In the episode entitled "Doomsday," Duryea was cast as a master criminal with a plan for a daring bank holdup that involves his posing as an insurance investigator, and while the holdup is successful, there's an ironic twist at the end. There are several things that distinguish this episode from some of Duryea's film roles. For one thing, he was the lead (his voice-over narration solidifies the noir connection), and it was an intelligent, perceptive character, given that he's a bank robber and reluctant killer. At one point, after his partner (Robert Middleton) gathers the gang (including Charles Bronson and Edward Binns), Duryea realizes that Binns recognizes him from the army, and since Duryea has prided himself on his anonymity, he decides to take

Binns "for a ride." On a bluff overlooking the ocean, Duryea's McDillard points his gun at Binns, allowing Binns the chance to live—so long as he refrains from giving Duryea away by calling him "Shoes," Binns's nickname for Shoemaker. Binns promises, but then calls him the dreaded "Shoes" a mere forty seconds later. Even in the grainy print available, one can see Duryea's despair at having to kill Binns—the first time he's taken a life. And, interestingly enough, the viewer sympathizes with Duryea's Shoemaker, as did reviewers at the time who found the robbers so erudite that the critics hoped they would get away.

Roles such as these would lead Duryea to turn increasingly to television series such as anthology shows and episodic dramas. Such programs were providing him with more complex parts than could be found in the film offers he was currently receiving. A prime example would be Duryea's next release for Universal (you have to say this for Universal-International Pictures: they certainly kept Duryea busy, even if the parts were slightly beneath him). *Slaughter on Tenth Avenue* was another example of the fact-inspired (it would be too much to say "fact-based") waterfront gang-busting melodramas that were popular in the 1950s. The most prominent of these was 1954's *On the Waterfront*, so it wasn't surprising when Universal attempted to cash in on that film's success, and if Columbia could use music by Leonard Bernstein, then Universal could certainly purchase prestigious composer Richard Rodgers's powerful "Slaughter on Tenth Avenue" as the film's main theme.

Slaughter on Tenth Avenue, directed by Arnold Laven with a script by Lawrence Roman, was loosely based on assistant district attorney Richard Keating's expose *The Man Who Rocked the Boat* (the film's working title as well); there is a small disclaimer at the beginning claiming that, in order to protect the identities of some individuals, "certain modifications had to be made." Richard Egan, lately from 20th Century Fox, was cast as the young crusading district attorney who tries to clean up the dirty doings on New York's waterfront and somehow avert a war between the longshoremen and the murderous racketeers (led by Walter Matthau, still managing to be amusing as the main heavy) who are trying to take over the whole waterfront. The case in question involves Solly (Mickey Shaughnessy), an honest boss who is shot and gravely wounded in the film's opening sequence. Initially willing to identify his assassins, Solly then changes his mind, mainly out of concern for his wife (Jan Sterling). Egan's inexperienced Keating is then entrusted with the task of trying to find someone willing to testify—which proves to be more difficult then he imagines since he is also faced with defending some possibly compromising actions on the part of the frustrated police detective (Charles McGraw).

Shaughnessy's deathbed decision to formally name his killers—made with Sterling's slightly wavering support—leads to a courtroom sequence that takes up the final quarter of the film. Duryea appears as Matthau's lawyer, someone who had once been on the other side of the fence and now spends his time defending gangsters such as . . . Walter Matthau. Duryea would see the role as "a sharp, suave lawyer moving into respectability. Then I read the reviews." It's true that Duryea is both smooth and sharp as John Jacob Masters, a polished but unscrupulous defense attorney who nearly succeeds in tarnishing both Keating's position and the credibility of Sterling's belated testimony. In fact, it is only an equally decisive (as the movie sees it) summation from Keating that enables the law to emerge triumphant—for now.

Slaughter on Tenth Avenue received a number of positive reviews upon its release in November 1957, with Kate Cameron of the *Daily News* writing that "the drama packs a powerful punch," while others called it a suspenseful and arresting picture of life on the waterfront. The film's documentary flavor was also praised (much of it was shot on location in New York). Duryea received several good notices, although some critics thought he was just marking time, and others thought the extended courtroom section marked the film's descent into mediocrity. In fact, even though Duryea did everything the part called for, there wasn't much to the role, other than a few speeches in court handled with proficiently if lacking inspiration. One could see Duryea's attraction to this "respectable" role, but one wonders why he wasn't offered the meatier role of the waterfront boss. Matthau is occasionally menacing but a little broad and somewhat comic, and Duryea would have brought both menace and charm to the part. Any Universal contract player could have played the part of the defense attorney.

On the basis of his undemanding (though fairly lucrative) appearances for Universal, it came as a surprise when the studio offered Duryea the lead in a heartwarming holiday comedy first called *Christmas in Paradise*, then *The Magnificent Brat*, and finally its release title *Kathy O'*. Duryea would play a happily married press agent in this comedy opposite the popular child star Patty McCormack, a very hot commodity since her success as that most malicious of children, *The Bad Seed*. Mary Fickett, recently Bing Crosby's ex in the decidedly non-musical *Man on Fire*, was cast as Duryea's wife, while Jan Sterling recovered from being mercilessly grilled by Duryea in *Slaughter on Tenth Avenue* to play his affectionate, sophisticated ex-wife.

While Duryea would often say that such-and-such a part was his best in years (he had done that with the very recent *Battle Hymn*, *The Burglar*, and *Foxfire*, and would do so again for *Kathy O'*), this was certainly the most unusual he had in years. He was the undisputed lead in a comedy, with two attractive women competing for his attention. He also had to play numerous scenes with children (his own character's, as well as the troublesome McCormack). As Duryea would say at the time: "I know I'm taking a chance with fans in this one. I'm nice to dogs, happy with my wife and I love kids." He seemed to acknowledge the possibility of disappointing his fan base—"I know some people will hate me for it but a man must gamble at least once in his life and this is my turning point"—although one might say the same for the low-budget *Chicago Calling*.

Kathy O' has Duryea as Harry Johnson, a harried publicity man who has more than enough trouble on his hands, what with some recent layoffs at the studio (the fictional Western National), as well as the antics of its most profitable asset, the temperamental title character, whose reputation as a hell-raiser causes grown men to tremble at the very mention of her name. When he learns his ex-wife, Celeste (Jan Sterling), now a magazine writer, is arriving to do a feature story on Kathy, Harry does all he can to ensure Kathy's cooperation, while trying to mend fences with the ex and maintaining the good graces of his loving and tolerant present wife (Mary Fickett).

The thing about Kathy is—and the film plays on McCormack's screen persona—she's not a malicious child. Kathy is really just an extremely hard-working girl who doesn't feel appreciated by the studio and is taken advantage of by her guardians, who promise her rest and then sign her up for some function (in this case, a parade that she has implored them not to make her attend). Various complications ensue: Kathy and Celeste genuinely come to care for each other, while Harry's kids take a fancy to Kathy, encouraging her to act like an "everyday child." Numerous movie reference books allude to Kathy taking part in a phony kidnapping to get attention, but this is the case of reference books not doing their homework; she only disappears to get away from her self-serving, venal guardians, while it's her studio that jumps to conclusions. There are some close shaves on the way to the upbeat, pleasing conclusion, as the guardians are told off, Duryea manages to keep his job and protect Kathy, and all fences are mended and maintained—on Christmas Day yet.

The filming of *Kathy O'*, from May through July, wasn't exactly uneventful for Duryea. He had injured his back while moving some boulders at Arrowhead, which means he had to film part of the movie while battling some intense pain. In addition, he attended son Peter's graduation from Harvard Prep School during the shoot; earlier, Peter had been diagnosed with mononucleosis and was therefore out of school for a long time prior to the ceremony. And proud papa Duryea got to see younger son Richard heading to Hollywood High after having graduated from North Hollywood Junior High.

Duryea would typically try to avoid filming during summer months. As he would tell an interviewer, "I have to be away from my family enough when I go on location, so I try to make it up by not working at all during July and August." In this case, however, he was not only filming during July but subsequently gave it his all when it came time for the film to be promoted in the months prior to its September 1958 release. Duryea would do extensive publicity for the film, not only in New York and Los Angeles, but anywhere the studio might want him to go. And it wasn't as if he was being compensated; to the contrary, he went all around the country despite the fact that he had no financial "participation" in the film's gross or profits, was not under contract, and was off-salary to boot. Duryea believed in *Kathy O'* and the possibility that this film would decisively alter how fans and the movie studios perceived him. He also would acknowledge to interviewers that even though he had just turned fifty-one, he hoped to be around much longer. Duryea had a rueful awareness that "audiences get tired of a face fast enough—without that face looking the same in the same kind of part."

As it turns out, Duryea, McCormack, and *Kathy O'* received some good notices at the time of its release, as many critics enjoyed McCormack's surprisingly sensitive child-star turn and the film's skillful blend of gentle humor and sentiment. Duryea received a great deal of praise, some of it from critics who "didn't know he had it in him." Ruth Waterbury of the *Los Angeles Examiner* wrote: "Until I saw Duryea here, warm, intelligent, sympathetic—I didn't know he had those qualities at his command." (Evidently, she had not seen *Chicago Calling* or *World for Ransom*—and she was not alone.) The *Hollywood Reporter* would note that "Duryea has his best part in years, and proves what a good actor he is by mining every contradictory nuance—loyal to family yet tempted by former sex bomb, jaundiced yet capable of sudden intuitive compassion." *Kathy O'* even made Kate Cameron's "10 Best Pictures" for the *New York Daily News*, as she praised the film's behind-the-scenes look at Hollywood and the natural dialogue.

Much to Duryea's regret, the hoped-for change in both the studios' perspective as well as audiences' didn't quite materialize, in spite of his winning presence in the film. Duryea is really quite good as the beleaguered, occasionally scheming (but only for the greater good—in this case, his job security and Kathy's welfare), yet generally understanding publicity man. In a rare comic and romantic lead, Duryea manages to be very appealing in his scenes with his on-screen wife. There's a sense of comfort between Duryea and Pickett; they seem quite convincing as a couple who are also friends. Duryea also exudes charm alongside the endearing Sterling, light years away from her mercenary turn in Billy Wilder's corrosive *Ace in the Hole*. The scenes between Duryea and Sterling in which they reminisce about happier times, with both managing to suppress their mutual attraction, benefit from their tender playing. Finally, Duryea and McCormack make an engaging on-screen pair, overcoming their own wariness toward each other and ensuring a modicum of eventual happiness (this is Hollywood as Hollywood sees itself—particularly in heartwarming holiday fare).

Yet despite Duryea's evident sincerity and obvious talent, moviegoers, whether they were your ordinary paying citizens or your Hollywood hiring types, would never fully embrace Duryea as the "nice guy." And maybe they had reason; no one could play it so entertainingly nasty as Duryea. He could be convincing as your ordinary good guy, but Duryea's best parts either allowed him to be more than slightly tarnished or gave him the go-ahead for unvarnished villainy unencumbered by thoughts of compassion or solicitude. Television would provide Duryea with an outlet for an array of more satisfying roles; moreover, the fast pace of filming would allow him opportunities to move from one fairly challenging role to another. For the next ten years, he would generally move freely between the mediums, and he even had a detour on Broadway. But, with a few notable exceptions, television is where Duryea would produce his most effective work.

A youthful Dan pictured in his Cornell University yearbook from 1928. Courtesy Dan Duryea Central.

Another pre-Hollywood Duryea photo, from his days at the Westport Playhouse. Courtesy Dan Duryea Central.

On Broadway in *The Little Foxes*, with Tallulah Bankhead, Charles Dingle, and Carl Benton Reid. Courtesy Dan Duryea Central.

The film of *The Little Foxes*: Duryea's Leo schemes with Oscar (Carl Benton Reid) in the bathroom. Courtesy Gregory Hines.

Duryea as comic gangster
Duke Pastrami in *Ball of Fire*
with Barbara Stanwyck.
Courtesy Dan Duryea Central.

Duryea and Joan Bennett
in *The Woman in the Window.*
Courtesy Richard Duryea.

From *Sahara*: listening to Zoltan Korda's direction along with star Humphrey Bogart and Bruce Bennett. Author's collection.

Duryea's Johnny blows smoke at Joan Bennett's Kitty in *Scarlet Street*. Courtesy Richard Duryea.

Duryea's Johnny hides from view in *Scarlet Street*. Courtesy Dan Duryea Central.

On the set of *The Great Flamarion*, with the director Anthony Mann, Erich von Stroheim, and Mary Beth Hughes. Courtesy Dan Duryea Central.

Black Angel: Duryea's Marty tries to be tough with unfaithful wife Mavis Marlowe (Constance Dowling). Author's collection.

Dan with Ella Raines in the frothy *White Tie and Tails*. Courtesy Dan Duryea Central.

Dan and Helen Duryea, circa early 1940s. Courtesy Richard Duryea.

The Duryea family at home, from left to right: Richard, Dan, Peter, and Helen. Courtesy Richard Duryea.

Dan with sons Richard and Peter at the piano. Courtesy Richard Duryea.

Duryea with June Vincent in
an atmospheric posed shot
from *Black Angel*. Author's
collection.

Dan in the mid-1940s. Courtesy Dan Duryea
Central.

Duryea, circa 1948. Courtesy Dan Duryea
Central.

Duryea with family, including Blackie the dog. Courtesy Richard Duryea.

Dan and Helen in costume at the Hollywood press photographer's costume ball at Ciro's, 1947. Courtesy Richard Duryea.

Dan landscaping at his home on Mulholland. Courtesy Dan Duryea Central.

As Oscar Hubbard in *Another Part of the Forest*, with Ann Blyth as Regina. Courtesy Richard Duryea.

Part of the preparations for the heist in *Criss Cross*, with Yvonne De Carlo, Burt Lancaster, and Stephen McNally. Author's collection.

Duryea posed with his trusty gun in *Manhandled*. Courtesy Richard Duryea.

Duryea in *Johnny Stool Pigeon*. Courtesy Dan Duryea Central.

Duryea is *China Smith*. Courtesy Dan Duryea Central.

Duryea with Lizabeth Scott in *Too Late for Tears*. Courtesy Dan Duryea Central.

Duryea with Gale Storm in *The Underworld Story*. Author's collection.

In *Terror Street*, Duryea's wounds are tended to by a sympathetic Ann Gudrun. Courtesy Dan Duryea Central.

Duryea on the phone again, only quite frantic in *Chicago Calling*, with Gordon Gebert in the background. Author's collection.

Dan and sons boating— Dan is in *Little Mink*. Courtesy Richard Duryea

Dan in the boat. Courtesy Richard Duryea

Christmas in Arrowhead:
Dan and Helen. Courtesy
Richard Duryea.

Dan and sons enjoying ice
cream while Helen is content
just watching the show.
Courtesy Richard Duryea.

Arrowhead: Dan and Helen
(holding mystery foot).
Courtesy Richard Duryea.

Duryea cackles and threatens in *Winchester '73*. Courtesy Dan Duryea Central.

Duryea on the oil rig in *Thunder Bay*. Courtesy Richard Duryea.

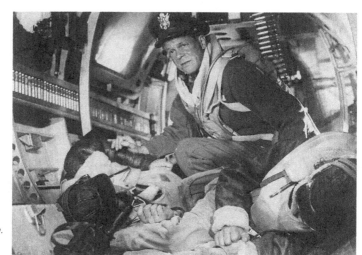

A somber and reflective Duryea in *Sky Commando*. Courtesy Dan Duryea Central.

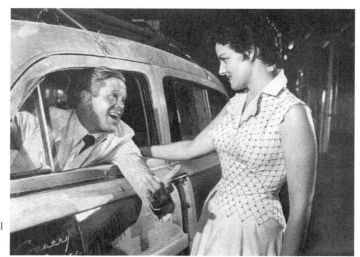

Duryea's doctor gets friendly with Jane Russell in *Foxfire*. Courtesy Richard Duryea.

Duryea in *Storm Fear* with Lee Grant, Steven Hill, Jean Wallace, and actor-director Cornel Wilde. Courtesy Dan Duryea Central.

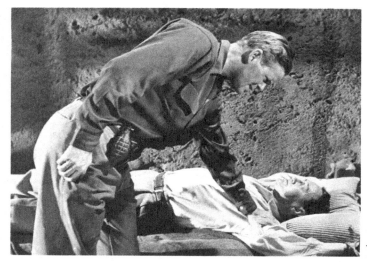

Duryea rescues scientist Arthur Shields in *World for Ransom*. Courtesy Dan Duryea Central.

A gleeful Duryea with Audie Murphy in *Ride Clear of Diablo*. Courtesy Dan Duryea Central.

Duryea and Jayne Mansfield in *The Burglar*. Courtesy Dan Duryea Central.

Duryea on TV and menaced by Harold Stone in "The Frightened Witness." Courtesy Dan Duryea Central.

Duryea in wardrobe on the set of *Night Passage*. Courtesy Richard Duryea.

Duryea in "The Cliff Grundy Story" on *Wagon Train*. Courtesy Dan Duryea Central.

Dan Duryea Fan Club cover photo, circa 1950s. Courtesy Dan Duryea Central.

Duryea with Patty McCormack and Mary Fickett in *Kathy O'*. Courtesy Dan Duryea Central.

Squire Dan at Arrowhead.
Courtesy Richard Duryea.

Three Duryeas in stripes,
circa late 1950s. Courtesy
Richard Duryea.

Dan with his dad. Courtesy Richard Duryea.

Dan at home, toasting the good life. Courtesy Richard Duryea.

Duryea with Terry
Moore in *Platinum
High School*. Courtesy
Dan Duryea Central.

Duryea with Hardy Kruger in *Flight of the Phoenix*. Courtesy Dan Duryea Central.

Duryea with Audie Murphy in *Six Black Horses*. Courtesy Dan Duryea Central.

That's Duryea under the clown make-up in "Tears on a Painted Face" on the series *Wide Country*. Courtesy Dan Duryea central.

Duryea's gentle, blind pianist bonds with Tommy Sands in "Blow High, Blow Clear." Author's collection.

Duryea with outlaw Buster Crabbe in *The Bounty Killer*. Courtesy Dan Duryea Central.

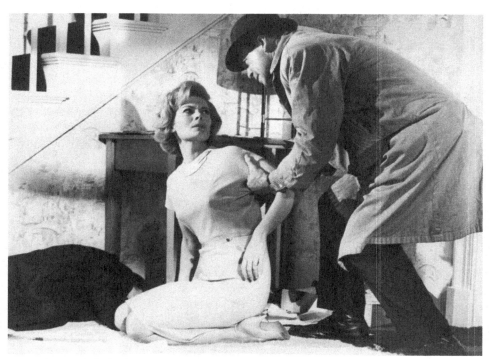

Duryea has just killed Patricia Owens's husband in *Walk a Tightrope*—and the fun is only beginning. Courtesy Dan Duryea Central.

Duryea as Eddie Jacks in *Peyton Place*. Courtesy
Dan Duryea Central.

Duryea with Jocelyn Lane in *Incident at Phantom Hill*. Courtesy Dan Duryea Central.

A smiling Duryea plays
hero in *The Hills Run Red*. Courtesy Dan
Duryea Central.

Duryea in the mid-1960s. Courtesy Richard Duryea.

Father and son: Duryea
with Peter in *Taggart*.
Courtesy Richard Duryea.

CHAPTER 11

Villainy and Valor in Film and TV

IT MUST HAVE BEEN FRUSTRATING FOR DURYEA WHEN HE REALIZED HIS role in *Kathy O'* wouldn't cause those myopic Hollywood executives to allow him the chance to expand his screen image. Perhaps they missed the favorable reviews that Duryea had garnered. Or perhaps they had seen some other reviews, like that of the *New York Times'* Howard Thompson, who referred to *Kathy O'* as "sticky treacle." Or perhaps they paid heed to many of the preview cards, especially those that marked the film as "poor" (or damned it with faint praise by noting it was better than another lighthearted Universal release, *This Happy Feeling*). In any case, it wasn't that the studios were beckoning him for villainous roles—once again, they simply weren't calling at all. Duryea's hopes and energies in getting behind *Kathy O'* only resulted in the same situation he was in during his lean period in 1951. This time, it wouldn't be a single producer or offer of a series that would grant him the opportunity to stretch; several series producers would enlist Duryea's services, and each successive Duryea television appearance would breed more appearances.

Between late 1957 and 1962, Duryea's career, except for two major roles in relatively minor films, would be centered on the small screen. There would be nights where you had your choice of watching Duryea in two hit television series. At first, these guest spots would catch the attention because Duryea was a film star who was "doing television." Later, the press would note the overall quality of his performances, and the probability that his appearances on these shows helped to raise that show's standards, resulting in a superior episode. Admittedly, not all of them were winners, and just as in the movies, there were occasions where Duryea seemed to be marking time (though even a Duryea walk-through could be more interesting than some presumably well-crafted portrayals from others), but many of these episodes contained some of his best work.

Take Duryea's first appearance as Cliff Grundy on the venerable *Wagon Train*. This classic series concerning settlers traveling westward under the watchful eyes of Major Adams and Flint McCullough (series regulars Ward Bond and Robert Horton) attracted many prominent film actors. These guest stars would appear in character-driven, self-contained dramas that centered on them, with subsequent episodes anchored by other major (or minor) stars. In the first season alone, stars such as Linda Darnell and Marjorie Main were among those providing conflicts along the wagon train's journey to its eventual destination. Duryea's episode, "The Cliff Grundy Story," features the actor as a likable, garrulous gold prospector more inclined to deliver a tale than to encounter gold. Grundy is a well-known windbag, but he is indulged by the leaders of the wagon train, notably Horton, who looks to Grundy with something akin to hero worship.

When Duryea's Grundy is severely injured after being trampled by buffalo, Horton offers to stay with him in order to help him recover—or to be there for Grundy's possible demise. Russell Johnson (who was a thorn in Duryea's side in *Ride Clear* of Diablo, but who considered him "a hell of a good actor and easy to work with") is a fellow cowboy who also offers to stay, mainly because he wants to discover the location of the gold mine Grundy has been blathering on about. Horton's character figures out Johnson's true motivations, but still leaves himself wide open to the butt of a gun, allowing Johnson to escape with the horses and guns, leaving Horton and the not–quite-dead-yet Duryea to face the elements (namely, Indians and hostile terrain, with no water in sight). Duryea manages his character's transitions seamlessly, as he moves from carefree and loquacious to gravely wounded and quietly brave. When he defies augury to recover (albeit unsteadily), Grundy prevails upon Horton to leave him and save himself, taking off when Horton refuses to do so. This action on Duryea's part only results in a fateful encounter with a bear, in which both men have to join forces in order to survive.

Duryea's appearance on *Wagon Train* was very well-received, with the *Hollywood Reporter* writing that "his portrayal as a gold prospector shows why he's in such demand as a character actor." The episode itself was seen by many as being "wonderfully gripping," and Duryea's efforts resulted in the actor being invited back later that season for the last episode, "The Sacramento Story," which depicted the fates of several of the passengers (Duryea's Grundy among them).

Duryea would become a favorite of the series' producers, subsequently doing a total of seven *Wagon Train* episodes. In 1959, Duryea would first appear in long hair and scraggly beard as "The Last Man," directed by James Neilson, who had previously indulged Duryea in *Night Passage*. Here, Duryea is the half-crazed sole survivor of another group of settlers who becomes a target when he is mistakenly identified as having contributed to the settlers' demise. He is finally exonerated by his own diary—only after the wagon-train passengers come perilously close to taking justice into their own hands. Duryea's acting remained free of overblown hysterics, and *Variety* wrote that he "carries off the role with subdued poignancy." The following year, Duryea would play another rescued traveler, only a more sinister one. "The Joshua Gilliam Story" has Duryea as an educated traveler who offers to "pay his way" by helping Bethel Leslie teach the young children. His attraction to Leslie is also helped by the fact that she is due to inherit a large tract of land—an inheritance that can be revoked should her suspicious mother think she is she marrying the wrong man. And since Duryea is laying on the charm while initially professing ignorance of Leslie's windfall—not to mention attempting the use of hypnosis, which Leslie's mother witnesses—the stage is set for a final confrontation, not between Leslie and Duryea, but Duryea and the mother. Duryea does a good job of "faking the sincerity" in the early stages, gradually becoming more sinister and deadly as the episode progresses. He plays in a lower key, with a lower pitch, beguiling the children with his tales of witches among us (their resultant fear transferred to the unwitting mother) and beguiling Leslie—that is, until he oversteps his bounds in a well-paced confrontation in a deserted mining town.

Besides *Wagon Train*, there were other Westerns lined up for his services; the genre was extremely popular on television, right up until the 1970s. Duryea did a couple of episodes for the long-running *Zane Grey Theater*, which adapted many of the prolific author's stories, in addition to attaching the author's name to homegrown Western fare. Duryea was well-cast in the tense half-hour episode "This Man Must Die," in which he played a wrongly condemned man who has escaped from prison on the eve of his hanging to corner the man whose testimony put him there—and to hopefully find the real killer, too. It's a stock situation, forced to a swift resolution by the demands of television, but Duryea does well by his single-minded character whose misplaced loyalty to his former partner (Karl Swenson) doesn't allow for the possibility he may be the real murderer. He is also more than serviceable in his tender scenes with the showgirl with a heart of gold (is there any other kind?) who helps him clear himself.

On multiple occasions in the West, Duryea played a flamboyant, corrupt, and murderous town boss who was more than a match (at least until the end) for the hero who has pledged to bring him down. On *Walt Disney's Texas John Slaughter*, starring Tom Tyron as an intrepid Texas Ranger, Duryea was his usual boisterous, smiling villain in an enjoyable episode entitled "Showdown in Sandoval." Duryea's outlaw leader conducts raids into Texas from his stronghold in Mexico, while Slaughter goes south (and undercover) in order to capture him. *Cimarron City*, a ninety-minute series starring George Montgomery, would cast Duryea as a cultured, cunning outlaw who has imprisoned our hero Montgomery among other undeserving, persecuted men. Spurred on by his own ambition and buoyed by the support of his loving wife (who adores him no matter what), the episode evolves into a battle of wits between Duryea and Montgomery, with the cat-and-mouse aspect well-developed throughout. Interestingly enough, Dan Blocker, soon to achieve stardom as Hoss on *Bonanza*, is a hoot as Duryea's enforcer.

In 1959, Duryea made the first of four appearances on the classic Clint Eastwood/Eric Fleming series *Rawhide*. This venerable series about the longest-running cattle drive nominally starred Fleming as the sturdy trail boss, but costar Eastwood captured the critics' and audiences' attention as his drover, Rowdy Yates. As with *Wagon Train*, the nature of the journey allowed the cowboys to have encounters with several name guest stars, who would often be here today, shot tomorrow. "Incident with an Executioner" makes full use of Duryea's star power, placing the actor in the role of a notorious and deadly horseman following the wagon train (from a not-so-respectful distance) in order to stalk and eventually execute his target, who happens to be unknown to the audience for most of the episode. Duryea and Eastwood share some good moments as the wary antagonists, while Martin Milner impresses as another traveler. *Hollywood Reporter* called it "a rare combination of mystery, suspense, and characterizations"—and it was noted by several reviewers that Duryea's biggest competition was himself, since he appeared in both *Rawhide* and *Texas John Slaughter* on the same night, meeting with the same violent demise.

Many of his Western roles had Duryea either on a quest for revenge or in the employ of those who want to use his hired gun to achieve a modicum of revenge on their part, or silence someone who might do them harm. In "Badge Without Honor," a 1960 episode of *Bonanza*, Duryea is dapper, smooth-talking deputy Gerald Eskith who ingratiates himself with the Cartwrights while seeking to transport their accountant friend, ostensibly so the friend can testify against a corrupt firm. It soon becomes clear that Duryea's badge is entirely without honor (hence the title) as Eskith is known to use it as an excuse to execute certain troublesome individuals who threaten his venal employers; in this case, he seeks to transport the "friend" with intent to kill him before they reach their destination. Duryea's role offers him the opportunity to be charming, brutal, and lethal—sometimes within the same monologue. The scenes in which he casually menaces the accountant and later berates the man's vulnerable wife have the intensity that Duryea brought to his 1940s noir efforts. Duryea is also given a memorable death scene; after being shot by Adam Cartwright (Pernell Roberts), Eskith laments that the only person he ever truly loved was himself.

It wasn't all sagebrush and tumbleweeds for Duryea during this remarkably prolific period. He starred in a one-hour drama, "Hour of the Rat," for the *U.S. Steel Hour*. Written by Arthur Hailey, it was a searing drama about an English civil servant (Duryea) with a deep hatred of the Japanese, brought on by his harrowing experiences in a prison camp during World War II. When he later sees his tormentor at a business meeting, he decides to exact his long-vowed revenge. (Whether in the West or in the present day, many of Duryea's characters were busy seeking revenge—is it any wonder he became so skilled at portraying the intensity and single-mindedness inherent in the wronged man?) Knigh Dheigh was the perceived captor, and critics believed that although Hailey's writing was a little formulaic, the piece was well-handled by the two actors. Another intense dramatic role, and a further opportunity to enact the vengeful protagonist, came by way of the series *Pursuit*. In the episode "Tiger on a Bicycle," Duryea was a cop whose policeman friend is killed in an armored-car robbery. He doggedly interrogates a child whom he suspects was used by his father in a holdup (by stalling his bike in front of an armored car).

After spending a great deal of time on the avenging side of the equation, Duryea found himself as the object of revenge in an episode of the short-lived anthology series *The David Niven Show*. The series attracted some notable stars (Niven himself was well-liked in Hollywood circles, and stars were willing to work on the series for less than their Hollywood fees), but the ratings were mediocre at best. In an episode called, fittingly enough, "The Vengeance," Duryea starred as a small-town justice of the peace who gets word that a mental case he had put away has escaped and is out to kill him. It's a reasonably taut episode, as Duryea's judge spends much of the time anxiously pacing in his home, gun at the ready (except for the one time he really needs it—a questionable development, to say the least), hoping to stop his assailant, but not necessarily hurt him, since he feels some responsibility for the disturbed lad's plight.

"The Vengeance" was initially meant be more than one episode of Niven's anthology series; it was intended to be the pilot for a drama called *Justice of the Peace*, but the series was never picked up. It would be one of a number of unsuccessful pilots that Duryea would make. Another pilot was for a prospective series to be called *Barnaby Hooke*, in which Duryea would play a newspaper columnist looking for stories. In the pilot, "Mystery in Malibu," Duryea's reporter is investigating a series of deaths connected with the expanding financial empire of a widow; his probe leads him to the widow's son (upset with mother for her role in father's death) and a greedy business partner who targets both Duryea and the son for elimination. After much speculation as to whether the show would be called *Barnaby Hooke* or *Confidentially Yours* for Revue Productions, the televised pilot was the recipient of apathetic audience turnout, and the series never materialized.

Around this time, Duryea discussed the frequency of his television work with Forrest Powers of the *Minneapolis Star*. He was grateful for the interest of television's casting agents and producers who enabled him to stretch his talents: "It's nice to have more of a variety of parts now. I couldn't buy a nice character in the movies." He also noted the less frenetic pace of current television, noting the first thirteen *China Smith* episodes were shot in twenty-one days, while the shooting schedule for *Barnaby Hooke* was a downright leisurely six days.

Another proposed Duryea pilot was a little comedy to be shot for Desilu Productions. The series was to have been called *The Holidays Abroad*, and it would costar Duryea and Margaret Hayes in a lighthearted series about a traveling newspaper writer with a wife and family. In the pilot episode, "Paris," he would travel with the family to interview a hard-to-see author, the concept being that the family would somehow foul up his interviews. After it completed shooting, Desi Arnaz (the *Desi* in Desilu) saw the finished product and halted the production of any further episodes (Duryea would appear under the Desilu banner again, with William Frawley in "The Comeback," Frawley's first role after playing Fred Mertz on *I Love Lucy*).

The fact that his pilots weren't being picked up did not deter producers from clamoring for Duryea to become a regular on an already established series. When *Riverboat* star Darren McGavin was recuperating from an injury, Duryea ably filled his shoes as the genial Captain Brad Turner. In "The Wichita Arrows," Duryea manages to get to the bottom of some trouble involving supposed Indians who are preying on the townspeople, ultimately discovering that the true culprits are some outlaws posing as Indians. Some elements stretch credibility, as in Duryea's rapid recovery from an arrow wound, but the Hollywood action veteran William Witney keeps things moving rather briskly. In his encore episode, "Fort Epitaph," Duryea's captain Turner unwittingly leads his crew into warfare between the Sioux and US soldiers. Captain Turner was a droll part, and Duryea was genial and thoroughly likable, but there wasn't anything especially memorable about the role or the efficient but uninspired episodes.

A more interesting offer from a long-established show came Duryea's way around the same time. Ward Bond, the wise, respected Major Seth Adams of *Wagon Train*, had died suddenly of a heart attack in November 1960. Bond had already completed a number of episodes for the 1960–61 season, (including Duryea's most recent stint, "The Bleymeier Story," one of his lesser appearances, as a fanatical farmer stirring up trouble with his belief in prophecies and his stubborn refusal to allow his daughter to go her own way). The producers approached Duryea about taking over as the new leader of the wagon train. Duryea considered it for a while before declining, saying he "wasn't quite right for the part." The role would subsequently go to John McIntire, but one wonders why Duryea turned it down—especially in light of his recent misbegotten pilots, and the fact he would be assuming the lead in an established, hit series as a heroic figure. It might have been that the part, as financially rewarding as it might have been, wasn't enough to satisfy Duryea—especially since quite often, the major has to take a subsidiary role, not only to the weekly guest star, but quite often to his second-in-command, Robert Horton. Perhaps Duryea wanted to build on his career as one of television's most reliable character actors by continuing to take on challenging roles in a variety of series, which would enhance his staying power both on television and eventually Hollywood.

It's not as if Hollywood executives were pounding at Duryea's Mulholland Drive door with significant offers. Duryea's only film between 1958 and 1961 was a negligible, low-budget endeavor at MGM for the producer Albert Zugsmith. *Platinum High School*—also known as *Trouble at 16* and *Rich, Young and Deadly*—would be a very loose remake of *Bad Day at Black Rock.* The original, made a scant five years earlier, pitted Spencer Tracy against Robert Ryan, as Tracy searched for answers in a hostile town (led by Ryan), regarding the whereabouts of a fallen comrade's father. *Platinum High School* has Mickey Rooney back at his old MGM stomping grounds to play a bereaved absentee parent investigating the mysterious circumstances surrounding his son's death at an island military school. The filming took place on Catalina Island, which stood in for the movie's sinister "Sabre Island." Duryea was cast as the menacing school superintendent who maintains the son's death was accidental, assisted by Terry Moore as Duryea's gal Friday and Richard Jaeckel as Duryea's prize cadet and enforcer. Yvette Mimieux also appeared as an island inhabitant who sympathizes with Rooney, while Warren Berlinger agonized convincingly as a guilt-ridden cadet who knows more than he's telling.

Platinum High School, while nowhere near as bad as its belittled stature might suggest, is not terribly good either. There is altogether too much talk and too little action as Rooney makes the rounds of the island, arousing the ire of Duryea and Jaeckel, while goading a conflicted Berlinger to do what's right. Rooney is actually quite good as the grieving father, trying to come to terms with the fact that his paternal concern has come a little too late; he's also quite handy with his fists (Mickey Rooney—action hero) as he takes on Jaeckel in a well-staged café brawl (reminiscent of Tracy's encounter with Ernest Borgnine in *Bad Day at Black Rock*). Duryea is on the sidelines for this scene, as he is in most of the picture. It is Jaeckel who gets plenty of chances to intimidate everyone, while Moore gets to cozy up to Rooney on Duryea's behest (like the unfortunate Anne Francis did for Ryan in *Bad Day at Black Rock*). Even the action-packed boating climax proved disappointing, both for viewers and for Duryea, since, as a skilled sailor, he saw his character's boating accident as "a blow to his pride." He may well have been speaking in jest, but there was no disguising the fact that Duryea was merely going through the motions throughout the recycled, uninspired proceedings. Not that the film was widely reviewed, but those who saw it, like the *New York Times* reviewer Eugene Archer, felt that "Duryea went through his paces with bored familiarity." Rooney was the only one to emerge unscathed, and he was in fact praised by several critics, including one who said his performance was "the only merit in this shoddy and obviously inexpensive exploitation melodrama."

If this is all that he could get in the movies, it's no wonder that Duryea became the busiest character actor on television. He was very fortunate to have been cast as the main guest star in the pilot episode of yet another long-running Western, *Laramie*. Robert Fuller and John Smith were the leads in this series and the pilot, called "Stage Stop," not only establishes their relationship, but provides Duryea with a meaty villain role. Smith and his younger brother own a ranch, but since they're strapped, they let their place be used as a stagecoach stop; Fuller is a roaming cowboy who initially butts heads with Smith, but as is the course of many series, their initial antagonism soon turns to mutual respect. Before the two leads are even introduced, the director and writer take advantage of Duryea's magnetism by introducing him as the threat du jour, an outlaw who plans to intercept a judge (Everett Sloane) on his way to a hanging. Once Duryea is introduced, the show proceeds to set up the character dynamics among the leads, until Duryea and his gang return to commandeer the stage stop, taking advantage of the leads' antagonism by forcing them to slug each other until one is knocked out. It's a tense, well-acted episode that makes good use of Duryea and his ability to ignite the action—and even the actors.

Laramie would be Robert Fuller's first important lead role in a series. In my research, I discovered a handwritten letter from Fuller to Duryea among Duryea's collected papers. In this letter, Fuller makes reference to what many have said about Duryea over the years; he not only brought his A game to everything he did, claimed Fuller, but also inspired others to do better work, and the finished product was better for it. In addition, Fuller found a great deal to admire about Duryea, the man: "You're my idea of what an actor should be on and off camera." When I contacted Fuller about my book, he was more than happy to contribute, and was effusive in his praise of his frequent costar. Fuller recalls being told that he would be working with a major motion picture star, saying, "I got a call from wardrobe one afternoon and standing there was Dan Duryea! He knew everyone in the business . . . Dan knew them all. He asked me to lunch in the commissary. We walked in . . . Dan knew all the waitresses by their first name."

Duryea impressed the younger Fuller with both his sheer professionalism and friendly, easygoing demeanor. Fuller remembered thinking": "This is the way to be if you're gonna be a star and a great gentleman." Duryea would have very few close friends in Hollywood, other than Jimmy Stewart, but he numbered Fuller among them and the feeling was mutual—not that the rising star necessarily listened to all of the older actor's pearls of wisdom. Fuller recounted some thoughts Duryea passed on to him after *Laramie* proved to be a hit: "Dan said to me, 'Now

Bob, I'm gonna give you the best advice. *Save* your money. Don't buy a new car. Put your money in the bank. There'll be time for that new car later.' Four days later, I showed up with a brand-new Thunderbird that I had bought two days before. Dan looked at the car and said, 'What did you do! So much for my advice' . . ."

Duryea would go on to make two more well-received appearances on *Laramie*. "The Long Riders," from 1960, has Duryea as a friendly but mysterious gunfighter who hires on at Smith's request. Fuller casts a suspicious eye toward the stranger, particularly as he is becoming friendly with Smith's younger brother, while mildly probing an incident from Smith's past. Duryea is so good as the would-be former gunman, who professes the desire to settle down, that the not-unexpected revelation that he is indeed in the employ of some vengeful gunmen adds emotional weight to the proceedings. "The Mountain Men," from 1961, was directed by Hollywood veteran Joseph Kane, and the cast featured Duryea as the patriarch of the rough-and-tumble Sanford family. After one of his sons is killed, Duryea, with the help of his other two sons, decides to circumvent the law and enact his own brand of justice on the convicted assailant. Duryea is forceful as the would-be avenger trying to cope with his hotheaded older son, his conscience-stricken younger son, and the entreaties of series regular Spring Byington to put a halt to his vengeful quest. The scenes between Byington and Duryea are the episode's best, but its ending leaves a little to be desired, as Duryea's fate is only spoken of, thus denying his central character a dramatically satisfying resolution. Taken as a whole, however, his episodes on *Laramie* would prove tremendously satisfying, giving the show's fans the chance to see different shades of Duryea.

Duryea's appearances on *Laramie* (as well as on other series) did not just ensure future employment for Duryea on a particular series; on occasion, his appearances, especially on pilot episodes, would help secure a place for the show on a network's fall schedule. Duryea's performance certainly helped *Laramie* earn its fall placement, and he was purposely sought out for another series pilot. *Frontier Circus*, from 1961, would cast Duryea as a buffalo hunter in conflict with gunslinger and star Dick York (a few years before becoming the first Darrin opposite Elizabeth Montgomery's Samantha on *Bewitched*). His appearance was acknowledged by the series producer, Dick Irving, as a major factor in helping to "sell it." More often than not, television producers or casting directors seeing Duryea on a particular show would use him on their show. Hedda Hopper would note that Duryea's appearance on *Laramie* (on its premiere episode, "Stage Stop") would result in him being immediately offered a part in "Tom and Huck" for *Shirley Temple Theater*, as well as a plum dramatic role in "Shadow of a Pale Horse" for the *U.S. Steel Hour*.

Adapted from a British television play by Bruce Stewart, "Shadow of a Pale Horse" is set in a remote colony in 1870 Australia and stars Duryea as a man whose son has been killed, allegedly by a drunken convict. Duryea wants to kill the convict but is urged to bury his son and wait until morning, particularly since the convict has been protesting his innocence—all the while referring to the existence of a mysterious pale horse. Frank Lovejoy costarred as the convict's employer who urges the men not to resort to mob rule. The story takes a turn when Lovejoy and Duryea are urged to switch roles—in order for the community to be as objective as possible. Duryea, as the unlikely defense counsel, comes to believe in the convict's innocence, even allowing for the possibility that the murder may have been committed by someone riding through; meanwhile, Lovejoy comes to take his own role seriously and becomes just as fervent as Duryea had originally been in proving the lad's guilt. The roles, then, are fully reversed, as Lovejoy's efforts lead to the lad being condemned to hang, in spite of Duryea's impassioned defense. Duryea embodies both fervor and forbearance as both the avenger and the advocate for compassion, while Lovejoy matches him as the initially unwilling prosecutor who ultimately breaks down in the aftermath of the trial. This is a lesser-known Duryea effort that deserves to be seen (like many anthology series, it has not been commercially released yet and was viewed in UCLA Arts Library's Special Collections). "Shadow of a Pale Horse" is also indicative of the satisfying roles Duryea was offered with regularity on television.

Although Duryea never received an Emmy, his efforts occasionally helped others to win theirs. Barbara Stanwyck, accepting an Emmy as Best Actress as the star of the anthology series *The Barbara Stanwyck Show*, took the opportunity to acknowledge Duryea as a prime reason why she won. Looking at their joint appearance, "Sign of the Zodiac," one can see why Stanwyck might have submitted this episode for consideration. Directed by the 1940s noir vet Jacques Tourneur, this is an atmospheric, suspenseful drama about a guilt-ridden woman (Stanwyck) who believes she has killed her husband and engages Duryea's spiritualist to drive out the spirit of her husband. Duryea is all smooth charm as the episode plays on his reputation as the crafty cad who may be trying to get Stanwyck to confess her guilt, but in reality wants to save her from the machinations of her supposed friend Joan Blondell—sister of Stanwyck's late husband. Stanwyck convincingly runs the emotional gamut (with some semblance of restraint on her part, which was not always the case), ably complemented by Blondell's turn as Stanwyck's duplicitous confidant and Duryea's intelligent rendering of the unexpected savior.

Perhaps Duryea's most enduring characterization during this period was his appearance on one of the most famous anthology series of them all, *The Twilight Zone*. Created and written in large part by the prodigiously talented and highly prolific Rod Serling (*Patterns, The Comedian, Requiem for a Heavyweight*, to name a few), the series would deliver half-hour episodes of a generally high quality (especially in the early seasons), usually with a protagonist caught up in circumstances which would warrant a journey into the netherworld known as "the twilight zone." Many of these episodes would contain twists leading to resolutions that could be disturbing but usually quite fitting; occasionally, these endings would also allow for a sliver of hope and even redemption.

Duryea's episode, "Mr. Denton on Doomsday," placed him once again in the West—only it's Serling's West, where characters are unwitting pawns, and events have their own twisted, inexorable logic. Duryea was given the bravura role of Al Denton, a former gunfighter turned hopeless drunk. When we first see Denton in the pre-credits sequence, he is cadging rinks from the amused populace, including a smiling town bully (Martin Landau, all in black) who forces Duryea to warble an off-key, admittedly pitiful rendition of "How Dry I Am" in order to wangle a drink. Despite the protestations of an adoring waitress, Denton continues his descent into the abyss—until he awakes after a binge to find a mysterious gun next to him. The gun seems to have a mind of its own since, after Landau taunts him once again, the gun goes off, winging the livid Landau. Denton follows it up with an unintentional, albeit well-placed, shot to the chandelier which prevents any further intrusions from Landau—and earns the respect of those who disparaged Denton in the past. News of Denton's renewed marksmanship spreads, much to Denton's despair; in an anguished monologue, Denton recounts how his past as a fast gun brought on the challengers and accelerated his drinking.

After hearing of yet another challenge, the newly sober (and cleaned-up) Duryea plans to flee, until a mysterious traveling salesman offers him an elixir—one which will give him speed and accuracy for ten seconds after he drinks it. Robert Fuller would recall the necessity for Duryea to be a very fast gun in this episode, and Fuller had a device used to help his own fast draw on *Laramie*, which he lent to Duryea for this episode.

The final showdown between Duryea and a very young Doug McClure as his boastful challenger brings about a clever twist that I won't spoil for those who have not seen it. Suffice it to say, Duryea is free to live his life in peace, with his supportive lady friend at his side.

"Mr. Denton on Doomsday" resonates for Duryea fans, as well as *Twilight Zone* and Western fans. A few reviewers noted that Duryea had never been in better form. Duryea captures the hopelessness and despair of the pathetic, drunken Denton and manages a seamless transition into a figure of integrity and a modicum of wisdom. Serling's script is skillfully developed without resorting to overstatement, supplying Duryea with the opportunity to etch a memorable character, while satisfying the *Twilight Zone* fans who have come to expect the heightened reality and ironic denouements essential to the show's success.

In the future, Duryea would get more of these full-fledged character parts, but these would generally be on television. The big screen would beckon occasionally—for starring and major supporting roles in low-medium-budget Westerns and crime dramas—but by and large his most fulfilling work would continue to be on the small screen.

CHAPTER 12

On the Tube, in the West, and a (Short) Trip to Broadway

AT A TIME WHEN MANY OF HIS PEERS WERE EITHER SLOWING DOWN or reduced to inconsequential supporting roles in film and television, Duryea was continuing to find solid work in quality TV drama, as well as the occasional meaty film role (even if the film itself was less than prime).

He played two different types of military men in two popular series from the early 1960s. In "Tight as a Drum," for the series *Checkmate*, Duryea would play the proud but compromised head of a military academy as series regulars Sebastian Cabot and Doug McClure investigate the possible murder of a gym instructor. While there is little doubt as to his involvement (Duryea's character is a reluctant participant in a smuggling scheme, along with the murder victim), Duryea contributes a thoughtful portrait of a conscientious but conflicted commander who cares about his young charges, eventually sacrificing his life to protect the student who had summoned the investigators in the first place.

Duryea's embittered army officer in the tense "Daughter, Am I in My Father's House," for the crime drama *Naked City*, is yet another example of Duryea's intensity being utilized for maximum effect on the small screen. *Naked City* was a popular show that made good use of the streets of New York to deliver gritty dramas of crime and punishment presided over by the detectives of the Sixty-fifth Precinct, led by Paul Burke, Harry Bellaver, and Horace McMahon. Barbara Harris was cast as Duryea's employed, sheltered daughter who lives with papa as he unsuccessfully tries to make a go of it as an insurance salesman. In the opening scene, Harris's attempts to silence some young hooligans at a movie house (where is an usher when you need him?) earn her catcalls from the ruffians and some manhandling outside the theater—fortuitously interrupted by the timely arrival of a helpful bystander.

After the encounter is brought to the attention of the police, Detectives Burke and Bellaver visit Harris and her father, and are immediately struck by all of Duryea's war souvenirs—as well as his unwillingness to trust the police with handling the situation, intimating that he'll take care of it himself. Duryea does this by dressing up his plainly attired daughter and using her as bait to find these miscreants—and, in a disturbing scene, he beats the hell out of some unwitting young fellow who happens to approach his daughter. In the meantime, one of her would-be tormentors—who has issues with his own father—is remorseful over his own actions and tries to strike up an acquaintance with a gradually thawing Harris. His persistence, in tandem with Duryea's use of Harris to draw him and his comrades out into the open, result in some unfortunate consequences—particularly for Duryea and his relationship with Harris.

"Daughter, Am I in My Father's House" is another example of the sterling work Duryea was regularly delivering on television. Duryea's characterization of an overly protective father trying to transpose his military successes of the past onto the mean streets of New York generate a certain degree of sympathy that nevertheless dissipates as he misguidedly uses his own daughter to further his own ends. Duryea has one chilling monologue toward the end where he justifies his tactics, as well as his own attitude toward the police. His tale of how he brutally disciplined his own men ("I believe I sent one to the hospital," he recalls with pride) when the local police were ineffectual sums up both the character's pride as well as his brutality.

Beginning in 1961, Duryea would portray troubled, aging father figures on *Route 66*, a popular series about two drifters (George Maharis and Martin Milner) and their various adventures as they travel the United States. "Don't Count Stars" has Duryea as an alcoholic uncle who has squandered a lifetime of second chances and runs a hotel for his loving, patient young niece—of whom he's a guardian. Early on, he falls off a boat and is rescued by the erstwhile heroes, who—motivated by their affection for the niece—try to encourage Duryea to change his ways and take responsibility for his actions. Since Duryea has made some questionable choices regarding the financial health of the hotel, and other parties have petitioned for him to be removed as guardian, time is of the essence. Duryea's drunken character is reminiscent of his turn as Al Denton; his first instinct is to drown his sorrows or flee from responsibility. Duryea and Maharis share a few good scenes as Maharis tries to browbeat Duryea, with Duryea resisting; and Duryea has a lovely rapport with his niece (well-played by Susan Melvin), making his expected change of heart understandable.

"A Cage in Search of a Bird" stars Duryea as an old bank robber opposite Stefanie Powers as his unwilling protégé, a drifter involved in fleecing naïve gamblers. The somewhat far-fetched plot has Duryea's aging robber driven by conscience to find the long-stashed takings of a past robbery, thus ensuring Powers's future by getting her to turn him in for the reward. Complicating matters is Powers's recent victim (a young Alex Cord). Motivated by revenge and a little greed, Cord tries to insert himself into the robber's plans. Powers and Duryea agreeably complement each other, with Duryea's weary, nostalgic robber serving as a welcome counterpoint to Powers's youthful, wary loner, who gradually grows to care about her unlikely mentor.

This string of successful television shows was interrupted by a call from Universal to take on a lead role opposite Audie Murphy in the 1962 Western *Six Black Horses*. Much had changed in the seven years since they starred together in *Ride Clear of Diablo*. Murphy's Westerns were no longer "shaky A" efforts and now fell decidedly into the B-movie category, with budgets to match. In the case of *Six Black Horses*, journeyman director Harry Keller was at the helm. Though Keller directed a number of features for Universal, he may be best known to cinema buffs as the director assigned to film additional "clarifying" scenes for Orson Welles's *Touch of Evil*.

For *Six Black Horses*, Keller was working from a screenplay by Burt Kennedy that resembled a warmed-over version of Kennedy's greatest hits, which had previously been enacted by Randolph Scott under the expert direction of Budd Boetticher. Drifter Audie Murphy, about to be hanged, is saved by gunman Duryea—*check*. The two new uneasy allies agree to escort a woman (Joan O' Brien) through dangerous country— for a price—*check*. Cue dangerous Indians and even more dangerous scalphunters—*check*. Have Duryea save Murphy's life during a gun battle— *big check*. Have the woman pit the two friends against each other—*double check*. End with a final confrontation between Murphy and Duryea who have been positioned as if by fate (or contrived plotting) to draw on each other ("There are some things a man can't ride around")—*checkmate!*

Though Kennedy's script is mainly a retread and Keller's direction just competent and no more (imagine what Boetticher might have done with the bursts of action or the framing in the dialogue scenes), both Duryea and Murphy, with an assist from O'Brien, are in good form, performing as if the dialogue and situations were newly minted. O'Brien did not have a long career, but she was an attractive, assertive presence in a number of 1960s-era films (including the Frank Tashlin-directed Jerry Lewis vehicle *It's Only Money*), and she does a fine job of holding the screen opposite her veteran costars. As for Audie Murphy, he had developed as an actor over the years, delivering his lines with more authority and a slight edge, becoming a more interesting, seasoned protagonist as a result. Murphy's increased assurance as a screen actor didn't allow him to necessarily enjoy the filmmaking process. Actor George Wallace (cast as a scalphunter) would tell the author Robert Nott: "I got the feeling he didn't enjoy acting. He was the opposite of Duryea, who was a sweetheart of a guy. A wonderful smile and glittering eyes all the time. Dan would just open up but Audie wouldn't open up."

Duryea's Frank Jesse (the name as shorthand for the character) is his patented likable hired gun with a past; he and Murphy build on the rapport they had developed in *Ride Clear of Diablo*. But Duryea's Jesse has committed a number of past sins; Jesse tries to justify his past killings by claiming those who hired him were really culpable, but he doesn't fool himself or the audience. What Duryea projects convincingly throughout the movie is cynicism laced with a shred of integrity and compassion—which is ultimately undone by his desire for quick money. It's not Duryea's fault that many of his lines, courtesy of Kennedy, came from earlier films. Duryea's tale of a passionate romp interrupted by a husband's arrival, leading to his admission that "you should never ride in another man's saddle," had already made its appearance in a few Scott/Kennedy films, while his nighttime chats with O'Brien are right out of 1960's *Comanche Station*, as is his climactic encounter with Murphy:

DURYEA TO MURPHY: I don't want to kill you. The truth is, I like
    you . . . I saved your life.
MURPHY: I remember.
DURYEA: I figured you would.

One can find similar exchanges throughout the Kennedy oeuvre, including *The Tall T* and *Ride Lonesome*. Here, Duryea and Murphy try to make it seem fresh, as the characters have developed a convincing bond as well as a mutual despair at how events have played out. It's not their fault that the situation, indeed the whole movie, was seen as one trip to the well too often.

While many critics noted the recycled nature of much of the proceedings, there was some praise for Murphy, and especially for Duryea. He was seen as so "uncommonly likable that the audience regrets to see him polished off." Duryea would also note the switch in his current villain roles in an interview with columnist John Scott, wherein Duryea would say that "the villain is a victim of circumstances, a basically all right character who took a wrong fork in the road . . . the film reprobate is more to be pitied than censured." This was certainly true of much of his television work, and he continued to be on the lookout for film roles that would at least include some humane traits for his villains.

In the meantime, Duryea, as a very happy family man who prided himself on his enduring marriage, took umbrage to a bishop who had written a widely read article on "the Hollywood image." This bishop had been perpetuating the notion (or, as Duryea would call it, the *myth*) that Hollywood is a haven for divorces, along with "the star morality . . . I know of no contemporary profession whose individual members are free to divorce and marry at will and maintain their good standing." As someone who was proud of his enduring (thirty-one years) marriage, and knowing others who maintained similar unions, Duryea took exception to the article. He further questioned why "actors and actresses should be singled out for retribution, when the same yardstick does not apply to members of any other profession." This would be another occasion of Duryea coming to the defense not only of his fellow actors, whom he feels have been unjustly pilloried, but of the sanctity of marriage and his (and Helen's role) in shattering supposed stereotypes of the licentiousness that was allegedly the norm in Hollywood.

While he was defending the morality of his fellow thespians, there was talk swirling around Hollywood about the possibility of reviving *China Smith*, only this time for a movie. Duryea would certainly be interviewed about the series over the years, given his increased television appearances; he also, deep down, wished for an opportunity to finally get it right, acknowledging the $17,500 budget and brisk shooting schedule made it "too hurried a process to get it right." Ultimately, Duryea decided against doing a *China Smith* movie, going on record as saying "the character would be indigestible to today's movie audiences." That might have been the case—or it might have been a graceful way out when financing didn't materialize.

Duryea would have to content himself with the television offers that were rolling in. There were well-received repeat appearances on both *Wagon Train* and *Rawhide*. In 1962's "The Wagon Train Mutiny," Duryea is a vocal member of the wagon train, pushing for justice to come to a young injured man who may have committed murder, while Jane Wyman (who is really the episode's focus) is another member of the wagon train driven by thoughts of retribution, but whose avenging ways become tempered by mercy. Duryea is convincing as one of the more vocal, bloodthirsty leaders of the aborted "mutiny," but in the end, it's a minor wagon trip for him.

He had better luck (though not with regard to his on-screen fate) on *Rawhide* with "Incident of the Wolvers." Duryea plays the patriarch of a family of wolf hunters who hire themselves out to Rowdy Yates's cattle drive when the presence of wolves threatens the stock. On this November 1962 episode Duryea was reunited with Patty McCormack (his youthful nemesis from *Kathy O'*), this time playing Duryea's impressionable daughter who has a hankering for Rowdy (Eastwood) while trying to find out what really happened to her mother, which has been a secret long held by Duryea. Duryea's mania in shielding his daughter from her mother's fate, as well as the believed romantic attentions of Rowdy, lead to a final confrontation and a fatal bullet, courtesy of his grieving daughter. Duryea is convincing, generating a degree of sympathy as a man burdened by his past mistakes and his misbegotten attempts to spare family members from discovering them.

Duryea would continue his run of television appearances as essentially good-hearted characters throughout November, opposite Gene Kelly's Father O'Malley in "Mr. Second Chance" for the likable but short-lived series *Going My Way*. Duryea guest-starred as a gambler who agrees, with O'Malley's blessing, to take over the role of "Mr. Second Chance," making amends for his former life by helping people start over. A week later, Duryea would appear as an aging rodeo clown with arthritis on "Tears on a Painted Face" for the series *Wide Country*. This series, set in the modern-day West, starred Earl Holliman and Andrew Prine as brothers who were making their living as rodeo riders, with some footage devoted to the challenges they meet every week, both at the rodeo and with the interpersonal relationships among their fellow ropers, as well as those whose paths they cross. It was an engaging show in general, carried by Holliman and Prine with their mutual affection and friendly rivalry, and supplemented by supporting veterans who knew their way around the West, and a convincing rodeo atmosphere.

Duryea's rodeo clown in "Tears on a Painted Face" (he is easily recognizable even under the heavy make-up) has his share of problems; he's a widower whose late wife didn't possess the most sterling character—particularly since she perished in a car crash with her lover. Duryea's aging clown has been a fixture on the circuit, known for his antics among the bulls, but he's been slowing down as of late. He is injured early on, but a doctor's examination reveals the onset of a crippling arthritis which could cause his knees to buckle at any time. Of course, clowning is the only life Duryea knows, and his efforts to hide his condition from his beloved wastrel son (Charles Robinson), as well as the riders and his employer, result in a good amount of personal turmoil. Further complicating matters is the fact that series regular Prine is falling for his son's disillusioned girlfriend.

Duryea has several good scenes as the all-too-fallible clown blinded by his misguided overindulgence toward his son—perhaps a way to make amends for his failed relationship with the lad's mother. After being caught in his misery by a concerned Holliman, Duryea reminisces about his late wife and his complicated relationship with his flighty son; it's a particularly telling moment and indicative of the subtlety Duryea was capable of. Holliman had fond memories of working with Duryea, whom he found to be not only generous to his fellow actors but also "down to earth and solid." According to Holliman, Duryea had always been an influence on Holliman's work: "When I was doing *Broken Lance*, my part [as a weakling son of Spencer Tracy's patriarch] reminded me of Leo in *The Little Foxes*. So I patterned my work after Dan's, and was happy to tell him so when I met him." For his part, Duryea was grateful for the role; in fact, as Allen Rich of the *Valley Times* would write, Duryea "jumped at the chance to do this sympathetic role," and as he played three different types on three networks, all aired within a few weeks, he was appreciative of the continued and varied employment.

During this period of late 1962 and early 1963, Duryea was busy in other areas as well. Once again showing a concern for civic affairs and public safety, Duryea joined other residents in protesting the construction of a power plant in the Hollywood Hills. This plant, which would have been on Mulholland Drive near Beverly Glen, might have proved a dangerous addition to what was already designated as a fire area, and the protesters were out in force to emphasize the fact that the high-tension poles in this area could result in disaster.

Duryea was also looking beyond his Hollywood career, and into the area of investments. One such investment (among many) was a ten-unit apartment building that he and Helen purchased in early 1963. Since Duryea considered himself to be a skilled carpenter and all-around handyman, he elected to do many of the repairs himself. Duryea's occasional visits to the building, tools at the ready, would delight his tenants and cause some unnecessary concern over his status, or lack thereof. As one tenant said to Duryea: "I'm sorry you're having such hard times that you have to do the plumbing yourself."

If that tenant had only watched television, she would have realized there was little cause for alarm. For the medical drama *The Eleventh Hour*, Duryea appeared in an episode called "Why Am I Grown So Cold?" as a phony psychiatrist who has been treating a young woman (an Emmy-nominated Eleanor Parker) for her drinking by the questionable means of hypnotizing her. The show's regular lead, Wendell Corey, wants to try a more conventional treatment, but Duryea's bogus doc perseveres, getting the young woman to say she loves and trusts him. But things go very awry for the not-so-good "doctor": when he kisses her, she strikes him with a bottle and kills him.

In February 1963, Duryea would appear in an unusual role on an episode of *Alcoa Premiere*. In "Blow High, Blow Clear," directed by John Brahm (he of such Fox horror/noirs as *The Lodger*), Tommy Sands starred as a troubled young horn player with a patient mother (Jane Wyatt), a yearning to go to sea, and a possible savior in freight captain John Anderson. Duryea appeared late in the episode as Sands's father. Long presumed dead, he surfaces as Charlie, a blind piano player in Louisiana. Duryea is understated, silent, and reactive, whether he is tickling the ivories (to the music of John Williams, then called Johnny) or reuniting with his son in a poignant scene at the conclusion. This episode was also briefly considered as the pilot for a spinoff series (not to feature Duryea, but starring Sands and John Anderson, who played Sands's mentor) but the executives were not too happy. Notes from the preview screening contained the following comments: "Production values, direction, script bad . . . Swinton's script makes no sense. Tommy Sands was quite wooden." The project was subsequently labeled "dead" and would go no further.

Duryea would make another well-received appearance for *The U.S. Steel Hour* in May 1963, with the sensitive drama "The Many Ways of Heaven." He's not playing a father here, but a father figure whose actions help reunite a broken family. As Captain Walker, a pipe-smoking retired pilot content to await the completion of a ship that he's designed, he becomes friendly with Teddy, a boy who feels neglected by his father. The father's desire to "be the top man in maritime law" and not coast on the family money necessitates a lot of travel on his part—and the possibility of permanent estrangement from his unhappy wife. Duryea is very appealing as he bonds with the boy or confronts the boy's Aunt Sissy, who is unaware of how much the boy misses his parents.

At a certain point in the story, Duryea counsels the boy to "pray when things are not going your way." This notion of faith spurs the impressionable young lad to send a message to his father (in Rome for an important business meeting), a note placed in a bottle which he expeditiously drops into the sea. Luckily, Duryea's character is there to witness this, and takes the necessary measures to ensure the message is delivered. The boy's faith is thus preserved, and the family is reunited. Duryea's role could easily have become treacly—and, in truth, some sections of this live drama are overwritten and a little maudlin. Duryea emerges not only with his dignity intact, however, but with his reputation somewhat enhanced through his delicate rendering of the compassionate captain.

A live outing like this, and in a generous, big-hearted role such as this one, must have once again rekindled Duryea's desire to do a Broadway play. He had been contemplating a return to the stage for some time now, though he thoroughly enjoyed acting for the screen and considered it just as challenging as acting for the stage. In a late-1950s interview, Duryea expounded on the differences between the two: "Acting on the screen requires more talent than acting on the stage. In Hollywood if you're lucky two scenes will be in sequence. Then you switch to another scene in another part of the script that must be done right then because it takes place on the same set . . . out of this disconnected jumping around you have to make a smooth picture . . . they say the stage is wonderful because there is a live audience . . . in movies there are fifty technicians and stage hands watching you. They're alive!" Despite Duryea's spirited defense of film acting technique, he actively began considering offers to return to Broadway.

The decision was motivated by both financial and artistic considerations; Duryea enjoyed doing the heavies, but he saw them as having a limited shelf life. It's true he had endured for over twenty years, but there was always the new rising young actor achieving a level of prominence; furthermore, Hollywood was no longer casting Duryea as the villain in anything approaching an important picture. Duryea felt that "Broadway would create a new demand for myself in movies . . . I'd really like sometime to do different things, to show that I can do them.

I would like to come to New York . . . not as a heavy, but something I haven't done before."

As television had been his previous career savior, he was now turning to the stage as a way of not only prolonging his screen career, but perhaps solidifying the bonds between father and son. Richard at this time was a twenty-year-old junior at Lewis and Clark College in Portland, Oregon, and as he would tell me later, "I had no ambition to get into acting—*at all*." But, by 1963, Duryea's other son, Peter, was a member of the Ford Foundation Players at Houston's Alley Theater, and proud papa Dan let on that "I'd like to find a good play for summer stock that has a leading role for father and son." Not that Peter would "flip over the chance to work with his dad. He wants to make it on his own and I haven't given him any help. . . . he's really quite good. He said he's not quite ready for Broadway and needs more training. But I think he'd agree to summer stock." Duryea had already seen Peter in such productions as *The Taming of the Shrew* and was proud of his son's work. Peter later thought that "Dad was secretly glad that someone was going to carry on the name in his profession."

Duryea started to make his theatrical intentions known not only in the print media, but also on television, such as when he was plugging his latest film or television project. When he appeared on Johnny Carson's show with the singer Julie Wilson, he told her he'd like to do summer stock. Later that night, her husband called from Chicago to offer Duryea a suitable summer engagement (which he subsequently had to decline when a film offer from Britain came his way). Duryea also admitted that while he would prefer the role not be a villain, if the playwright had a good lead for a sniveling rat, he would consider it: "I sent two kids through college and paid for two homes and a lot of groceries by being a rat. How can I knock it?" On the one hand, Duryea could be wistful about extending his range, and on the other, be thoroughly pragmatic about his fixed place in the Hollywood universe.

Why the constant talk about Broadway when he had all the roles he could handle on television? One possibility (purely commercial, mind you) is the higher paychecks afforded those working in the "important films." Duryea was doing pretty well, but his Universal contracts from the 1940s to the early '60s, reflect his diminished value. For example, the relatively minor 1949 effort *One Way Street* netted him the princely sum of $10,000 per week, while more recent efforts earned him $5,000 a week. Television salaries, as frequent as his appearances were, would be hard put to approach *that*. Another consideration was that, as prolific and versatile as Duryea had been (and would continue to be throughout the mid-1960s) television was still viewed, despite its so-called golden age, as the inferior medium, a placeholder for actors looking to regain their footing in film or seeking refuge after a film career flamed out. While actors like Henry Fonda, David Niven, and Robert Taylor had found some success on television, they were also chastised for abandoning movies and embracing the small screen. Television had nowhere near the cachet it now holds.

It was with no small degree of pleasure that, in August 1963, Duryea announced he had finally obtained a leading role on Broadway (his first time back since Leo in *The Little Foxes*, twenty-three years earlier). The play was *Slander*, by Henry Deniker, who was known for his hard-hitting screenplays such as the James Stewart/Anthony Mann collaboration *The Far Country*. *Slander*, which would eventually be retitled *A Case of Libel*, was based on Louis Nizer's bestselling book *My Life in Court*. It was a fictionalized version of the events surrounding a case where columnist Westbrook Pegler wrote a scurrilous column attacking the war correspondent Quentin Reynolds for his personal life, professional life, and patriotism. This would form the basis for a well-publicized libel action, wherein Nizer served as counsel for the plaintiff Reynolds. In Denker's retelling, Duryea would play the columnist, now called Boyd Bendix, with Van Heflin as Robert Sloan (i.e., Nizer) and Larry Gates as the plaintiff Reynolds, the libeled party.

Duryea was extremely excited about *Slander*, informing columnist Hedda Hopper, with whom Duryea had remained friends, often going to her first with "breaking news." Duryea enthused about his role, and the company he would soon be keeping: "I met Louis Nizer yesterday at rehearsal—just to say hello and shake hands. Of course I've read the book and think it's great. And I think we're getting a great play . . . Henry Denker wrote this. Roger Stevens and Joe Shenker are producing—I couldn't come back under a better banner."

Conspicuously absent from this praise was the director of the play, Sam Wanamaker. Wanamaker began his Hollywood career in the 1940s as an actor in such films as *My Girl Tisa*, with Lilli Palmer. He also had become a member for a time in the Communist Party. Wanamaker subsequently gave up his membership, but was quite vocal in his support for the recently imprisoned Hollywood Ten, making an impassioned speech on their behalf when some were released from prison. It came as no surprise to Wanamaker that the vultures were circling around him; he was in England filming when he learned he had been blacklisted, and he opted to remain in England. There, Wanamaker established himself as an actor on stage and screen; he also became a director of note, primarily for the stage. It was this Wanamaker who had returned to America in the late 1950s.

About a week after the company entered into rehearsals, and two days after Duryea (via press release) proclaimed how happy he was with the play, the producers released this statement to the media: "Due to a feeling on the part of the producers that Dan Duryea cannot play the heavy, he is leaving the show." Dan Duryea could not play the heavy? Was there something else going on? A spokesman for the show said: "We were reluctant to see him go, but the actor was coming across as a nice guy." Had the producers and director Wanamaker not seen that Duryea, despite being an all-around nice fellow in real life, had consummately portrayed scores of heavies, producing some of the most indelible depictions of depravity yet seen on the screen? Evidently no, since Wanamaker would inform Duryea that he wasn't familiar with Duryea's film or television work.

Duryea was understandably dumbstruck by his sudden release. He called his old friend Hedda with his take on the unfortunate developments: "I was getting ready for some publicity shots when the producers and director came in and said they were sorry but they thought I was too inherently a nice guy to play this part. I was amazed at this reaction because after a week . . . the director had offered no suggestions on interpretation of the part [Duryea had said earlier that he wasn't going to pattern his portrayal on the real Pegler—maybe that was a factor]. I said, 'We did the 3rd act three times yesterday—why didn't you say something about the interpretation—or tell me what I did wrong.' The director said, 'You didn't do anything wrong, but you're just not the picture of what we thought the part should be.' So they sent this wire this afternoon to the New York papers: 'Due to feeling on part of producer . . . ' So I'm flying home." Two years later, Wanamaker's dismissal still cut deeply: "This came as a surprise to me, after all the mean parts I played, and it broke my heart not to come on in the play. . . . he told me I don't ooze evil. I told him I've been oozing evil in pictures and TV since 1940. He said he hadn't seen me—he never watched television and won't go to American movies."

After Duryea's release, some of the actors were reconfigured into other roles. Heflin remained as Sloan, but John Randolph assumed the role of Quentin Reynolds, while Larry Gates was shifted from the part of Reynolds into Duryea's vacated role as Bendix. A number of cast members spoke anonymously to reporters, some agreeing that Duryea was fired "at the hands of the worst director I ever saw." The play would open under the title *A Case of Libel* in October 1963, and while the writing and direction would receive mixed reviews, Gates would be cited by the *New York Times* for "his brilliant portrayal" and also receive a Tony nomination. *A Case of Libel* would run for six months on Broadway, so there was at least one tangible benefit for Duryea. As Duryea recounted a few years later to columnist Dick Kleiner: "I showed them I could ooze evil. I had a run of the play contract and made them pay me every cent while the play ran."

Duryea did indeed go back to California, chastened somewhat by his recent experience, but the theater bug hadn't entirely left him. Soon after he returned, he took part in *Brecht on Brecht*, a stage adaptation based on Bertolt Brecht's works, incorporating scenes and dramatic episodes from his memoirs. This was a production for the professional theater group of the UCLA extension, with Nina Foch and Kevin McCarthy costarring. It turned out to be a staged reading with some songs, one of which Duryea performed. Duryea did a solo turn in "The Parable of the Burning House," and acted with Foch and McCarthy in "Solomon's Song," in which the characters pondered the price of success. The *Hollywood Reporter* was mixed about the results, noting that "Duryea, with his American simplicity, was miscast for the harsh realism of German theatre." His best moment came in his recitation of "The Memory of Maria," the final phrases of which he sang with "a beautifully horrible voice" (in the words of *Westwood Press'* Dan Hunt).

Although his recent theater experience didn't produce the desired results, Duryea found his talents still in demand; not only was television constantly calling, but the film roles were again coming his way. Granted, most of them were what one might generously call B movies, yet Duryea would rarely find himself at a loss for work, and movie audiences would again discover he could be the meanest cuss around.

CHAPTER 13

Gunmen and Killers, Occasionally alongside Son Peter

WHEN THE OPPORTUNITY TO APPEAR IN SUMMER STOCK FIRST CAME Duryea's way, he had considered it, especially since it would have meant acting with his son Peter. However, this anticipated working relationship was not to be, as Duryea ventured off to London in July 1963 to shoot a very low-budget drama called *Walk a Tightrope*. It was the first time he had been back to work in London since *Terror Street* twelve years before. Now he was back playing opposite another American, Patricia Owens (known for her histrionics in *The Fly*), in an initially intriguing drama with Duryea as a down-on-his-luck gunman who kills Owens's husband at her behest, only to find himself thwarted when an unexpectedly grieving Owens refuses to come through with a promised payment. Duryea pushes his luck, however, when he sees that Owens's deceased husband was well-to-do, so his demand for even more money earns him a meeting with Owens—who, by this time, has summoned the "bobbies" to place Duryea under arrest.

All of this happens in the first half of this brief-but-dragged-out meller, as Duryea is allowed to dominate a trial scene where he demands that if he is to be punished, then Owens must be punished, too, for hiring him to do the deed in the first place. His fervent admission of his own (relative) guilt and condemnation of Owens (in front of a somewhat disbelieving court) earns him a quick one-way trip to prison. Meanwhile, the film does have time to throw in a twist: while the hard-luck Duryea did in fact murder Owens's husband, he wasn't the husband she wanted murdered. Instead, her real target was her bounder of a "first husband"—whom she did not divorce and who was now seeking to blackmail her. This revelation reveals her true motives, and validates Duryea's wild protestations, resulting in a well-deserved trip to prison for Owens.

Walk a Tightrope, a J. Arthur Rank release shot in a mere two weeks for Parroch-McCollum Productions, and directed by Frank Nesbitt, had more than its share of problems, the least of which was its low budget. The script by coproducer Neil McCollum (who would have more success as an actor) is almost split in two, seeming unnecessarily padded to reach the seventy-five-minute mark. Yet the film has its share of moments, courtesy of an intense turn by Duryea as a man prone to violence while justifying his actions in terms of his relative hard luck. The courtroom scene, which might have offered an opportunity for overdone histrionics, is instead effectively modulated, as Duryea summons up the requisite outrage without alienating the viewer. The film is a shoestring affair, but Duryea shows why his talents were still in demand.

Duryea was such an immense hit with his peers and producers that he was immediately signed for a second picture with Parroch-McCollum Productions, this one a distinct cut above *Walk a Tightrope*. *Do You Know This Voice?* was another low-budget British noir, directed by Frank Nesbitt, again written by Neil McCollum, who based his script on a novel by Evelyn Berckman. Perhaps the source material contributed to an improvement in quality, because *Do You Know This Voice?* is a tense, fairly suspenseful drama dealing with child kidnapping, battered spouses, and murder.

In *Do You Know This Voice?*, Duryea was cast as another American expatriate down on his luck, married to a long-suffering wife and eking out a living as an orderly—with very little in the way of savings to show for it. Before the credits roll, a muffled voice (which could be either male or female) is calling from a phone booth, telling the unfortunate people on the other end that their son has been kidnapped. Soon after, the viewer discovers the parents are working class, and that the child has been discovered dead. What the police are banking on is that the kidnappers don't know the body has been discovered.

Duryea's first appearance makes it seem that he might be used as a red herring; he is at ease with his neighbors, friendly to all he meets, especially his foreign next-door neighbor, who is missing her family. He even encourages her to call her daughter from a local phone booth. Taking her kind friend's advice, the woman proceeds to drop her change outside the booth and is distracted enough not to really notice the person exiting the booth, although she does take note of the man's coat and shoes. After the police inform the woman that the kidnapper made the call from that booth, she still can't identify the caller. Nonetheless, the civic-minded woman tells the newspapers she can, hoping (with the police's grudging cooperation) to lure the kidnapper/murderer into trying to silence her.

How could this wicked kidnapper be her friend and occasional confidant Duryea? He even sent her to the same phone booth . . . as it turns out, his wife (British actress Gwen Wittford) had made the calls, as she and good neighbor Dan had kidnapped and, to hear Duryea tell it, he accidentally killed the boy, saying "the boy was lucky to have died clean." In a moment of good fellowship, he did indeed send the woman to that dreaded phone booth, not realizing what might occur. These plot developments unfold within the first twenty minutes, setting up the subsequent cat-and-mouse game between the kidnappers and the neighbor, with the police as interested bystanders. Duryea is naturally perturbed but comes to the realization that the woman doesn't really know the caller's identity, especially since the police haven't been knocking on his door. He proceeds to visit her in the guise of the good neighbor, but in reality he hopes to assuage his own fears; yet, although she confides she couldn't identify the caller, her belief that one day something will come to her makes Duryea decide to kill her.

What make this little thriller percolate are the dimensions given to the central characters, as well as the suspenseful situations resulting from Duryea's not-too-neighborly resolve. Duryea's early attempt to strangle his neighbor is interrupted by the presence of a young detective (in the guise of a visiting relative), while the later use of poisoned milk is aborted by the timely suffering of the woman's kitty. In addition, Duryea and Wittford are convincing and unexpectedly poignant (especially Wittford) as the desperate kidnappers. Wittford pleads with Duryea to not kill the woman, getting on the receiving end of one of Duryea's patented slaps (not the first time, the film suggests) but still surrendering to him when he apologizes; throughout, she comes off as achingly credible. For his part, Duryea delivers a multilayered portrayal, conveying the conflicts that tear the character apart, from his frustration with his lack of success to his desire to be someone, as well as his belief that his own cleverness will prevail. At fifty-seven, Duryea could still be the most outwardly confident, cunning guy in the room, traits that will prove to be his own and his wife's undoing in a twist ending that is no less effective for being telegraphed. *Do You Know This Voice?* has achieved a cult status over time, but it deserves to be more widely seen. It stands as a good example of later British noir.

Back in the States, and following his tepidly received theatrical sojourns, Duryea was hard at work on the small screen; this being Hollywood, an occasional opportunity for an interesting on-screen reunion might occur. This was certainly the case in January 1964 on *The Alfred Hitchcock Hour*, on which Duryea would costar opposite Teresa Wright (of *The Little Foxes* fame) in the droll, very entertaining "Three Wives Too Many." Wright, normally the spirited, if virtuous leading lady, was cast as Duryea's loyal wife who discovers that her husband's frequent business trips are really opportunities for him to see his three other wives—hence, the title—so she decides to remove the unwanted competition, permanently. The first scene plays on the audience's familiarity with Wright's warm, considerate persona as she befriends one of Duryea's younger wives, only to poison her and make it look like suicide. Later, she feigns helplessness in dealing with the boiler (as well as the coffin-like hole that has been dug in which to place it), leading Duryea (if not the audience, whom she lets in with a smile) to believe how much she depends on him.

Nevertheless, Duryea is more the bemused victim in this one than he is a victimizer, a self-proclaimed happily married (!) opportunistic ladies' man who, with each successive poisoning (Wright gets around to each in turn) and subsequent interrogation by the local police, comes to realize how powerless he really is. Duryea's reactions to the murders are priceless, as his allegations that his wives were indeed the victims of murder (as opposed to suicide, because his wives were indeed quite happy) seem to ignore the possibility of his being perceived as a murderer. The still-attractive Wright proves to be a different kind of femme fatale; her best scene involves Wright's realization that, as Wife #3, she indeed "stole" Duryea from Wife #2—although that does not stop Wright from giving the younger #2 a lethal cocktail.

Two weeks later, Duryea could be seen as a detective on the suspense anthology series *Crisis* in a nifty little drama called "Who is Jennifer?" Brenda Scott stars as an eighteen-year-old runaway in police custody, whom Detective Duryea believes may be Jennifer, a girl who went missing twelve years earlier. When he brings the "mystery girl" to the sunny California beachfront home of her mother (Gloria Swanson, playing it moderately big but still credible), the mother's insistence that she can't possibly be her daughter leads Duryea to think there is only one reason for this certainty: that Swanson herself murdered the girl years before, and quite possibly buried her on the grounds. This leads Duryea to prevail upon Scott (with the aid of a little blackmail, since the girl is wanted in Nevada) to remain with Swanson, until a fingerprint match can be established. The cat-and-mouse game that ensues results in a bittersweet, open-ended finale in which Swanson realizes, after discovering the girl's supposed grave to be empty and that she has spent years covering up for a crime purportedly committed by her now-deceased husband, but in reality may never have happened. Duryea and Swanson are in fine form as, respectively, the calculating, humane detective and the mother with a conscience over her late husband's alleged misdeeds, while Scott almost steals the proceedings as a young rebel who grows to care for her would-be mother.

It had been a couple of years since Duryea played an out-and-out baddie in a Western, but that was about to change when Universal offered him the lead villain role in *The Gun Hand*, which would soon be rechristened as *He Rides Tall*. Tony Young would play the lead; he was being given the star treatment from Universal, having made an impression on television in the short-lived series *The Gunslinger* but in this film and others, he would prove to be a rather colorless, wooden lead. After a few more leading roles (including a reunion with Duryea), he would find himself in supporting parts in such films as *Black Gunn* and *The Outfit*, and later, on television.

In this R. G. Springsteen-directed black-and-white Western (reflective of the diminished budgets Universal was parceling out for their Westerns), Young is a sheriff who is about to leave law enforcement and marry the local tenderhearted bar gal. However, his last day is interrupted by the arrival of some rowdy members of a cattle drive, including longtime nemesis Duryea and the worthless son (Carl Reindel) of a longtime friend, ranch owner R. G. Armstrong. When Young is forced to kill the murderous Reindel in self-defense, he takes it upon himself to personally deliver the news to friend Armstrong. Duryea follows the wary Young out to the spread with murder in his heart, his distinctive laugh at the ready as he tries to counter Young's justifiable suspicions, all the while figuring out the best way to kill Young.

Of course, Armstrong doesn't take the news of his son's death too well, and emboldened by alcohol urged on him by his faithless wife (who is burning for Duryea), as well as a bravura plea from Duryea to put down "Mad Dog" Young, orders his reluctant doctor to slice Young's gun hand so as to render Young forever useless with a gun. After Young is incapacitated, Duryea takes off with the wife and the cattle, while Young is left to face the world deprived of his quick draw—or so it seems until the doctor confides that he has cut the hand just enough so as to avoid permanent damage. It remains for Young to pacify Armstrong and to take action against a now supremely confident leader of men, Duryea.

In truth, *He Rides Tall* is no great shakes as a Western, as it is severely hampered by the dead wood that is Tony Young; in many ways, especially vocally, Young resembles Robert Francis of *The Caine Mutiny*, whose deadening blend of stolidity and sincerity threatened to bring *that* movie to a halt whenever he took precedence in a scene. *He Rides Tall* is one of those films that would have no afterlife if it weren't for the presence of Duryea. He is all exuberant malevolence as the smiling villain, feigning a grudging affection for Young, professing to change his ways, and all the while planning to exact some form of revenge for Young's having sent him up. Throughout, he is cheerfully unapologetic, whether he is making early attempts on Young's life while professing indignation at being accused, initiating a stampede in order to kill the pursuing rancher, or, in the most striking scene, sending Morrow into the hands of the Indians, who after encountering some understandable resistance from Morrow, swiftly kill her. "Sorry, you ain't got no vote," he says when explaining his willingness to sacrifice her in order to save his own skin. The final sequence, wherein Duryea and cronies take over ex-Marshal Young's small town, is actually well done, with a taut final shootout between Young and Duryea, wherein Duryea memorably refuses to go quietly.

Duryea's gleeful villainy earned him the only good notices received by *He Stands Tall*. Though he is the bad guy, audiences were bound to root for him (well, perhaps not at the very end, but certainly up to that point) since the hero was colorless in comparison with Duryea. The flavorful role showed off Duryea at his best, though it was a shame it had to be confined within what many reviewers would dub "a program Western." One critic would echo the thoughts of Duryea fans as well as moviegoers in general when he wrote: "Duryea's character, though outrageously exaggerated, provides a necessary dose of levity and color."

Universal's other 1964 attempt to propel Tony Young to stardom was *Taggart,* based on a novel by the prolific Louis L'Amour, and Duryea was once again engaged to play the main villain. He told an interviewer that he was "trying to say goodbye to villainy, but movie menaces make money. They are also ageless and in demand. Once in a while, I do get to play a sympathetic role, so I'm not a mountain of frustration . . . let's face it, the audience remembers the killer a lot longer than they do the hero."

Duryea neglected to mention that he would be most certainly remembered longer than the oak-like Young, but it was apparent to viewers nonetheless.

For *Taggart*, R. G. Springsteen would once again direct, this time with the benefit of Technicolor and some scenic locations (although the skimpy budgets can be detected in the cheap-looking interiors). Notwithstanding Young (a little less wooden than before) and his female lead, Springsteen had a good cast at his disposal; apart from Duryea, the cast included Bob Steele, Emile Meyer, Harry Carey, Jr., Dick Foran (in his last film role), and making their film debuts, David Carradine and Duryea's son Peter (working for the first time alongside his father). Although Peter's screen time was fairly short and included none with his father, it pleased both to be in the same film.

Duryea would also be working with imposing contract actor Tom Reese, one of the more reliable heavies in the Universal stable. They rode alongside each other here (for a short time), as well as the later *Stranger on the Run*. Reese enjoyed working with Duryea; he would tell author Boyd Magers in the valuable collection *Best of the Badmen* that the actor was "a very nice man. He wasn't well the second time I worked with him but he invited me over to his dressing room and we hung out. Heavies in person are usually nice guys."

The plot of *Taggart* is fairly simple; in fact, it shares some similarities with *He Rides Tall*. Young isn't a marshal in this one, but he is a peace-loving, law-abiding citizen named Taggart whose family is unfairly attacked for being squatters. A land baron (Emile Meyer) and his son lead a raid on his family's wagons, a violent encounter which leaves Taggart's family and friends dead. He then returns the favor by confronting Meyer's son (Peter Duryea) as Meyer lies on his deathbed, and killing the son in self-defense, arousing the ire of the dying Meyer, who wants to see justice (that is, revenge) done. The elder Duryea is the gunman hired to do the dirty deed (along with Tom Reese and Carradine). He has already passed Taggart on the way to town, as Taggart had been been allowed to flee by an understanding lawman. Armed with the sunny notion that luck will always come his way, Duryea gets Meyer to describe his target, and the realization he knows the man sets him and his (unwanted) partners in hot pursuit.

This sets in motion a chase that lasts much of the film, as Taggart manages to elude Duryea and his men (after Carradine's early exit, Duryea hastens the wounded Reese's departure via a bullet to the heart), while they both try to avoid becoming the Indians' next victims. Taggart eventually gains sanctuary with miner Dick Foran, who has a small fortune in "rocks," a lovely daughter, and a scheming second wife (Elsa Cardenas)—who is quick to latch on to the equally mercenary Duryea. Motivated by greed and lust (in that order), Duryea forgoes killing Taggart and instead runs off with both Cardenas and the loot. This leaves Taggart and the cuckolded, grieving Foran (who has an altogether different picture of his younger bride) to pursue *them*. If these similarities to *He Rides Tall* weren't enough, Duryea's gunman abandons his unfortunate female conquest—again—to Indians on the warpath, leaving her without the goods—and her life.

Once again, Duryea steals the proceedings as the cold-blooded killer; even though the part is not as colorful as that in *He Rides Tall*, he manages to elevate the film with his sly humor and his ever-convincing displays of exuberant nastiness. The *Hollywood Reporter* would put its finger on Duryea's value, especially in films like this: "Duryea is theoretically the heavy, but by infusing the role with rich, fascinating character, giving the lines a lift, he seizes the whole film and makes it interesting and memorable." It's strange and perhaps fitting that these low-budget affairs would showcase Duryea at his best; in both of his Young/Springsteen endeavors, the energy and precision are just right. The cackling is present and never overdone, and Duryea's characterizations are liberated by the trend toward more "adult violence"; he could go places with his character's brutality that he could only hint at before.

Duryea would continue with his villainous streak on television, returning to *Wagon Train* for the seventh time in "The Race Town Story." By now, John McIntire was firmly entrenched as the wagon master, while Duryea's friend Robert Fuller assumed the role of second-in-command, as Robert Horton had left the series for the greener pastures of movies. However, in this episode, most of Duryea's interactions were not with Fuller (who must have been dealing with other members of the train), but with Terry Wilson's Bill and a young Michael Burns as Barnaby, a new regular, and an impressionable one at that.

Duryea's Sam Race runs a popular outdoor combination of casino and dance hall, complete with a bevy of beauties and some strong-arm types who are apt to relieve certain patrons of their funds should they become too "burdened" with the fruits of winning. Burns's naïve Barnaby has taken a fancy to one of Race's girls who would like to join the wagon train but is prevented by Race's insistence that she unduly compensate him for "expenses incurred." Barnaby and staunchly reliable series regular Bill (who is well-acquainted with Race) venture to Race's tent city, and while Bill manages to win some money, he is quickly relieved of his funds—after being drugged and beaten by Race's minions. When Barnaby tries to intervene, he is also beaten and publicly humiliated; in these scenes Duryea, smile predominant, is chilling as he maintains that he is giving these victims some valuable life lessons.

Barnaby's disillusionment after this unfortunate turn of events leads him to disregard Bill's advice (he had cautioned the lad to just walk away) and return to Race Town and confront the seemingly avuncular Race, who once again delivers another life lesson in the form of a beating from his henchmen; however, Bill arrives and confronts Race (after incapacitating his head henchman), and after a savage battle incorporating whips and axes (well-choreographed, and almost stuntman-free), Bill takes his money back and gives a bloodied Race a lesson of his own. One of the strengths of this episode—besides the fact that it's one of Duryea's more satisfying turns in small-screen Western villainy—is the twist at the end. Barnaby offers the girl money to leave Race Town, but she refuses, as she is quite happy with her lucrative new job (apparently Race's venality doesn't extend to underpaying his employees). This would be the last of Duryea's appearances, as *Wagon Train* would cease its journeys at the end of the season.

Later in 1964, Duryea would make a return trip to *Bonanza*, appearing in "Logan's Treasure." In contrast to his previous appearance on *Bonanza* as a mercenary killer, now Duryea's character was the one being hounded. He portrays Logan, an ex-convict who had been in jail for twenty years after stealing some gold from Wells Fargo. His release doesn't sit well with a former agent who wants to recover the gold, but Duryea's character is afforded a rare happy ending as he begins life anew (after depositing the aforementioned gold at the agent's feet) with the son (Tim McIntire) of his dead partner. The episode is a little disappointing for Duryea fans as it concentrates more on the vengeful agent than on Logan; furthermore, Logan's redemption lacks development and comes off as a little too abrupt.

Duryea would also make two appearances on *Burke's Law*, starring Gene Barry as a smooth police detective blithely navigating his way through murder and other unsavory doings on the boulevards of Manhattan. The sophisticated tone of the show as well as the liberal inclusion of guest stars (quite often used as red herrings) helped to give it a distinctive feel, quite unlike the gritty realism of, say, *Naked City*. In "Who Killed the Paper Dragon?" Duryea is Hop-Sing, of both Irish and Chinese descent, who owns the Paper Dragon Club, as Burke investigates who might want his lead singer Lotus Bud dead. "Who Killed 711?" would also be chock-full of Hollywood heavyweights, with Burgess Meredith, Broderick Crawford, Hans Conreid, and Rhonda Fleming joining Duryea in this tale of a murder trial's key witness who is himself murdered in his hotel room ("711" being his room). Staying at the same hotel with him are several other prospective witnesses—and possible suspects. Though Meredith's character is arrested early on, savvy viewers will realize he can't be the murderer; Duryea's character is a crafty lawyer who enjoys baking as a diversion, and his scene with Gene Barry's Burke provides the occasion for some enjoyable light banter. Once again, Duryea is well-used as a rather prominent red herring (the culprit being Conreid), but both appearances are minor entries in the Duryea canon.

It would be like father, like son in two of Duryea's 1965 appearances, as Peter would join his father—and interact with him on-screen in some surprising ways. One of Duryea's most memorable roles on the small screen would be on *Daniel Boone*, in which he played a calculating, unregenerate traitor clashing with Fess Parker's Boone and Ed Ames's wise Indian sidekick, Mingo, in "The Sound of Fear." As the sturdy, well-established stars, Parker and Ames would play second fiddle to Duryea, who takes no prisoners as Simon Gore, an Indian killer who wants Boone's help in starting an Indian war, holding Boone and his family captive (as Mingo had been injured by Gore in an earlier massacre). As the savage warmonger Gore, Duryea is in fine fettle throughout, oozing so much menace that even a simple line like "pleasant dreams, son" comes off as a threat. Veteran heavies Jack Elam and Robert Wilke provide strong support as Duryea's henchmen, though Wilke's character has grown quite conflicted about his own role in the dubious exploits, bringing in Gore's son (Duryea's son Peter) to surprise Gore and perhaps dissuade him from further bloodletting.

The episode develops into a battle of wills among the peace-loving, resourceful Boone, the idealistic son, and the villainous father—who still has a soft spot for his boy, even though he's not a "chip off the old block." Needless to say, Duryea's plans are all shot to hell by the end (aided in no small way by Boone's wife, a strong female character who helps engineer their defeat). Originally, Duryea was to be killed in the ensuing carnage. However, Duryea suggested that it might be more memorable if the innocent son were to be killed instead. The scene was reshot, and what remains is a memorable image of the fatally wounded Peter dying in his father's arms. Duryea would say this death scene "was almost impossible to play," and it comes across as a powerful conclusion to a gripping episode.

Duryea's last appearance with son Peter would come in another 1965 release, the very low-budget Western *The Bounty Killer*. It's not a particularly good film, but it's a fascinating one in many ways, and a terrific showcase for Duryea. In the mid-1960s, a number of producers had the notion of corralling former stars and putting them together in B Westerns; A. C. Lyles was perhaps the best known, with such efforts as the Dana Andrews/Jane Russell opus *Johnny Reno* among his credits. Alex Gordon, a British producer who emigrated to America and had produced such B classics as *The She-Creature* and *Atomic Submarine*, decided to try his hand at the Hollywood old-timers' reunion Western. Earlier that year, Gordon would produce *Requiem for a Gunfighter*, starring former sagebrush star Rod Cameron under action veteran Spencer Gordon Bennet's direction. Bennet had previously helmed a number of Republic serials such as *Zorro's Black Whip*, as well as several recent Gordon productions, including *Atomic Submarine* and *Submarine Seahawk*.

For *The Bounty Killer*, Gordon would reunite with Bennet, whose last finished picture this would be, with a script by the veteran character actor Leo Gordon, who would rattle off genre scripts when he wasn't acting the tough guy in films like *Riot in Cell Block 11*. The budget would be extremely low, with some of the most blatant use of indoor stages and painted backdrops substituting for outdoor sets you will ever see. It appears as if whatever money there was went to Duryea and a recognizable supporting cast including Rod Cameron, Buster Crabbe, Bob Steele, Richard Arlen, Grady Sutton, Audrey Dalton (as Duryea's love interest), and Peter (as a gunfighter). In addition, the ten-day shooting schedule would leave little room for error (and more likely would allow the errors to go unchanged). Yet this schedule seemed almost luxurious to Duryea, who had grown accustomed to the more hectic pace of television. Moreover, he enthused about playing opposite his son, as well as his own role: "I really like this part. I start out all right, I'm actually human, a puritanical easterner but then, as it must in all Duryea films, I wind up a villain again."

Duryea's naïve Willie Duggan in *The Bounty Killer* is an Easterner making his way out West to earn a living. He runs afoul of a local ruffian after engaging the attentions of attractive, warmhearted saloon girl Audrey Dalton (those saloon girls with hearts of gold certainly did get around). Duggan's fumbling attempts to engage this bully in the gentlemanly art of fisticuffs result in a beating (as said bully was unfamiliar with the marquis of Queensbury rules)—and the timely intervention of solicitous but deadly gunman Rod Cameron, who quickly dispatches the bully and offers Duryea the use of his room (since Cameron is a wanted man and now must skedaddle). Cameron is quite good in this scene (probably the best he's ever been throughout his long career), as his worldly gunman tells the green Duryea that, out in the West, "fighting with your hands is a losing game." He also offers the still-dazed Duryea the dead man's gun. Duryea laments the loss of life ("He was a human being") but grudgingly accepts the gun. At fifty-eight, Duryea is a little too old to be an impressionable tenderfoot, but he plays these early scenes with unquestionable sincerity.

It's not too long until the idealistic Duryea, seeking to make good in order to win the smitten Dalton, signs on with Fuzzy Knight (another Western old-timer brought out of semiretirement) to guard a payroll. After successfully defending it and killing the would-be robbers—and learning of the reward they're entitled to—Duryea and Knight decide to become bounty hunters. This is where the script becomes somewhat preposterous, since in no time at all (I mean this literally) Duryea goes from uneasy Easterner to seasoned Westerner, with attire to match. Here, and in other parts of the choppy script, no time is given for the transition; more often than not, Duryea must lend credibility to the arbitrarily constructed hoops which his character must jump through.

Duryea's next encounter is with dangerous gunman Buster Crabbe and his pals, a meeting that initially goes Duryea and Knight's way, since they manage to surprise and apprehend the boastful desperado. Having failed to heed Crabbe's warnings of possible gang reprisal, they are waylaid on the trail by Crabbe's comrades. After toying with Knight for target practice, a departing Crabbe kills both Knight and delivers what he believes is a fatal bullet to Duryea. But the severely wounded Duryea manages to find his way to the home of Dalton and her father (Arlen). The recovering, increasingly mercenary Duryea is not the same Willie Duggan as the wistful soul Dalton was so enamored of; moreover, his tailoring a shotgun into a more easily handled, deadlier weapon concerns Dalton's father, who warns Duryea never to see his daughter or set foot on his property again.

Again, Gordon's script leaves no room for graceful transitions, since no sooner than Duryea departs does he become the most fearsome bounty hunter in the West, killing rather than capturing. In one tense night scene, we see the full power of Duryea's reconfigured gun, as he takes out three men (including Crabbe) with one double-barreled shot. Duryea becomes known as a legalized killer, and he more and more takes refuge in the bottle. In a sensibly scripted exchange with son Peter and another townsperson, the merits of what Duryea has accomplished are debated, with Peter favoring the bounty hunter, while the townsperson notes that "he's done more killing than the men he's gunned down." In a scene that's been foreshadowed earlier, Duryea runs afoul of his now-imprisoned mentor Cameron when Cameron discovers his protégé has killed his brother. Cameron's rage is altogether understandable, leading to another taut scene as Cameron breaks jail (it's suggested with the local law's tacit consent) only to find himself at the wrong end of Duryea's scatter gun.

Somewhat ironically, the instrument of Duryea's success leads to his destruction. After drunkenly haranguing some "good people" for hypocritically treating him as a pariah while desiring him to clean their towns (an intense scene helped by Grady Sutton as the pastor), Duryea accidentally shoots the bartender with his hair-trigger gun, making him a wanted man. The now-chastened Duryea flees to Dalton's farm, where a forgiving Dalton defies her father and runs off with the sincerely contrite Duryea. Their hopes for the future are shattered, however, by a shotgun blast from none other than Duryea's son Peter, who tells a grieving Dalton he did it "for the $500 bounty." Duryea would remark later that Peter's shooting of his "old man" was probably a first in the history of nepotism, at least as far as Hollywood was concerned. Although the ending is not altogether unexpected (and variations of which had been used in earlier films), the convincing playing of Duryea and Dalton gives it a degree of poignancy that the writing doesn't quite earn on its own.

Of course, *The Bounty Killer*, with its low budget and relegation to the lower half of double bills, didn't garner much critical attention on its release. Even so, it's fascinating since it encompasses many aspects of the Duryea persona within one compact film: his erudite, romantic idealist segues to wounded avenging angel and then to cold-blooded killer, who makes a belated gesture toward reformation. The screenplay provides little help in smoothing over the abrupt transitions, so Duryea has to do it all himself. It comes down to Duryea's ability to add stature to any film (or television series, for that matter) because of the sincerity and intensity of his performance, no matter what was on the printed page. While his efforts may not have been recognized by the public at the time, they did not go unnoticed by his employers; *The Bounty Killer*'s executive producer, Pat Rooney, would send Duryea a letter thanking him for his dedication to his part, "and consequently everyone made efforts to up-grade themselves to your acting level."

Following Duryea's work in *The Bounty Killer*, the film's producer, Alex Gordon, issued a press release announcing his intention to star Duryea in a film called *War Against Crime*. Duryea's name was also bandied about for an adaptation of Joseph Conrad's *Heart of Darkness*; the possibility of see-ing Duryea enact Conrad's Kurtz was indeed intriguing, but the project never secured the necessary financing. Another project that hadn't yet come to fruition in spite of Duryea's efforts had nothing to do with a part in a film, but everything to do with movies themselves. He had long been a proponent for the construction of a Hollywood museum, and found himself frustrated with the lack of progress. Duryea saw the museum not only as an informative place for families to learn about our film heritage, but also as a place to draw tourists and enhance Hollywood's prestige. Though Hollywood is now strewn with a number of worthy institutions (as well as some that merely trade on the Hollywood name for some dis-tinctly low-level amusements), Duryea and some of his contemporaries were among the first in pushing for their creation.

Duryea's long involvement with *Laramie* and subsequent friendship with star Robert Fuller paid dividends when Duryea was cast opposite Fuller in Universal's Western *Incident at Phantom Hill*. It was Fuller's first lead role in a (medium-budget) major motion picture, and Duryea was cast as the villain opposite Fuller's stalwart hero. The veteran director Earl Bellamy would be guiding the action from a script with no fewer than three writers: Harry Tatelman (also producer), Frank Nugent, and Ken Pettus, with shooting to be done mainly on location in northern California. Fuller was pleased to be working with Duryea and had ac-tively lobbied for his casting; in addition to Duryea's acting skills, Fuller noticed how hard he worked with horses and guns.

Incident at Phantom Hill is set a few years after the Civil War, as Full-er's Union officer reluctantly enlists the aid of imprisoned rebel officer Duryea, since Duryea knows the whereabouts of $1 million in stolen gold—and especially since Duryea was one of the rebels who had am-bushed the Union convoy and buried the gold. Since Fuller's brother was one of the Union officers killed, he has a vested interest in recover-ing the gold, even if it means trusting the duplicitous Duryea (who, as viewers might have guessed, is only leading the men in order to get the gold for himself). Fuller rounds up some men for the journey, including Indian-hater Claude Akins and likable "Irish" rogue Noah Beery (whose accent must be heard to be disbelieved). They are also saddled with the unwelcome presence of a very attractive young woman (Jocelyn Lane) who has outstayed her welcome in town (much like Claire Trevor's Dallas in *Stagecoach*) and has been forced by the local law to join these out-of-uniform travelers.

Of course, a trip like this has its share of expected hazards, ranging from Indians (in whose territory the gold resides), nosy reprobates who suspect the party's gold-seeking intentions, and mutual distrust among the motley group's members, especially as Duryea is either fomenting rebellion or covertly seeking allies for his own larcenous schemes. In spite of the predictable nature of the enterprise, *Incident at Phantom Hill* remains a serviceable, action-packed drama bolstered by its veterans, as well as some good work from Fuller and Lane, who are granted a lot of screen time for their distrust to turn to something resembling love. Duryea's Joe Barlow is not among his most memorable villains, but he is still a strikingly menacing figure throughout, beginning with a train ride in which Duryea tries to end his and Fuller's partnership early, courtesy of a wild fight between railroad cars. Like many other Duryea Western villains, he justifies his actions by saying he's just trying to test the hero. He also claims that since the war is over, the gold should go to whomever finds it. The writing doesn't provide Duryea with as many layers as one would like, but he is still the standout in this efficient drama.

Although *Incident at Phantom Hill* would be Duryea's last major role as a villain, he still had a few good films left, as well as some solid television appearances. The next few years would see Duryea reunite with some acting buddies and the introduction of a few new grace notes into his cinematic repertoire. These years would also be marked by devastating loss and immense hardships.

CHAPTER 14

Reunion with Aldrich; Duryea Does the Italian West; A Sad Parting

ALTHOUGH DURYEA WAS NEARING SIXTY, HE KEPT UP A WORKING PACE of someone half his age. He was continuing do some fine work in a host of television shows. Duryea was a troublemaking relation on the series *The Long Hot Summer*, inspired by both the William Faulkner novel and the popular 1958 Paul Newman film version. In the episode "Return of the Quicks," Duryea was Chuck Quick, conman cousin to Roy Thinnes's Ben Quick (Newman's role), who stirs up trouble while trying to take over Ben's farm as the next of kin. Chuck is forced to leave town after one too many cons (and trying to get cousin Ben killed). Duryea was well-received as the requisite scoundrel and the producers wanted him for return for future appearances, but the series only lasted for one season.

Duryea would also make two guest appearances, in 1965 and 1967, on the World War II drama *Combat*. The series was fairly popular in the mid-1960s (as was another World War II adventure, *The Rat Patrol*), as it focused on a squad led by Vic Morrow's intense, quietly heroic Saunders and their various encounters in and around the battlefield. Duryea's two characters were similar in that they were both struggling to overcome a strain of cowardice that threatens them and those round them. In 1965's "Dateline," Duryea is Barton, an imprisoned American war correspondent, and it has fallen upon Saunders and his men to rescue him from a German prison camp, by way of a supposed tunnel. But Duryea's injured correspondent is reluctant to risk his neck, momentarily endangering

Saunders and company through his protestations. Throughout, Duryea projects a sense of weary resignation laced with self-disgust, making his climactic choice all the more gratifying. For 1967's "A Little Jazz," Duryea was again looking to save his own skin, rules of war be damned. He's the leader of a motley little touring jazz combo that has seen better days (among the "players" are Noah Beery and Dennis Hopper). After an impromptu jam session attracts the attention of a German squad, the band and Saunders's small group have to take shelter in a farmhouse, where Duryea's Bernie covertly waves an improvised white flag (not seen by Saunders). This causes even more problems when Saunders's unsuspecting men fire upon the advancing Germans—in retaliation, the Germans vow to kill everyone in the farmhouse, soldier and civilian alike. Duryea's character elicits less sympathy than his prior *Combat* role, since Bernie's misguided actions have immediate and fatal results. Any feeling one might have toward his character is due to the defenses made for Bernie by his fellow musicians. Still, both Duryea's appearances were well-regarded and the episodes themselves are top-notch.

Duryea would not neglect the West, finding himself back in the saddle for a variety of roles. For the short-lived series *The Monroes*, Duryea was a mountain man in "Gold Fever," stealing from the Monroes, then dropping a pouch of gold and being followed into the mountains by Clayt (series lead Michael Anderson, Jr.) as well as by other crooks who desire the rest of the gold. Duryea would then be reunited with Rod Serling, as well as Lloyd Bridges (one of his tank comrades from *Sahara*), on the Western *The Loner*. This was Serling's first series after *The Twilight Zone* had concluded its successful run, and another opportunity for the prolific writer to explore serious issues within the genre format. Set in the post-Civil War West, Bridges played a former Union officer searching for some meaning, and offering his expert gun in the service of those who need it.

On *The Loner*, Duryea was cast in "A Little Stroll to the End of the Line," playing yet another released prisoner (around this time, Duryea cornered the market in either released or escaped convicts). He's not the villain, though; that role belongs to Robert Emhardt as a so-called preacher who has offered Bridges, now a deputy, a great deal of money to protect him from Duryea's "devil." It doesn't take long for Bridges to see through Emhardt, and when a peaceful Duryea arrives (nursing a persistent cough, for those on foreshadow alert), Bridges protects Duryea from another gunman who had been hired by the preacher. In a riveting monologue, Duryea tells Bridges he has not come to kill the preacher but to confront him, as the preacher bears responsibility for the death of

Duryea's son. Years earlier, the preacher had convinced Duryea's beloved son to encourage the wanted Duryea to surrender peacefully—only to arrange for a bloodbath that claimed Duryea's son and earned the preacher a big reward. In the climactic confrontation, an unarmed Duryea allows himself to be killed by the preacher, but not before drawing the town's attention to the preacher's evil ways. It's a fine episode, allowing time for Bridges and the two guest stars to register strongly while addressing the themes of justice, faith, and redemption. *The Loner* would only last one season because of low ratings, but it's yet another series from this period that deserves to better known.

There would also be Duryea's one and only appearance on the long-running ninety-minute Western drama *The Virginian*. In the deliberately paced episode "The Challenge," Duryea is Clayton, a peaceful rancher who helps an amnesiac Trampas (Doug McClure), even though he is afraid for his daughter (Barbara Anderson) because of her growing attachment to him—to say nothing of the corrupt and murderous deputy (Don Galloway) who has also come a-courting. In addition to Duryea's presence, it's interesting to see Galloway and Anderson play opposite each other—particularly with Galloway playing such an unsavory character—a year or so before Anderson and Galloway costarred with a wheelchair-bound Raymond Burr, in the popular crime drama *Ironside*. In addition, Michael Burns (from *Wagon Train*) was prominently featured as Duryea's restless son, acquitting himself in a creditable manner, alongside Duryea's sensible, reputable rancher torn between the dictates of the law and his desire to help the haunted, pursued Trampas.

Amidst this flurry of quality small-screen outings, Duryea would get a call from his old friend, director Robert Aldrich, to appear in a big studio picture. In the years since their collaborations on *China Smith* and *World for Ransom*, Aldrich developed quite a reputation as a real man's director with such muscular action films as *Vera Cruz* and *Apache*, the Atomic Age noir *Kiss Me Deadly*, as well as tense war dramas like *Attack*. For a time, there was no one better than Aldrich in taking a disparate group of individuals (usually male) and plunging them into dangerous, often life-or-death situations, where they were more apt to fight each other than against any enemy. For 20th Century Fox's *Flight of the Phoenix*, Aldrich and the screenwriter, Lukas Heller, would place their characters at the mercy of the elements, notably an unforgiving desert, amidst their own internal squabbles, dwindling supplies, and diminished strength, in a gripping, all-star, big-budget adventure.

For this drama of a cargo-passenger plane that crashes in the North African desert, and the effort to remodel the wreck into a single-engine working plane, Aldrich would assemble an international all-star cast, as befitting a drama with teamwork and cooperation at the very core. James Stewart was the aging pilot Frank Towns, while Richard Attenborough was cast as his alcoholic navigator Lew Moran. Hardy Kruger was Dorfmann, a plane designer who comes up with the idea of salvaging the wreck, while Peter Finch is a proper British officer who is all too willing to risk his life to search for water or assistance—as remote as that might be. These actors, along with Ronald Fraser (Oscar-nominated as Finch's second-in-command) and Ernest Borgnine (cast against type as an inherently gentle soul recovering from a breakdown), were the most prominently featured members of the cast. Also making appearances were Christian Marquand as a compassionate doctor, and Aldrich's own son, William, and son-in-law, Peter Bravos, for two brief, ill-fated roles, as they both perish in the crash that opens the movie.

So, where does this leave Duryea? He was cast in the relatively minor role of Standish, a devout accountant who is worried about what his extended absence might mean for the financial health of his employers; together with a subdued George Kennedy and Aldrich's two relations, they are perhaps the most underused members of the ensemble. However, Duryea was extremely grateful for the opportunity for a number of reasons. The role of mild-mannered Standish was a substantial supporting role in a big studio picture, and one where he could play "a meek man, for a change." Duryea was also thrilled to be working for Aldrich, and equally excited about acting with his old buddy Stewart. He and Stewart liked playing practical jokes on each other; one running gag involved who could outdo the other as to who could say "good morning!" first, with Stewart calling Duryea at four in the morning, and Duryea having a loudspeaker announce the greeting. Additionally, when the actors were in Yuma (standing in for the African desert, and exuding just as much oppressive heat, with temperatures reaching 120 degrees in the shade), Duryea was among the few actors whose trailers were equipped with working air-conditioning (the others were Stewart and Attenborough). Consequently, several of the actors would gather in Duryea's trailer, and Duryea was in fine form throughout the shoot, regaling his peers with Hollywood war stories, fortified with much liquid refreshment.

Besides the harshness of the Yuma location, reality intruded on *Flight of the Phoenix* in a devastating manner. Respected stuntman Paul Nantz was killed late in July during the filming of the plane crash that opens the film; as Duryea pointed out later to reporter Rebecca Franklin on Stage 6 at 20th Century Fox studios, "Nantz was flying the plane you see here on the stage. It was a terrible thing." The film would eventually be dedicated to Nantz. Later in the filming, after their return to the studio (tons of sand were dumped there to give the Fox soundstage that "desert appearance"), Duryea was injured in a mock-up plane crash when the plane slipped off its supports (he had been on the wing, along with George Kennedy and make-up man Jim White). While Duryea's injuries weren't life-threatening, it only served to enhance the perception that this *Flight* was a jinxed endeavor.

I'll admit that I was not too enamored of *Flight of the Phoenix* when I first saw it around the time of its initial release in early 1966. However, I've seen it several times since (in addition to viewing it again in preparation of this book), and it's a film that impresses more with each subsequent viewing. What makes it work so well is the convincing severity of the situation juxtaposed with a fierce battle of wills involving Stewart's rigid pilot, Attenborough's receptive navigator, and Kruger's haughty designer—or, as many critics were to mention, the cooperation between the Americans, British, and Germans. Stewart's Towns is an "old-school" veteran who has little use for his reduced circumstances (namely, "the cruddy outfit" he flies for) and even less use for Kruger's air of superiority based on what Stewart perceives as a far-fetched scheme that involves rebuilding the wrecked aircraft and getting it airborne. Furthermore, Kruger's insistence on being in command is seen by Stewart as a direct threat to his own standing. Because of their intransigence, Attenborough is forced to act as mediator, motivated by his belief that he'd rather have the men focus on survival then watch them die. This conflict is skillfully developed throughout, right up to the point immediately prior to their hoped-for departure, when Stewart and Attenborough discover that Kruger is really a model airplane designer (or, as Attenborough laughingly puts it, a maker of toy planes).

While this three-way tension and the building of the aircraft (christened *Phoenix* by Duryea's Standish) take up much of the running time, several other situations contribute to the suspense or provide humanizing moments amidst the parched surroundings. Borgnine's unstable, music-loving survivor allows his radio to be used to help ease the pain of a dying man—as well as the hopelessness of his fellow survivors; later, his violent insistence on joining Officer Finch in the search for water leads him on a futile quest of his own. Meanwhile, Finch's noble, idealistic officer has problems with his craven insubordinate (Fraser) who fakes injury to avoid joining Finch on his treacherous trek—and who later flatly refuses to accompany Finch when it comes to ascertaining the intentions of a band of Bedouins.

Duryea's Standish is a gentle, conscientious man who eventually is able to summon his own inner strength while retaining his essential humanity—even if it sets him apart from some other, more callous survivors. He progresses from a meek accountant frantic at the thought of missing a deadline (as his Standish puts it, "Insurance companies work in mysterious ways—like God, but not as generous") to a merciful caretaker for the severely injured passenger. In one delicately played scene, he tries to ease the dying man's pain with words of encouragement. Another lovely moment comes when he tries to explain to a churlish Foster (and, by extension, the viewer) the significance of the *Phoenix*. His wistful description is so well done that one regrets Foster's brusque response. As author Tony Williams points out in his excellent study of Aldrich, *Body and Soul*, Aldrich allows Duryea a beautiful, private moment with his rosary as the *Phoenix* rises, giving the character the respect he has earned. Duryea's role is not as showy as the others, but he invests Standish with a great deal of dignity and compassion.

Perhaps there was more of Duryea in the original cut of the film. There was probably more of everybody, as the initial *Flight* was substantially longer than the finished product. Aldrich wrote to Duryea explaining his (and perhaps others') reduced footage after the film was whittled down to its final 145-minute length: "The first cut ran over four hours. Many little things were lost along the way. Some of these things you'll miss and be sad about . . . it's been sheer hell for me." Duryea must have been disappointed to see his role even further diminished in the final release, but he still quickly accepted when Aldrich invited him and his wife for the world premiere in London. At the event, Duryea received a happy surprise in the form of a huge sign proclaiming "Good Morning Dan!"—a fitting and greatly appreciated conclusion to his and Stewart's running gag.

Flight of the Phoenix would certainly be the last Duryea film to be considered truly "major," but his services were very much in demand. His next role took him back to Europe—namely, Italy. The spaghetti Western, originating in "the Italian West," complete with symphonic scores (courtesy of Ennio Morricone among others), rivers of blood, loquacious villains, and laconic heroes (personified by that former *Rawhide* star, Clint Eastwood) was making big strides in both Europe and America.

Quite a few were directed by Sergio Leone, but several were helmed by talents such as Sergio Corbucci. Lee Van Cleef became a star on the basis of his two outings with Eastwood and Leone. No longer were American actors looking down on these foreign ventures, especially after Eastwood's worldwide success in a role turned down by actors like James Coburn and Charles Bronson. Indeed, they looked to European Westerns to jump-start their flagging careers, much like fading movie stars had previously turned to television. From 1966 on, one would not be surprised to see actors such as Eli Wallach, Cameron Mitchell, Lex Barker, Jeffrey Hunter, Stewart Granger (poorly dubbed as Old Surehand in the "Winnetou" Westerns), Gilbert Roland, John Ireland, and Burt Reynolds. Even Henry Fonda, Jason Robards, and Charles Bronson joined the carnage in Leone's epic *Once Upon a Time in the West*. Leone (as producer) also managed to pair Rod Steiger's sweaty Mexican bandit with James Coburn's Irish mercenary in a sprawling epic of the Mexican Revolution, *Duck You Sucker*.

Duryea's sole entry in the spaghetti Western sweepstakes was originally called *River of Dollars*, but would end up being released as *The Hills Run Red* (a far better, more evocative title). The direction wouldn't be by Leone, but instead would be credited to Lee Beaver, who, in reality, was the renowned Italian filmmaker Carlo Lizzani. Lizzani had established himself in Italian cinema, first as a writer on such classics as Rossellini's *Germany Year Zero* and Giuseppe de Santis's *Bitter Rice*, then as a documentary filmmaker, and finally as a director of solid genre films. The producers had hoped to enlist Burt Reynolds for the lead role of the avenging hero, but it finally fell to an up-and-coming actor, Thomas Hunter. The spaghetti Westerns were nothing if not operatic in scope, and generally had room for more than one cutthroat since the main villain—often a powerful, bloodthirsty rancher—usually had at least one psychotic henchman. For *The Hills Run Red*, the evil landowner was portrayed (in a smarmy manner) by Nando Gazzolo, while the flashy, smiling psycho of a gunman was played by Henry Silva, who had perfected his own version of the dangerously unstable killer in *The Tall T* and *Johnny Cool*.

While the laughing villain in black might have suited Duryea to a tee, occasionally the spaghetti Western would grant actors an opportunity to reinvent themselves. This was certainly the case here, with Duryea cast as a rather enigmatic gunman whose true motives aren't revealed until the end. This uncertainty, especially on the part of audiences accustomed to seeing Duryea as the villain, works in the film's favor, giving *The Hills Run Red* more of a sense of ambiguity throughout.

This fast-paced (for an Italian Western—see Leone's languorous opuses for comparison), post-Civil War horse opera begins in the wake of the South's defeat, as two rebels are trying to flee with a pile of Union money. Gazzolo's duplicitous Seagull beats Hunter's Brewster in a card draw, which results in Brewster's being apprehended by the pursuing army, after diverting attention from the escaping, loot-carrying Gazzolo (who by the way has promised to look out for Brewster's wife and child). Upon Brewster's release, he discovers his house is now a shack, and his wife has been abandoned by his avaricious pal, who now calls himself "Milton" and lives quite lavishly (later he'll learn that Milton has killed her). Moreover, Milton has learned of Brewster's release and has sent a welcome party in the form of some hired gunmen. Duryea's Winny Getz (that's his name) appears as the under-siege Brewster is hiding out in a barn and supplies Brewster with some firepower—or, rather, a gun with two shots.

After Brewster dispatches of his would-be assassins, Duryea's Getz offers to help Brewster by allowing him to pretend to be dead—with the aid of some proof, supplied by the removal of a tattoo (along with the surrounding skin) from Brewster's forearm. Getz then insinuates himself into Seagull's good graces with said tattooed skin, and secures a job as a hired gun, while "Houston" (as Brewster calls himself) discovers his old pal Milton/Seagull has been terrorizing other landowners. Ironically, he winds up being hired by the vicious Mendez (Silva) after impressing him with his ability to take on four tough hombres in hand-to-hand combat.

Getz and Houston help the oppressed ranchers in their revolt against Mendez and Milton, while Houston manages to find time to romance Milton's relatively innocent sister (the very lovely Nicoletta Machiavelli). It all winds up in a showdown, with Getz and Brewster (his intentions becoming known to "Milton") taking on Mendez and Milton's minions in a protracted but exciting encounter on the deserted streets of Austin, making expert use of a horse-drawn carriage bearing an empty coffin laden with dynamite.

Because this was Duryea's first film in Italy, the ways of local filmmaking were somewhat new to him. He had seen Clint Eastwood's latest spaghetti Western (probably *For a Few Dollars More*) to get the feel of how things are done. There were no microphones on the set, and Duryea discovered "the Italians don't shoot picture and dialogue at the same time." Duryea also realized that both the production and pay were a little slow; he was at work for six weeks before he received his first check. And the forces of nature proved to be a factor when a spell of bad weather caused all involved to remain on location longer than expected.

While *The Hills Run Red* is certainly not the finest spaghetti Western to come out of Italy (there are some critics, then and now, who thought it was impossible to produce even a fair-to-middling spaghetti Western), it has come to be regarded as among the better ones—and was, in fact, one of Italy's highest grossing cinematic exports for 1966. The action sequences are top-notch and plentiful, and the plotting and motivations fairly credible for this kind of genre picture.

The acting is also of a fairly high caliber, notwithstanding the occasional distracting dubbing. Silva's maniacal killer steals scenes, and Thomas Hunter is convincingly anguished and determined as the avenging hero—though he would soon become disenchanted with the movie business and desert Hollywood to become one of the founders of the New England Repertory Company. Although Winny Getz is not the most challenging of Duryea's later roles, as he is made to cede screen time to the younger, more volatile characters, it is worth looking at for the little variations it makes on Duryea's established persona. Duryea's Getz (he pronounces the name "Winny . . . *Getz*," as if even he is not sure how he was stuck with it) is a little world weary and seemingly opportunistic, capitalizing on Brewster's circumstances to negotiate the possibility of a little nest egg. As had been the case in earlier films, Duryea is utilized partly to keep the audience in the dark about Getz's true intentions; this little misdirection helps make the conclusion that much more satisfying. At the end, after all has been revealed, Duryea was allowed a moment in an Italian Western that would always be denied him in an American Western: the opportunity to heroically ride off into the sunset, after a lovely moment of bonding with the hero's rediscovered son, to the accompaniment of Ennio Morricone's lilting score.

Duryea's next experience with foreign filmmaking would not be nearly as satisfying. He signed to make a cameo appearance in *Five Golden Dragons*. It was part of a then-popular subgenre in which ordinary Americans abroad would find themselves unwittingly involved in some foreign intrigue, often accompanied by a beautiful woman (or two, one of whom might be a femme fatale). Actors like James Garner and Tony Randall, normally associated with light comedy, would have the leading roles. For *Five Golden Dragons*, Robert Cummings (perhaps a belated nod to Hitchcock's *Saboteur*) would be the lead, in his last film role. The cast would include a number of prominent actors as the leaders of this international crime cartel known as the Golden Dragons. Removing their heads near the end of the film to signify their participation would be such purveyors of villainy as Brian Donlevy, Christopher Lee, George Raft (well . . . a part-time purveyor), and Dan Duryea. When asked about this occasionally entertaining hokum, Duryea would cheerfully admit he did it for the money and a first-class trip to Hong Kong, joined by his wife, Helen.

Duryea's villainous reputation—especially his prowess at realistically slugging his female costars—also might have interfered with getting steady employment stateside. He had been up for a part in Jean Arthur's forthcoming television series, but the producers decided to cast someone else, much to Duryea's dismay—and Arthur's relief. Duryea lamented: "I heard she was glad I didn't get the part because she was frightened of me." Once again, the intensity of Duryea's screen image would blind narrow-minded producers to the fact that Duryea was simply a very good actor. In spite of this presumed setback, Duryea was still grateful to television for "the chance to do many different kinds of things I could not do in pictures."

For one thing, Universal-International was happy to have Duryea play on their team, offering him a contract to make more appearances on both their television shows, as well as their upcoming slate of television movies. What television was doing in the mid-1960s was the equivalent of what cable and video-on-demand are doing now: films that might not have deemed worthy enough to make it into the commercially cruel world on their own were instead granted a cushion of a first run on television. These movies were made on trim budgets but were able to attract some name talent, much like today's cable or video-on-demand releases, with no shortage of top-tier talent participating. The first intended television movie was to have been Universal's 1964 remake of *The Killers*, starring no less than Lee Marvin, John Cassavetes, and, in his last role before entering politics, Ronald Reagan—but it was deemed too violent and was released as a feature instead.

By 1967, Universal had already completed a few of these made-for-television features, occasionally burrowing into their rich cinematic past for inspiration. A case in point is the 1967 remake of *Winchester '73*. The 1950 original was a tough, lean Western starring a very determined James Stewart as a cowboy who spends the entire film trying to reclaim the prized rifle, with Duryea as the scene-stealing, cheerfully psychotic Waco Johnny Dean. The 1967 version would star Tom Tryon as the rightful owner of the rifle, John Saxon as his bitter first cousin who covets the Winchester, and, in a prominent supporting role Duryea himself—only not as any grinning gunman. This time, Duryea would play Saxon's troubled father, trying in vain to make up for his own perceived past transgressions.

The temptation is to write off Universal's second trip to the *Winchester* well as a failed effort, and while this *Winchester '73* is a minor offering, there are a number of things worth noting about it. The remake is nowhere near as episodic as the original, focusing primarily on the Tryon-Saxon rivalry, with a side trip involving John Dehner's gun seller—and one who would like the rifle himself (this sequence also features John Doucette, another original cast member, as a gun-toting tavern owner who doesn't care who shoots whom, as long as it's not in his bar). The biggest change involves Duryea's role as the remorseful father and the misguided steps he takes to make things right with his alienated son. After the initial shooting contest that opens the film (revealed to be at Duryea's instigation, in order to attract wayward son Saxon), Saxon's very sore loser guns down Tryon's father, Paul Fix, to claim the rifle as his own. Duryea then allows Saxon to get away, passing the shooting off as self-defense. Though Sheriff Tryon would prefer to kill Saxon, he decides to try to apprehend him and let the courts decide (as opposed to the vengeful desires of his own hotheaded brother). When the eventual showdown comes, it's not in the mountains but inside and around a mission, with Saxon expiring—but not before Tryon tells him about Duryea's valiant attempt to protect Saxon from the hangman's noose. Duryea is forceful opposite Saxon in an early scene in which the father tries to justify his own actions to his disbelieving son, and later in a coach with Saxon and Barbara Luna, attempting to rationalize the errant Saxon's actions. When *Winchester '73* was telecast in March 1967, a few critics lamented Duryea being relegated to an "elder statesman" role, but in truth, the resigned, weary nature of the role fits Duryea rather well at this stage of his career.

When Duryea wasn't working, he and Helen were still happily together, and their nearly thirty-six-year union proved to be a generally unattainable model by Hollywood standards. By now, Peter was a working actor who had been away from home since the early 1960s; having shared the screen with his father, Peter was now busy shuttling between television roles and some film work. Richard, though he was still living in the family home on Mulholland Drive, spent a great deal of time away as the manager of the Beach Boys. The Beach Boys, as Richard recalls, were fans of his father's, and the first time he had the group over to the family home, Richard remembers a usually confident Dennis Wilson being quite nervous the first time he met the elder Duryea. Helen and Dan were proud parents, with both sons enjoying success in their chosen fields.

Despite the passing of the years, the topic of death had really never been addressed among the Duryeas, although they had seen their share of it in the last decade or so, especially in the passing of Duryea's parents. While the idea of death was downplayed in the Duryea household, occasionally Helen would tell her husband and sons that "you'll miss me when I'm gone." Early in 1967, there would be a family reunion of sorts; the occasion was a wedding and both Peter and Richard, who had both been on the road, would be present. It was especially significant since the whole family had not been together for some time. In the parking lot after the afternoon reception, Helen fainted and was immediately taken to the hospital. She had suffered a massive brain hemorrhage and died on the night of January 21.

Helen's unexpected death had a devastating impact on the entire family. While both Peter and Richard felt the loss, Peter felt particularly guilty because of his own extended absence. As for the widower, it would take a while for Dan to speak openly about Helen's death, and many who were close to him believe he never really recovered. Robert Fuller would say that when he subsequently would see Dan, "it was if the light went from his eyes." Fortunately for Duryea, there would be work to keep him occupied—even as he would subsequently battle health issues of his own.

CHAPTER 15

Twilight; Not Going Gentle into That Good Night

THERE WOULD BE MANY CHANGES IN DURYEA'S LIFE FOLLOWING Helen's death. One of the first things he did was to telephone close friends; in these calls Duryea shared an anecdote or two in which the friend had figured with Helen. And, with Richard and Peter's assistance, he wrote hundreds of thank-you notes to those friends and fans who had wired, written, or sent cards and flowers. While Duryea comforted others, he also carried his personal grief alone.

It became a daily activity for Duryea to go to the cemetery and place flowers on Helen's grave. He would later reflect on his routine to interviewer Sylvia Resnick: "I can't think of the cemetery as a morbid place. Instead, I see the beauty of the green lawns, the vivid colors of the flowers and I feel a certain peace within myself." After one of these visits, Duryea had driven home to see his son Richard come out the front door. As Duryea would recall, "We both smiled a little as he opened the gate and it squeaked familiarly. Then Dick said something that touched me deeply. 'You're not going to sell the house, are you, Dad? This is our home. It's the only place I know.'"

Whether or not to hold on to the house on Mulholland was something that indeed weighed on Duryea. His son Peter was to be married later in the year, leaving Duryea and his son Richard to rattle around together in the big house. They had no domestic help at this time—indeed, they hadn't had anyone for twelve years, since the last young woman they employed had left to get married. Helen had not wanted to hire someone else, which left the Duryeas to maintain the home on their own—which, given Helen's domestic skills and Duryea's generally handy nature, wasn't exactly a daunting proposition. In the end, Duryea decided to keep the house on Mulholland, but to engage someone to look after it. This decision pleased Duryea and both sons, especially Richard. As Duryea said at the time, "Dick is the tour manager for the Beach Boys, which requires his being away a great deal of the time. But when he's in town this is the home he wants to come to."

This meant that Richard and his father would have to interview several couples sent by the employment agency. The first couple they hired quit after a few weeks, mainly because they couldn't handle the relatively remote location. Duryea said, "Where our home is located, it's necessary to drive or you're stuck in the mountains. Neither of them knew how to drive, so I had to let them go." Their replacements would be a motorbike-riding couple, Richard and Else Samuel, who became welcome additions to the Duryea household—especially Else, who was an excellent cook.

Duryea also had a yen to get back to work, since he enjoyed the creativity and the camaraderie of being on a film set. He also believed that Helen, with her zest for living, would want him to get out of the house, and get on with his life. Fortunately, Universal, with Grant Tinker as its vice president, was still regularly producing made-for-television movies. Tinker felt more television movies were inevitable, in order to meet the demands of those who preferred to watch films in the comfort of their own homes. Universal would hire Duryea in a major role for his second television movie, announced as *Death Dance at Banner*.

The talent behind and in front of the camera for *Death Dance at Banner* would be a significant improvement over Duryea's previous made-for-television foray, *Winchester '73*. Instead of journeyman Herschel Daughterty as the director, the project would be helmed by Donald Siegel, a year before discovering his cinematic alter ego in Clint Eastwood, via *Coogan's Bluff*. The script was an original by Reginald Rose, and the cast was impressive, including Henry Fonda, Michael Parks, Anne Baxter, and Duryea, with strong support from Lloyd Bochner, Sal Mineo, and two actors who had acted opposite Duryea before, Tom Reese and Michael Burns (as Anne Baxter's son).

Death Dance at Banner would eventually be renamed *Stranger on the Run*, but under any title it generally succeeds in its goal, as espoused by Tinker, of combining traditional Western action with contemporary psychological examination. There's even a slight similarity to *Bad Day at*

Black Rock, as the protagonist has come to a one-horse town in search of one of its inhabitants. This time, however, the arriving train passenger isn't a fedora-sporting Spencer Tracy, but a drunken, unshaven, beaten-down Henry Fonda who is first seen being thrown off the train at Banner (it's clear he wasn't a paying passenger). Banner is a tiny railroad town with a small group of deputies on just this side of the law to protect the workers and to contain those who are upset with the mining interests. Reluctant "company man" Michael Parks is the head of this rather ragtag group of deputies, with Reese and Mineo among its more unstable participants, while Duryea acts as Parks's mentor and sounding board.

Parks and Duryea share a degree of mutual respect, which manifests itself in an early scene in which Parks defends Duryea against the railroad boss (Bochner) who wants to fire him in order to "defuse the tension." Duryea's appreciation receives a response of "no charge" from Parks, a comment which is echoed throughout by Duryea in different contexts. Parks's main concern is that his deputies will become even more unstable since they have too little to do in this parched, remote town, and might need to relieve the tension in some socially unacceptable ways. Duryea tells Parks of something he had done earlier with his own men: a game of "bear dog" where they set loose a wild animal and hunt it, both for sport and the release the ensuing pursuit offered.

Into this tense tableau comes the pathetic, disheveled Fonda, who attracts the attentions of concerned widow Anne Baxter, as he inquires about a mysterious woman named Alma (Madlyn Rhue). Unbeknownst to Fonda, Alma is a person of substantial interest among the "lawmen"—namely, Parks and Reese—and one who has recently been beaten by one of them. She has also told Parks of her intention of embarrassing the railroad by naming one of his deputies as the guilty party. When Fonda finally gets around to locating Alma (after having been discouraged by some of Parks's men), he discovers her corpse; as he is running from the scene, Parks and his lawmen come upon him. Rather than allowing Fonda to take his chances in court, Parks decides to offer Fonda a horse and a sporting chance—as the unwitting human prey in a sport called "bear dog."

The cat-and-mouse pursuit that takes up the remainder of the film charts both Fonda's redemptive journey toward manhood and Parks's gradual descent into obsessive near-madness that threatens both Fonda's life and Parks's tenuous hold on his men—and his own humanity. Fonda is offered some assistance from Bernie Hamilton's rebellious homesteader, later risking his own life to save Hamilton, in the process temporarily incapacitating Parks with a lucky shot. He has also earned the affections of the widow Baxter, whose son Michael Burns is now part of the deputies, having been encouraged to join by the well-intentioned Duryea.

One of the film's highlights comes after Fonda has been apprehended by Burns and Reese. He is tied and later guarded come nightfall by Duryea; in a precisely timed moment, with his back turned to Fonda, Duryea warns him not to even *think* about trying for Duryea's gun. Duryea's solicitude means little at first to Fonda, who has seen Parks's eyes and knows he'll never make it to trial. Duryea knows it, too, and lets Fonda go (echoing Parks by saying "no charge" in response to Fonda's gratitude), in order to catch the early train out of Banner. The scene dissolves to a late-night talk between Parks and Duryea, in which Duryea tells Parks of his belief in Fonda's innocence, while also letting on that he is indeed getting old, with deteriorating eyesight—a malady that Duryea's concealed spectacles do little to remedy. When Parks asks him, "What good are you?" there is both wounded dignity and resignation in Duryea's response: "No good, no good at all."

In the climactic gun battle at Banner (presumably the so-called "death dance"), Fonda and Baxter face down the deputies, who proceed to be their own worst enemies as they decimate their own ranks, including a mortally wounded Reese who reveals to Duryea that he is the guilty party in poor Alma's death. The determined Parks plans to burn the hotel down if Fonda doesn't show himself, in spite of Duryea conveying Reese's dying declaration to an increasingly unhinged Parks. Fonda's decision to step into the street to face the bloodthirsty Parks (or "bear dog" meets "rabid dog") and the eventual resolution proved to be a huge concern for Siegel and Rose. One possible, if conventional conclusion had Fonda overcoming Parks in a grueling fistfight, but Siegel thought it extremely unlikely that a tired Fonda could best Parks's younger deputy.

In fact, Siegel had an altogether different finish in mind, considering that he appraised Fonda's character as not being physically capable of beating Parks in a fight. Instead, Siegel filmed this confrontation so that after Parks knocks Fonda down, there would be "a duel of big close-ups. They look at each other. Very different from the kind of ending people would see." This would prove to be an effective finish, with quickly edited close-ups among Parks, Fonda, and finally Duryea—as he observes Parks's bloodlust subsiding.

Siegel was proud of this somewhat unusual climax, but he still felt some pangs from the loss of Rose's original conclusion, since it was predicated on his own fondness for Duryea's character—and Duryea the actor.

As Siegel would tell Peter Bogdanovich in a 1968 interview: "I thought Dan Duryea was marvelous. Wonderful part. In a way, I was heartbroken we didn't have the old ending . . . Fonda and Parks had a tremendous fight. Parks is knocked to the ground. Fonda walks away. Parks reaches for his gun to kill him, when Duryea kills Parks. There's nothing wrong with that ending. As a matter of fact, it would work quite well but that's what everybody was expecting to happen, which was one of the reasons I didn't do it." Siegel was not quite as enamored of Parks, though he thought Parks was good in the role. Luckily, both Siegel and NBC liked the result, a film that worked as "one-twenty" (the term for these two-hour made-for-TV movies). *Stranger on the Run* would be a well-reviewed premiere outing for NBC's *Tuesday Night Movie*. Regrettably, the film hasn't been officially released on video to date (although it has surfaced on streaming services such as YouTube). It contains fine, thoughtful work from Fonda, as well as a sublime contribution from Duryea as the aging, ethical deputy.

It's too bad that *Stranger on the Run* couldn't be Duryea's last movie, as he managed to invest the part with a great deal of dignity, and he appeared alongside some seasoned Hollywood pros. His last film release would instead be a low-budget sci-fi/Cold War drama, *The Bamboo Saucer*, released in late 1968. The saucer in question appears from outer space and manages to land, somewhat intact, in Red China. Duryea represents the military brass; it is he who persuades reluctant pilot John Ericson (his brother-in-law was killed in an ill-fated collision with the saucer) to join a team, including Bob Hastings and Bernard Fox, to retrieve the alien aircraft despite anticipated Chinese (and Russian) interference.

In China, Duryea and his team eventually locate the saucer—as well as a Russian team (including Lois Nettleton as an attractive Russian interpreter) vying for access to the saucer's advanced technology. After some ill-fated attempts to fly the aircraft, the Russians attempt to forcibly take possession of the saucer. A brief skirmish between these US and Russian rivals is interrupted by the arrival of Chinese forces, leading to the joint decision that these opposing ideologies (minus the Chinese) will have to join forces in order to fight the advancing Chinese, with the Americans and Russians sacrificing their lives, leaving Nettleton and Ericson to work together in order to fly the craft out of the country.

The Bamboo Saucer has been out of circulation for several years, but a recent video release (from Olive Films, known for restoring classic, hard-to-find films) confirms that the movie is indeed a lackluster affair. The script is by the book, and not an interesting one at that, eschewing any

attempt at espousing a semi-original idea—aside from the occasional ut-
terance by either Ericson or Nettleton that in order to succeed "we have
to work together." The action scenes are rather perfunctory, the characterizations rather cardboard, and the special effects—namely, those of
the saucer's travels and the climactic escape—wouldn't have been out
of place in an Ed Wood movie. Duryea's military man isn't thoroughly
exempt from the cinematic carnage; he is competent but gives no more
than the shallow scripting allows.

It would take approximately a year for this *Saucer* to land on Earth; in
the meantime, Duryea considered himself lucky to be fielding two very
attractive and lucrative offers. One was to appear in Francis Ford Coppo-
la's big-budget movie version of the Broadway hit, *Finian's Rainbow*, with
the already-cast Fred Astaire, Petula Clark, and Tommy Steele. Duryea
was offered the part of the Southern senator, a fairly juicy role that would
have given him the opportunity to sing for the first time on screen. However, Duryea was also given the chance to play an even meatier role on
the popular prime-time soap opera *Peyton Place*. The character was Eddie
Jacks, a charmer and a conman who had deserted his wife, Ada, and
their daughter, Rita, eighteen years earlier. It was a difficult choice, especially since the *Peyton Place* producers had to know right away, so Duryea
opted to join the denizens of *Peyton Place*. He would sign for twenty out of
the upcoming twenty-six episodes, with an option for more. There were
several reasons why this was a good move for Duryea. As Duryea put it,
"The money is good, the material is good, and the people are great. My
only reservation was whether I should get into something which already
had started."

Another factor was that, for a sixty-year-old actor, the opportunities
to maintain prominence (not to mention employability) dwindle over
the years. Duryea had for years made a good living as the go-to guest star
in episodic dramas, or as a star in segments of anthology series. However,
as he saw it, "the guest star business has gone to pot, more prime-time
hours have been given to old movies." In addition, the anthology shows
had been disappearing, while salaries had steadily been going down for
guest spots.

The casting of Duryea (along with the relatively recent addition of
Gena Rowlands) meant an infusion of new blood for the series, which
was in its fourth year. It had premiered in 1965 with Mia Farrow (who
left after the first season), Ryan O'Neal, Patricia Morrow, Barbara
Parkins, and Christopher Connelly, among others, enacting the various conflicting relationships among the inhabitants of the fictional town

called Peyton Place. Duryea's Eddie Jacks, intent on insinuating himself into his daughter's life (for reasons unknown, but probably having to do with money), would be a very welcome addition to what had been a fairly harmonious cast. Patricia Morrow, who played Rita since the series' inception, would remember it as a show in which "everybody saw each other . . . it was a well-integrated cast where everyone worked with everybody." For Morrow and the rest of the cast, Duryea was "a big deal for everyone connected with the show." If anything, Duryea's work ethic and overall demeanor exceeded their expectations. "Duryea was such an artful actor," Morrow says, "when he's in a scene, you're thinking how can *I* learn what *he's* doing." Morrow would remember Duryea as "always fun, devil-may-care, a rogue, a flirt, and always a class act." Morrow would also be grateful that "Dan treated me like the daughter he never had. He was always right where he needed to be as an actor."

At this time, the series would contemplate moving from two episodes per week to three episodes per week. The plotlines would focus on the constant intrigue among the various members of the Peyton clan, consisting of the fabulously wealthy and avaricious Peyton; his son, Leslie Harrington; Peyton's rebellious grandsons, Norman and Rodney Harrington; and the women in their lives. Ada Jacks and her daughter, Rita, were from "the other side of the tracks," yet Norman would take Rita for his wife, a union that posed some difficulties, given Rita's fragile health (being tended to by another series regular Dr. Rossi, portrayed by Ed Nelson).

Enter Duryea's Eddie Jacks, who is given the movie-star entrance at the beginning of his first episode with his carefree stroll down the main street. Eddie has returned to Peyton Place to renew his acquaintance with Leslie Harrington. Eddie is well-versed with Leslie's unsavory side—and sees some potential profit in it. He's also there in order to get to know Rita, especially now that she's married into money. Never mind the fact that hotheaded husband Norman (Christopher Connelly) has spurned Grandpa's money and support—if there's an angle Eddie will find it. Then there's the matter of Eddie's ex-wife, Ada (Evelyn Scott), who still hasn't gotten over his desertion of them (without leaving them so much as a cent), and Old Man Peyton's fiancée, Adrienne (Gena Rowlands), whom Eddie knows previously as a gal of uncertain moral fiber. It's not long before Eddie has ingratiated himself with Rita, finagled a job tending bar at Ada's saloon, scuffled with Norman over Rita's growing affections, and gotten himself tangled up in a scheme to murder Old Man Peyton himself (George Macready).

Duryea would see Eddie as someone who "doesn't have class, but thinks he does . . . He's an out-and-out scoundrel, but a charmer with the ladies." Soon after Duryea began filming, he told a reporter how his new role helped rejuvenate him: "An actor lives for good scenes, and in the two weeks I've been with *Peyton Place* I've had several." Patricia Morrow believes that Duryea excelled as Eddie because "he knew the character since he played it before but he brought a different twist to it . . . he added a dimension of emotion as well."

While filming his initial episodes, Duryea read something in the paper that, as a proud actor, he felt compelled to publicly respond to. William Holden had gone on record saying, "The actor is not a creative artist, he is an interpretive artist. The man who conceives the idea is the most important. The actor comes last, after the producer, director and the writer." While others, including actors and columnists, brushed off Holden's remarks, Duryea fired off a letter in which he would challenge Holden, declaring: "Isn't it true that the performer, with more frequency, has rescued a colorless story from obsolescence rather than the other way around?" Duryea recognized Holden as "an actor with an unusual talent . . . I am certain he has salvaged more than one inferior property by his expertise in moments of need." Duryea acknowledged the genius of creative forces like Hellman, Wyler, and others, but he also never denigrated the worth of his profession and the ability of a gifted actor to transcend his material—a talent Duryea himself possessed.

After viewing the sixty or so episodes that Duryea appeared in (having originally being slated for about twenty), one sees that *Peyton Place* was a polished, well-written, well-acted *continuing drama* (producer Paul Monash's term for the series, as opposed to "soap opera") featuring a uniformly high level of acting and an appropriate level of theatrics (occasionally amplified by Macready's melodramatic relish in devouring his role as the universally disliked Peyton). Duryea's Eddie is at the center of many of these episodes, and he has many memorable moments, especially in the first thirty episodes.

Many of those episodes involve his furtive, late-night meetings with the also crafty Harrington, as Eddie tries to parlay his knowledge into a paycheck. At first this entails spying and simply keeping his eyes open. When it comes to the prospect of murdering Peyton, Eddie is all due diligence in extracting a "promissory note" for services to be rendered, implicating Leslie (as well as himself) should things go south. Eddie justifies his actions through his desire to do right by Rita, yet finds it hard to convince anyone of his alleged good intentions. Duryea also has some strong scenes clashing with Connelly's Norman, especially when an attempted rapprochement winds up with Eddie slugging Norman in the ribs. There is an element of guilt and self-disgust in Eddie that creeps into his dealings with others. When called on his motives by a caring if unbelieving Dr. Rossi, Eddie deflects by declaring no one could know how he feels as a father. He then turns the tables on Rossi by saying, "Practicing medicine in this state takes in a lot of territory, *doesn't it.*" Duryea's scenes with Ada resonate as well; watch his character talk even faster (and slightly higher) as he tries to assure Ada of his sincerity. She doesn't buy it, based on her knowledge of Eddie, and neither do we, given our long association with Duryea.

The only character who believes in him throughout (barring a few doubts) is Rita. The first meeting between Rita and Eddie is delicately played by Morrow and Duryea; the two characters quickly develop a bond as perpetual outsiders looking for some validation. Rita's innocent affection touches Eddie, bringing home just how much he has hurt himself and the family by running away. It even raises some long-dormant paternal sensibilities, as Eddie expresses outrage with Ada's supposed neglect of Rita, while being put in his place by Ada's allegation that his leaving didn't do much to alleviate their situation. Eddie's desire to provide for Rita—admittedly bogus when he first arrives—credibly evolves into real affection, leading to Eddie's admission to Les (after brokering some $50,000 out of him) that "I want to just *like* myself a little before I die."

After Eddie is implicated in Adrienne's death—eventually revealed to be an accidental fall—Duryea has some spirited confrontations with Macready's Peyton, as he offers to give up Les and the promissory note in exchange for freedom. The battle of wills between Macready and Duryea—two classic Hollywood heavies—delivers a real jolt to the proceedings. After Eddie was released and exonerated, his involvement in the series' action diminished; *Peyton Place* began to focus on other visiting characters (Duryea was by now renewed beyond his initial twenty-six episodes), including Joe Rossi, a character who revives some suppressed feelings in Rita, as well as paternal outrage from Eddie. The complications stemming from Eddie's misguided feelings lead to Eddie's eventual departure from Peyton Place, but there was another factor as well.

Patricia Morrow would remember that the shooting schedule was pretty hectic, complicated by the fact it was a single-camera show, often shooting two to three episodes at once, with three sound stages going at the same time. The sixty-year-old Duryea was beginning to show some signs of malaise and fatigue, which he attributed at first to the grueling schedule; his son Richard would also recall his father having difficulty keeping down his meals around this time. Richard took Duryea to St. Joseph's Hospital, where they did some exploratory surgery; the doctors found that Duryea had pancreatic cancer. This was in early February 1968; Richard would also remember that the doctors gave his father about three months.

Duryea wanted to continue to work, but the onset of chemotherapy would make working difficult in the foreseeable future, so he was given the opportunity to make an early, graceful exit from *Peyton Place*. Morrow fondly recalled that "he was tough to the end; he managed to retain his vitality and both the cast and crew loved him." Nearly everyone in *Peyton Place* showed up for the shooting of Duryea's final scene in which Eddie leaves town on the bus, acknowledging to the bus driver (and to the audience) that, like the bus, he has always been a little behind schedule. According to Morrow, the writers inserted this scene "to give him a proper goodbye" and when Duryea's character departed, "the crew was in tears . . . he was like a second dad to me. It was a very poignant moment."

After Duryea left *Peyton Place*, he went about the business of following doctor's orders in an attempt to outlive the original diagnosis. He began taking oral medication, then agreed to a new treatment involving electrical therapy, which would involve being attached to an outlet and a 100-foot length of cord for fourteen hours a day. He would tell friends that his only trouble was trying to live a reasonably normal life in spite of having to manipulate this lengthy cord.

Word of Duryea's illness was kept a secret from the general public, but there were Hollywood insiders and close friends who knew; they responded in unexpected ways. Duryea was signed for a bad-guy role in Andrew Fenady's *No God in Saguara*. He had told Fenady to find a replacement, but Fenady waved him off, saying they could wait for him: "You'll be ready in a month or two and I don't want to go ahead without you." As for the top columnists, while they knew of the severity of Duryea's illness, they respected him—and stood by him. If they published anything connected to Duryea, it was in the form of blithe public relations items furnished by Duryea's representative, David Epstein.

Duryea would bounce back occasionally during his difficult final months. He spent a weekend at Lake Arrowhead and managed to eat and regain some of the forty pounds he had lost. However, after experiencing some recurring pain, it was found he had developed a gastric ulcer, possibly caused by the medication.

As a proudly independent man, Duryea insisted on functioning as well as he could on his own. Patricia Morrow would remember Duryea's son Richard as "always being there for his dad." Still, the elder Duryea wanted to maintain his routine of driving himself to the doctor every other day. As he would tell a friend, "I don't know how much longer I can make those trips, but I can't bear the thought of becoming a burden to anyone. To me, that would be the ultimate humiliation. But then . . . maybe some of this therapy will begin to take hold."

Finally, on the morning of June 7, Duryea collapsed in his bathroom. Richard was home at the time, later recalling, "I called out to him and there was no answer. I thought to myself should I open the door or go get someone to do that for me. I decided to open the door alone by myself. I saw my father on the floor and watched his last breath being released from his mouth. I know this sounds hard to believe and I am not a very religious man, but I saw the wrinkles of time in his face smooth out. I also saw and felt his spirit leave his body. I am so glad I made the decision to open that door at this time. That experience has had a profound effect on me through my life and I will never forget this moment as long as I live." Duryea had died before the doctor's arrival. The news of his death reached the airwaves the same day of Robert Kennedy's assassination, with all its repercussions. As a result, Duryea's passing was considered almost inconsequential to a nation that had been stunned by Kennedy's death. As many would later discover, Duryea had a greatness all his own.

This would not be apparent right away, at least if you were reading the newspapers carrying news of Duryea's death. One of the more neutral obituaries featured the headline: "Film Star Dan Duryea Dies After Long Illness." Other newspapers carried such headlines as "Dan Duryea, Girl Slapping Villain of Movies, Dies at 61" or "Dan Duryea, Actor, Dies at 61; Played Unsavory Characters." Obscured within the attention-grabbing headlines were his other activities and interests; just about all eventually mentioned he was a dedicated father and ever-faithful husband.

Duryea would be buried at Forest Lawn next to his beloved Helen. Her headstone would read "Our Little Mama, We Love Everybody," while Dan's read "Our Pop, A Man Everybody Loved." A number of Hollywood notables attended the services, including Jimmy Stewart, a coterie of cast mates from both movies and television, as well as the crew members who adored him, and his close friends outside the business, for whom he was always a regular fellow.

Duryea would leave his six-figure estate to his two sons. Following his father's death, Peter would continue to act into the early 1970s. He would also develop some unwanted fame for being cast in the original *Star Trek* pilot ("The Menagerie," with Jeffrey Hunter) only to see the show recast for its second pilot. In 1973, Peter would move to Kootenay Lake in British Columbia, where, with his partner Jan Bryan, he would develop a production company specializing in ecological and social awareness; Peter passed away in 2013. Younger brother Richard would continue his career in show business as a theatrical manager with his successful association with the Beach Boys. Under the banner of Duryea Entertainment, Richard would also manage Chicago, Billy Preston, and Mary Wilson of the Supremes, among others. Richard is still active today, continuing to produce live theatrical presentations. Richard's and Peter's success in their chosen fields would have gratified Duryea, always the proud father.

Despite the occasional career frustrations, Dan Duryea had a pretty good life—and I'm hoping his screen and television work will have a long afterlife. I'd like to let Duryea have the last words: "Look, I'm no saint and I don't want to sound that way. I like to belt a few every now and then and have fun. It seems like too perfect a life, and I don't mean it that way. . . . I'm very happy and content to go along, without any great ambition to be the top star in the United States. I am happy the way I am. Don't forget the heavies work pretty regularly, too. I would not rather have done anything else except acting. I absolutely would not. It has been a wonderful life for me."

ACKNOWLEDGMENTS

A FEW YEARS AGO, MY FRIEND BARRY LIEBMANN TOLD ME ABOUT A program at the New York Public Library for the Performing Arts, and for that, I'm very grateful. Carl Rollyson, editor of the University Press of Mississippi's Hollywood Legends series, had written a biography of Dana Andrews and would be discussing the book and holding a signing afterwards. After the program, I spoke to Carl about Dana Andrews and the Legends series, and I asked in passing, "Would you consider a book on Dan Duryea?" As there had not been a biography yet on the actor, he said, "Possibly." He gave me his card and some pertinent information. Since then, Carl and the good people at the University Press of Mississippi, especially Leila Salisbury, Valerie Jones, and Lisa McMurtray, have been nothing short of wonderful, offering all kinds of encouragement and assistance along the way. I'm also deeply appreciative of Peter Tonguette and his copyediting expertise. Special thanks to Carl, too, for encouraging me to *never* lose sight of Duryea, the man.

In doing research for an actor's biography, there are places you have to go. My thanks go to many: Sandy Garcia Meyers and Ned Comstock at the Cinematic Arts Library at the University of Southern California. Sandy was a great help in facilitating space and materials, while Ned was incredible in furnishing me with the desired memorabilia and relevant clippings. My gratitude knows no bounds. Jenny Romero from the Margaret Herrick Library of the Academy of Motion Picture Arts and Sciences provided assistance in locating some needed material. The UCLA Arts Library Special Collections had a number of rare Duryea films and television work. There was also much information to be found at the New York Public Library for the Performing Arts. The Hollywood Book and Poster Shop was one of several then-thriving memorabilia shops along Hollywood Boulevard that provided all kinds of valuable merchandise, especially for the collector of classic movie photos. I also found some rare videos at Eddie Brandt's Saturday Matinee in Burbank, still going strong and an invaluable resource for movie and television buffs.

I'm very grateful to the actors who took the time to speak to me or send their recollections. Jerry Mathers and Piper Laurie helped with Duryea, the actor. I'm especially grateful to Robert Fuller, Gordon Gebert, Earl Holliman, and Patricia Morrow. All worked with Duryea, generally during the latter part of his career, and spoke to me at length regarding his professionalism and standing as a true gentleman. I cannot thank them enough.

I'm sorry I never got to meet Duryea's son Peter, who passed away in 2013, but I'm happy to have gotten to know Duryea's only living son, Richard. He's still busy as a manager and producer; he also sat with me to discuss his father's life, clearing up misconceptions that had found their way into print. Richard also supplied a number of family photos, which are appreciated as Duryea was very much a family man. And he put me in touch with three of his friends who gave me some insights into Duryea in his Arrowhead retreat. Thanks to Mary Bernard, Sharon McDaniel, and Rich Baughman for helping me to fill in Duryea, the man.

There are several people with websites devoted to Dan Duryea. Sarah Garcia from Dan Duryea Central has posted a great deal of valuable material, while Gregory Hines has several Facebook pages of Dan Duryea photos within his Peyton Place Revisited site, as does Laura Wagner. Arthur Harvey from Movie Memorabilia also helped me locate some useful Duryea photos. Thanks to all for your assistance, insights, and the use of relevant photos. Sarah, in particular, has been extremely generous, providing many photos from her own vast collection of Duryea memorabilia, especially the areas where mine has been lacking. Sarah has done a tremendous job preserving Duryea's legacy, and her Dan Duryea Central website is well worth visiting.

My colleagues at Bishop Loughlin High School also deserve my appreciation. Thanks to those in administration, especially Cecilia Gottsegen, Brother Dennis Cronin, and Ed Bolan, who have been thoroughly supportive of my endeavor in all kinds of ways. Abby Walthausen not only supplied assistance with technology, but she also suggested a few years back that I write a book. A huge thanks to Desta Moe, Nat Emmanuel, Luis Montes, and Kathleen Burns for being patient as they explained the vagaries of Microsoft Word. Thanks to my friends in the English department led by the delightful Regina Bratichak—especially for allowing me to make the Computer Lab my "second office." There were many others at Loughlin who have been encouraging, but I want to single out Ted (Teddy) Frank for his technical assistance (and moral support), Bill Mason, and the good folks of 219, namely, Richie McGuire, Vinny Visco, Tom Pettersen, Cindi Cericola, Angela Proce, Sean Cunningham, Ed Bowes, and Chester Bartnikowski.

My friend and fellow author Bob Herzberg provided some help in terms of my research. I'm indebted to Nancy Bianconi of the valuable website NoHoArtsDistrict for allowing me time and space to practice my craft. The very knowledgeable Dennis Bartok helped me locate some actors and others who might be of help; Daniel Madigan provided some worthy insights into Duryea's appeal. These are some (among many) who either read earlier works or encouraged me at some point along the way: Carrie Gordon Lowrey, Yvette and Alex Pons, Jeannette Sachs, Jim Hayes, Robin Roy, Neil and Robin Wilensky, Kyle Levitt, Marilyn Kirshen, Christopher Caliendo, Mike Yadzyn, Joe Kuhr, Debbie Mercer, Tim Conlon, Eric Vetter, Kathy Becker, Colleen Herzberg, Anne Bass, Alex Farrill, Lori and Keith Halop, Chris Aguda, Joe Fedor, Walker and Lisa Rice, Fred Velez, Mike Fass, Michael Dale, David Mackler, Hernan Poza, Stephanie and Ted Ayvas, Greg and Ming Ayvas, my godmother Irene Ayvas, Barbara Rosene, Rich Condelles, Carmen Sorvillo, Bill Peabody, Bill Morton, Cathy Sigal, John Sharp, Harold Vaughn, Mary Ann Hand, Jeff and Patty Lesser, Susan Dorsey-Nelson, Howie and Sandy Lewengrub, George and Herlita Garfield, Felice and Leon Cohen, Richard and Alice Weiner, and my oldest friends, Curtis Davenport, Dave Orkin, and Dave Peiser. If I missed you (and I certainly may have), I hope you'll forgive me.

Thanks to brother John who supplied the title *Heel with a Heart*— everyone liked that title more than any title I had come up with. He and his talented partner, Jim Braswell, have been a constant source of encouragement all along the way. A very big thanks to brother Steve for years of lively discussions and somewhat spirited debates over movies, quite often conducted during our yearly trip to the San Diego Comic-Con; Steve's lovely and talented bride Sybil Darrow also helped jumpstart my writing by getting me the gig with NoHoArtsDistrict. I'm also grateful for all the times they let me stay in their West Hollywood home, especially when I was doing my research. A huge thanks to my parents, George and Tessie Peros, who took me to the movies from a young age, encouraged me to purchase (or bought for me) biographies of movie stars like Cagney and Bogart, and often let me stay up way past my bedtime to watch many classic movies on television. They have always been there for me and I am eternally grateful.

Finally, my wife, Barbara Trueson (whom I met through Steve), also deserves my gratitude and love. Barbara has helped in the research, she's been patient when we've had to adjust our plans, and she's been great in helping me format and locate things I might have missed. Thank you so much, now and always.

FILMOGRAPHY

MANY OF DURYEA'S FILMS ARE NOW AVAILABLE ON DVD, AS WELL AS on various streaming sites such as Amazon Instant Video (referred in this filmography as "Amazon") and YouTube, at least as of this writing. There are numerous vendors offering films that have not been officially released, but for now, I have referred to these films as "hard-to-find." Many of Duryea's films are broadcast with some regularity on Turner Classic Movies, as well as on such new movie channels as GetTV and the Movies.

YEAR	TITLE	STUDIO	DIRECTOR	VIDEO
1941	*The Little Foxes*	Goldwyn/RKO	William Wyler	DVD
1942	*Ball of Fire*	Goldwyn/RKO	Howard Hawks	DVD
1942	*Pride of the Yankees*	Goldwyn/RKO	Sam Wood	DVD
1942	*That Other Woman*	20th Century Fox	Ray McCarey	DVD
1943	*Sahara*	Columbia	Zoltan Korda	DVD
1944	*Man from Frisco*	Republic	Robert Florey	Amazon
1944	*Mrs. Parkington*	MGM	Tay Garnett	DVD
1944	*Ministry of Fear*	Paramount	Fritz Lang	DVD
1944	*None but the Lonely Heart*	RKO	Clifford Odets	DVD
1944	*The Woman in the Window*	RKO	Fritz Lang	DVD
1945	*Main Street After Dark*	MGM	Ed Cahn	hard-to-find

1945	*Along Came Jones*	RKO	Stuart Heisler	DVD
1945	*The Great Flamarion*	Republic	Anthony Mann	DVD
1945	*Lady on a Train*	Universal	Charles David	DVD
1945	*Scarlet Street*	Universal	Fritz Lang	DVD
1945	*The Valley of Decision*	MGM	Tay Garnett	DVD
1946	*Black Angel*	Universal	Roy William Neill	DVD
1946	*White Tie and Tails*	Universal	Charles Barton	hard-to-find
1948	*Another Part of the Forest*	Universal	Michael Gordon	hard-to-find
1948	*Black Bart*	Universal	Gordon Douglas	hard-to-find
1948	*Larceny*	Universal	George Sherman	hard-to-find
1948	*River Lady*	Universal	George Sherman	DVD
1949	*Criss Cross*	Universal	Robert Siodmak	DVD
1949	*Johnny Stool Pigeon*	Universal	William Castle	hard-to-find
1949	*Manhandled*	Paramount	Lewis Foster	hard-to-find
1949	*Too Late for Tears*	United Artists	Byron Haskin	DVD
1950	*One Way Street*	Universal	Hugo Fregonese	hard-to-find
1950	*Winchester '73*	Universal	Anthony Mann	DVD
1950	*The Underworld Story*	United Artists	Cyril Endfield	DVD
1951	*Al Jennings of Oklahoma*	Columbia	Ray Nazarro	DVD
1952	*Chicago Calling*	United Artists	John Reinhardt	DVD
1953	*Thunder Bay*	Universal	Anthony Mann	DVD
1953	*Sky Commando*	Columbia	Fred Sears	hard-to-find
1953	*Terror Street*	Lippert	Montgomery Tully	DVD
1954	*World for Ransom*	Allied Artists	Robert Aldrich	DVD
1954	*Ride Clear of Diablo*	Universal	Jesse Hibbs	DVD
1954	*Rails into Laramie*	Universal	Jesse Hibbs	YouTube
1954	*Silver Lode*	RKO	Allan Dwan	DVD
1954	*This Is My Love*	RKO	Stuart Heisler	hard-to-find

1955	*Foxfire*	Universal	Joseph Pevney	hard-to-find
1955	*The Marauders*	MGM	Gerald Mayer	DVD
1955	*Storm Fear*	United Artists	Cornel Wilde	DVD
1957	*Battle Hymn*	Universal	Douglas Sirk	DVD
1957	*The Burglar*	Columbia	Paul Wendkos	DVD
1957	*Night Passage*	Universal	James Neilson	DVD
1957	*Slaughter on Tenth Avenue*	Universal	Arnold Laven	hard-to-find
1958	*Kathy O'*	Universal	Jack Sher	hard-to-find
1960	*Platinum High School*	MGM	Charles Haas	hard-to-find
1962	*Six Black Horses*	Universal	Harry Keller	hard-to-find
1964	*He Rides Tall*	Universal	R. G. Springsteen	YouTube
1964	*Walk a Tightrope*	Paramount	Frank Nesbitt	hard-to-find
1964	*Taggart*	Universal	R. G. Springsteen	hard-to-find
1965	*Do You Know This Voice?*	British Lion	Frank Nesbitt	Amazon
1965	*The Bounty Killer*	Embassy	Spencer G. Bennet	hard-to-find
1965	*The Flight of the Phoenix*	20th Century Fox	Robert Aldrich	DVD
1966	*Incident at Phantom Hill*	Universal	Earl Bellamy	hard-to-find
1967	*The Hills Run Red*	MGM	Carlo Lizzani	DVD
1967	*Winchester '73* (TV)	Universal	Herschel Daugherty	DVD
1967	*Five Golden Dragons*	Commonwealth	Jeremy Summers	Amazon
1967	*Stranger on the Run* (TV)	Universal	Donald Siegel	YouTube
1968	*The Bamboo Saucer*	World Entertainment	Frank Telford	DVD

It has been speculated that Duryea made an unbilled appearance in *El Tango en Broadway*, a 1934 Spanish-language musical. I was able to view the film during the final editing stages of this book. Indeed, it is Duryea asking (in English) the actress Bianca Vischwer for a dance . . . and that's it. He was very nondescript.

TELEVISION CREDITS

1951	*The Kate Smith Show* "Land's End" (dramatic sketch)
1952	*The Affairs of China Smith* (twenty-six episodes, syndication)
1952	*Schlitz Playhouse of Stars* "P.G.," "The Souvenir of Singapore" CBS
1953	*Ford Theater* "Double Exposure" NBC
1955	*Schlitz Playhouse of Stars* "O'Brien" CBS
1955	*The Star and the Story* "The Lie" NBC
1955	*Fireside Theatre* "Nailed Down" NBC
1955	*December Bride* "High Sierras" CBS
1955	*The Jack Benny Show* "The Lunch Counter Murders" CBS
1955	*The New Adventures of China Smith* (twenty-six episodes, syndication)
1956	*Schlitz Playhouse of Stars* "Repercussion" CBS
1956	*20th Century Fox Hour* "Smoke Jumpers" CBS
1956	*Star Stage* "The Marshal and the Mob" NBC
1956	*General Electric Theater* "The Road That Led Afar" CBS
1957	*Cavalcade of America* "The Frightened Witness" ABC
1957	*Suspicion* "Doomsday" NBC
1957	*Wagon Train* "The Cliff Grundy Story" NBC
1958	*Cimarron City* "Terror Town" NBC
1958	*Zane Grey Theater* "This Man Must Die" CBS
1958	*Climax* "Four Hours in White" CBS
1958	*Pursuit* "Tiger on a Bicycle"
1958	*U.S. Steel Hour* "Hour of the Rat" CBS
1958	*Wagon Train* "The Sacramento Story" NBC
1959	*Walt Disney Presents* "Texas John Slaughter: Showdown at Sandoval" ABC
1959	*Rawhide* "Incident with an Executioner" CBS
1959	*Wagon Train* "The Last Man" NBC
1959	*Desilu Playhouse* "The Comeback" CBS
1959	*David Niven Theater* "The Vengeance" ABC
1959	*Laramie* "Stage Stop" NBC

1959	*The Twilight Zone* "Mr. Denton on Doomsday" CBS
1960	*Adventures in Paradise* "Judith" ABC
1960	*Riverboat* "The Wichita Arrows" NBC
1960	*Riverboat* "Fort Epitaph" NBC
1960	*Wagon Train* "The Joshua Gilliam Story" NBC
1960	*G.E. Theater* "Mystery at Malibu" CBS
1960	*U.S. Steel Hour* "Shadow of a Pale Horse" CBS
1960	*Bonanza* "Badge Without Honor" NBC
1960	*Shirley Temple's Storybook* "Tom and Huck" NBC
1960	*Laramie* "The Long Riders" NBC
1961	*The Barbara Stanwyck Theater* "Sign of the Zodiac" NBC
1961	*Zane Grey Theater* "Knight of the Sun" CBS
1961	*Route 66* "Don't Count Stars" CBS
1961	*Checkmate* "Tight as a Drum" CBS
1961	*Frontier Circus* "The Shaggy Kings" CBS
1961	*Laramie* "The Mountain Men" NBC
1962	*Tales of Wells Fargo* "Winter Storm" NBC
1962	*Naked City* "Daughter, Am I in My Father's House" ABC
1962	*Wagon Train* "The Wagon Train Mutiny" ABC
1962	*Going My Way* "Mr. Second Chance" ABC
1962	*Rawhide* "Incident of the Wolvers" CBS
1962	*Wide Country* "Tears on a Painted Face" NBC
1963	*Eleventh Hour* "Why Have I Grown So Cold?" ABC
1963	*Alcoa Premiere* "Blow High, Blow Clear" ABC
1963	*U.S. Steel Hour* "The Many Ways of Heaven" CBS
1963	*Rawhide* "Incident of the Prophecy" CBS
1964	*The Alfred Hitchcock Hour* "Three Wives Too Many" NBC
1964	*Kraft Suspense Theatre* "Who is Jennifer?" NBC
1964	*Burke's Law* "Who Killed the Paper Dragon?" ABC
1964	*Wagon Train* "The Race Town Story" ABC
1964	*Bonanza* "Logan's Treasure" NBC
1964	*Burke's Law* "Who Killed 711?" ABC
1965	*Daniel Boone* "The Sound of Fear" NBC
1965	*Combat* "Dateline" ABC
1965	*The Long Hot Summer* "The Return of the Quicks" ABC
1966	*The Loner* "A Little Stroll to the End of the Line" CBS
1966	*The Virginian* "The Challenge" NBC
1966	*The Monroes* "Gold Fever" ABC
1967	*Combat* "A Little Jazz" ABC
1967	*Winchester '73* (made-for-television movie) NBC

1967   *Stranger on the Run* (made-for-television movie) NBC

1967   *Peyton Place* (fifty-nine episodes airing from August 1967 through May
         1968) ABC

NOTES

DAN DURYEA LEFT HIS PERSONAL PAPERS TO THE UNIVERSITY OF Southern California, where a researcher can find a lifetime's worth of clippings. Some are from his White Plains school days, and a box or two contain Cornell memorabilia, including some programs and notices. There is also a great deal of material relating to his career. Included not only are some letters to and from Duryea, but also reviews, publicity material, candid shots, movie stills, as well as a number of published articles. Some of these are from newspapers, while others are from the Hollywood magazines of the day. Almost from the onset of his career, Duryea was known around town among columnists as a good interview, gladly granting practically every request that came his way. He also contributed a number of articled under his own byline. When I asked his son Richard about some of this published material—particularly the articles that looks like they could only have emerged from a publicity man's head—he vouched for their veracity.

If one visits the USC campus, one can also find a treasure trove of clippings from Universal, including a great deal of relevant information pertaining to Duryea's Universal output. Time and again, I would see while poring over this material such items from publicity men as "Talk to Dan" or "Dan's a good interview, take advantage of that!" I also found several letters at the Academy of Motion Picture Arts and Sciences' Margaret Herrick Library, particularly one in which he gave his side of being released from *A Case of Libel*.

CHAPTER 1

"The Egg and the Eye": Balling, "Dan Duryea—When They Said He was Nice They Meant It."

CHAPTER 2

The opening quote is from Duryea's "The Faith No One Could Teach Me."
The high school programs and Cornell material can be found at USC.
Reflections on his father from "Scully's Scrapbook."
Duryea's son Richard spoke to me about the relationship between Dan and his brother.
Dan would tell the story of his courtship of Helen several times. Some material was taken from "Happy Anniversary" and "Heel With Sex Appeal."
Duryea's early pre-Broadway theater days: USC.
"I wish I could have Hellman's words come out of my mouth": Rebecca Franklin, "Duryea, That Famous Old Film Villain, Earned Bad Guy Tag on Broadway."
Reflections on being hated and Carl and Dan's dressing room: "Dan Duryea Likes to be Hated."

CHAPTER 3

"Bette Davis is a great gal . . .": Morehouse, "'Villain' Dan Duryea Affable Guy."
Duryea's voice: Patricia Morrow, interview with author.
Duryea's leaving Goldwyn: press release, USC.
Duryea' memories of *Sahara* found their way to several news organizations, and are included in Jeffrey Meyers's fine biography of Humphrey Bogart.
Duryea would speak of his problems with horses in several articles including Balling, "Dan Duryea—When They Said He was Nice They Meant It"
Much material concerning *Valley of Decision* and *Mrs. Parkington* came from the Greer Garson biography, *A Rose for Mrs. Miniver*.

CHAPTER 4

Some of the Lang material concerning *Ministry of Fear* and *The Woman in the Window* comes from McGilligan's biography of Lang, as well as Grant's *Fritz Lang: Interviews*, and Paul Jensen's *Cinema of Fritz Lang*. For his own part, Lang was dismissive of *Ministry of Fear*.
I also consulted Edward G. Robinson's autobiography; he really liked *The Woman in the Window* but was displeased with his work on *Scarlet Street*.
Anthony Mann conveyed his dislike for *The Great Flamarion* in a number of books dedicated to his career; he also rarely failed to mention the sole compensation was meeting Duryea.

CHAPTER 5

Universal material at USC contains copies of correspondence over the censorship battles.

Duryea as a bandit was reported in the *New York Times*, found in USC's clippings.

Francis Nevins discusses *Black Angel* and Woolrich in his fine biography of Cornell Woolrich, excerpted in the excellent noir anthology, *Film Noir Reader 2*.

White Tie and Tails or *The Swindlers*—under any title, most major papers, and Duryea himself, lampooned or lambasted it.

The Man from Nowhere: Duryea papers at USC.

Black Bart—most thought Duryea was miscast, even longtime supporters: Duryea's contract for this film courtesy of Universal papers at USC.

Another Part of the Forest: Universal collection at USC.

CHAPTER 6

James Mason dismisses *One Way Street* in *The Films of James Mason*.

Winchester '73: it is worthwhile to seek out Basinger's *Anthony Mann* biography, as well as Kitses's *Horizons West*.

Manhandled: Duryea gave several interviews noting that the lackluster response to his likable presence in *Black Bart* gave Paramount added impetus to making his already slimy character even slimier.

The Underworld Story tidbits concerning Duryea's attempts to harden his character come from interviews with Hedda Hopper, as well as reporters from the *Herald Tribune* and Silver's *Film Noir Encyclopedia*.

Arrowhead material comes from Sharon McDaniel and Richard Duryea.

CHAPTER 7

Chicago Calling: Duryea granted interviews to Erskine Johnson and the *Mountain News* about his participation; he would also give slight variations in several articles.

Gordon Gebert, interview with the author, about his recollections working with Duryea.

Duryea's radio work can easily be found (and played) via various online outlets.

China Smith and *World for Ransom* material comes from Duryea himself in "Look Who's a Hero," as well as Silver and Ursini in *Whatever Happened to Robert Aldrich?*

Thunder Bay: some relevant essays courtesy of Basinger, as well as Frank Kogan in the very readable anthology *OK, You Mugs*.

Terror Street: a good section on the films in *Hammer Films*, a book that also liberally discusses the studio's early noir efforts, prior to the horror classics that made its name.

Ride Clear of Diablo: Nott's *Last of the Cowboy Heroes*; Universal press releases at USC.

Rails to Laramie: Universal press releases at USC.

CHAPTER 8

Lake Arrowhead: courtesy of Sharon McDaniel, Mary Benard, and Rich Baughman.

Foxfire: Universal press releases and essay by Kogan.

This Is My Love: e-mail message from Jerry Mathers.

CHAPTER 9

Storm Fear: *The Film Noir Encyclopedia*.
Information on Duryea's early television appearances comes from Duryea papers at USC.
"The Road That Led Afar": Laurie, e-mail to author.

CHAPTER 10

"The cigar-smoking sergeant . . .": "Dan Sheds Meanie Role in *Battle Hymn*."
The Burglar filming and producer Kellman: Bland, "Made in Delaware Valley."
Night Passage. Universal collection at USC, Eliot, Nott.
Slaughter on Tenth Avenue: Universal collection at USC, Duryea papers at USC.
Kathy O': Duryea provided interviews to many news outlets, including the *New York Herald Tribune*, *Variety*, *Daily News* (Wanda Hale was a champion of his work); more material found amidst Universal clipping files and Duryea papers at USC.

CHAPTER 11

Russell Johnson, as quoted to Gene Blottner about Duryea.
Information about Duryea's unsold pilots comes from Kitses's *Unsold Television Pilots* and Duryea papers at USC.
Possibility of Duryea starring in *Riverboat*: Duryea clippings at USC.
"You're my idea of what an actor should be . . .": letter from Robert Fuller, who also spoke to me at length about his friendship with Duryea.

CHAPTER 12

A Case of Libel: clippings at USC, the Performing Arts Library at Lincoln Center, the Margaret Herrick Library (with copies of letters in Duryea's handwriting regarding his dismissal); Franklin, "Duryea, That Famous Old Film Villain, Earned Bad Guy Tag on Broadway."
Six Black Horses: Universal and Duryea clippings at USC; Nott, *Last of the Cowboy Heroes*.
Wide Country: Earl Holliman, interview with author.
The possibility of working with son Peter: Pack, "Duryea Looks Toward Broadway."
Brecht on Brecht: Duryea papers at USC, *Hollywood Reporter*.

CHAPTER 13

Duryea in London: much material found in Duryea papers at USC.
He Rides Tall, *Taggart*: Universal clippings, Duryea papers at USC
Duryea on *The Bounty Killer*: letter from producer Pat Rooney, Duryea papers at USC; *Hollywood Reporter*; Balling, "Dan Duryea—When They Said He was Nice They Meant It."
Incident at Phantom Hill: Robert Fuller, interview with author; Universal and Duryea collection at USC.

CHAPTER 14

Flight of the Phoenix: Silver and Ursini, *Whatever Happened to Robert Aldrich?*; Franklin,
"Duryea, That Famous Old Film Villain, Earned Bad Guy Tag on Broadway";
Richard Duryea, interview with author; Williams, *Body and Soul* (a fine book on
Robert Aldrich).

The Hills Run Red: Hughes, *Once Upon a Time in the Italian West*.

Helen Duryea's death was reported in many papers; specific information came from
Richard Duryea, "Duryea recovering from Tragedy"; Resnick, "The Haunting
Memories that Guide His Life"; Muir, "Dan Duryea Recovering."

CHAPTER 15

Stranger on the Run: Duryea papers at USC; Don Siegel, interview in Bogdanovich,
Who the Devil Made It.

Duryea's work on *Peyton Place*: Patricia Morrow, interview with author; "Return of
the Con Man."

Duryea's last months: Richard Duryea, interview with author; Balling, "Dan
Duryea—When They Said He was Nice They Meant It."

"Look, I'm no saint": Bill Roberts column, *Houston Post*.

BIBLIOGRAPHY

AP. "Dan Duryea, Actor, Dies at 61; Played Unsavory Characters." *New York Times,* June 8, 1968.

Balling, Fredda Dudley. "Dan Duryea—When They Said He was Nice They Meant It." *Motion Picture,* September 1968.

Baltimore Sun. "Return of the Con Man." July 9, 1967.

Basinger, Jeanne. *Anthony Mann.* Wesleyan University Press, 2007.

Beck, Robert. *The Edward G. Robinson Encyclopedia.* McFarland, 2002.

Bland, Steve. "Made in Delaware Valley." *Philadelphia Inquirer,* January 8, 1956.

Blottner, Gene. *Universal-International Westerns, 1947–1967: The Complete Filmography.* McFarland, 2011.

Bogdanovich, Peter. *Who the Devil Made It.* Knopf, 1997.

Buford, Kate. *Burt Lancaster: An American Life.* Da Capo Press, 2000.

Canfield, Alyce. "Heel With Sex Appeal." *Liberty,* December 1946.

Cox, Jim. *Radio Crime Fighters.* McFarland, 2002.

Crowther, Bosley. "White Tie and Tails." *New York Times,* November 8, 1946.

Duryea, Dan. "The Faith No One Could Teach Me." *Modern Screen,* 1951.

———. "Look Who's a Hero." n.d.

Eliot, Marc. *Jimmy Stewart: A Biography.* Harmony, 2006.

Film Daily. "You Can have Good Old Days." February 1967.

Franklin, Rebecca. "Duryea, That Famous Old Film Villain, Earned Bad Guy Tag on Broadway." *Birmingham News,* August 8, 1965.

Goldberg, Lee. *Unsold Television Pilots, 1955–1988.* McFarland, 1990.

Gossett, Sue. *The Films and Carer of Audie Murphy.* Empire, 1996.

Graham, Sheilah. "When I Read of You Digging Dirt, It Spoils My Dream." *Boston Globe,* September 7, 1947.

Grant, Barry Keith. *Fritz Lang: Interviews.* University Press of Mississippi, 2003.

Greene, Alice Craig. "Happy Anniversary to the Duryeas." *Screen Stars,* August 1951.

Hansberry, Karen Burroughs. *Bad Boys: The Actors of Film Noir.* McFarland, 2003.

Herman, Jan. *William Wyler: A Talent for Trouble.* G. P. Putnam and Sons, 1995.

Hirsch, Foster. *Dark Side of the Screen.* DaCapo Press, 1981.

Hirschhorn, Clive. *The Films of James Mason.* Citadel Press, 1977.

———. *The Universal Story.* Octopus Books, 1983.

Hopper, Hedda. "What's in Fans' Minds Astonishes Duryea." *Baltimore Sun,* June 12, 1949.

Hughes, Howard. *Once Upon a Time in the Italian West*. St. Martin's Press, 2004.

Hunt, Dan. "Brecht on Brecht." *Westwood Press*, October 28, 1963.

Jensen, Paul. *The Cinema of Fritz Lang*. Zwemmer/Barnes, 1969.

Johnson, David. "Dan Duryea had Sense Enough to Know His Limitations." *Films in Review*, 1975.

Johnson, Tom, and Deborah Del Vecchio. *Hammer Films: An Exhaustive Filmography*. McFarland, 2012.

Kaminsky, Stuart. *Don Siegel Directs*. Curtis Books, 1974.

Key, Ty. "Villainous Duryea Wants to be Good Guy." *Hartford Courant*, December 22, 1957.

Kitses, Jim. *Horizons West*. British Film Institute, 2004.

Kogan, Frank. "Dan Duryea." In *OK, You Mugs: Writers on Movie Actors*, by Luc Sante and Melissa Holbrook Pierson. Vintage, 2000.

Larkins, Bob, and Boyd Magers. *The Films of Audie Murphy*. McFarland, 2004.

Lebenthal, Joel. *Tallulah: Life and Times of a Leading Lady*. Harper Collins, 2004.

Louisville Times. "Dan Duryea Likes to be Hated." 1941.

Loy, Philip. *Westerns in a Changing America: 1955–2007*. McFarland, 2012.

Lyons, Arthur. *Death on the Cheap*. DaCapo Press, 2000.

Magers, Boyd, Bob Marcus, and Bobby Copeland. *Best of the Badmen*. Empire: 2005, n.d.

Malnic, Eric. "Dan Duryea, Girl Slapping Villain of Movies, Dies at 61." *Los Angeles Times*, June 8, 1968.

McGilligan, Patrick. *Fritz Lang: Nature of the Beast*. Faber & Faber, 1998.

Meyers, Jeffrey. *Bogart: A Life in Hollywood*. Houghton Mifflin, 1997.

———. *Gary Cooper: American Hero*. William Morrow, 1998.

Morehouse, Ward. "'Villain' Dan Duryea Affable Guy." *Boston Globe*, February 24, 1957.

Morning Call. "Storm Still Rages Over Film Credits." December 1967.

Muir, Florabel. "Dan Duryea Recovering from Tragedy in Family." *Times-Picayune*, September 3, 1967.

Muller, Eddie. *Dark City: The Lost World of Film Noir*. St. Martin's Press, 1998.

Nevins, Francis. "Translate and Transform: from Cornell Woolrich to Film Noir." In *Film Noir Reader 2*, by Alain Silver and James Ursini. Limelight Editions, 1999.

Nollen, Scott Allen. *Three Bad Men: John Ford, John Wayne, Ward Bond*. McFarland, 2013.

Nott, Robert. *Last of the Cowboy Heroes: The Westerns of Randolph Scott, Joel McCrea and Audie Murphy*. McFarland, 2000.

Pack, Harvey. "Duryea Looks Toward Broadway." *Herald Statesman*, May 1963.

Resnick, Sylvia. "The Haunting Memories that Guide His Life." *Movie Life*, February 1968.

Roberts, Bill. "Visiting Fireman." *Houston Post*, April 17, 1963.

Rollyson, Carl. *Lillian Hellman: Her Legend and Her Legacy*. St. Martin's Press, 1988.

Ross, Don. "Dan Duryea on Sensitive Roles." *New York Herald Tribune*, June 1, 1958.

Screen Guide. "Dan Duryea, Hollywood's Most Likable Villain." 1951.

Scully, Frank. "Scully's Scrapbook." March 25, 1959.

Server, Lee, and Ed Gorman. *The Big Book of Noir*. Carroll and Graf, 1998.

Shadoian, Jack. *Dreams and Dead Ends*. Oxford University Press, 2003.

Silver, Alain, Elizabeth Ward, James Ursini, and Robert Profirio. *The Film Noir Ency-clopedia*. Overlook, 2010.

Silver, Alain, and James Ursini. *Whatever Happened to Robert Aldrich?* Limelight, 1995.

Sunday News. "Dan Sheds Meanie Role in Battle Hymn." February 1957.

Swinkels, Gilles. "Veteran Villain Dan Duryea has an Utterly Pleasant View of Life." *Houston Chronicle*, April 12, 1963.

Terrace, Vincent. *Encyclopedia of Television Pilots*. McFarland, 2011.

Terrace, Vincent, and James Robert Parish. *The Complete Actors' Television Credits, 1948–1988*. Scarecrow, 1989.

Todd, John. "Duryea Regards Self as Good Businessman." *Phoenix Gazette*, June 1947.

Troyan, Michael. *A Rose for Mrs. Miniver*. University Press of Kentucky, 1998.

Wagner, David, and Paul Buhle. *Blacklisted: The Film Lover's Guide to the Hollywood Blacklist*. Palgrave MacMillan, 2003.

Walker, Michael. "Robert Siodmak." In *The Book of Film Noir*, by Ian Cameron. Continuum, 1993.

Williams, Tony. *Body and Soul: The Cinematic Vision of Robert Aldrich*. Scarecrow, 2004.

World Telegram. "It's Tough on Duryea Always Playing Heels." January 15, 1939.

The author also consulted publications such as *Variety, Hollywood Reporter, New York Herald Tribune, New York Daily News, Los Angeles Times*, and the *New York Times* for reviews of Dan Duryea's film and television work. Many of these could be found within Duryea's clippings at USC. The following websites proved especially useful: Dan Duryea Central, Escape and Suspense, Peyton Place Revisited (on Facebook), and the Internet Movie Database (IMDB).

INDEX

Printed in the United States
By Bookmasters